First World War

and Army of Occupation

War Diary

France, Belgium and Germany

32 DIVISION
14 Infantry Brigade
Lancashire Fusiliers
19th Battalion
21 November 1915 - 30 June 1916

WO95/2394/1

The Naval & Military Press Ltd
www.nmarchive.com
Published in association with The National Archives

Published by

The Naval & Military Press Ltd

Unit 10 Ridgewood Industrial Park,

Uckfield, East Sussex,

TN22 5QE England

Tel: +44 (0) 1825 749494

www.naval-military-press.com

www.nmarchive.com

This diary has been reprinted in facsimile from the original. Any imperfections are inevitably reproduced and the quality may fall short of modern type and cartographic standards.

Contents

Document type	Place/Title	Date From	Date To
Heading	WO95/2394 Nov 15-July 16 19 Lancashire Fus		
Heading	32nd Division 14th Infy Bde 19th Bn Lancs Fusiliers 1915 No-Jly 1916		
Miscellaneous			
Heading	32nd Division 96th Infy Bde 19th Bn Lancs Fus. Nov-Dec 1915		
Heading	32nd Division 19th Lancs. Fus. Vol I 96/32 Nov. & Dec 15 Transferred to (95th=14th Bde Dec. 31st		
War Diary	Codford	21/11/1915	21/11/1915
War Diary	Havre	22/11/1915	23/11/1915
War Diary	Neuville	24/11/1915	26/11/1915
War Diary	Flexicourt	27/11/1915	27/11/1915
War Diary	Rainneville	28/11/1915	29/11/1915
War Diary	Albert	30/11/1915	27/12/1915
War Diary	Senlis	28/12/1915	31/12/1915
War Diary	Albert	01/12/1915	10/12/1915
War Diary	Trenches E 3	11/12/1915	12/12/1915
War Diary	E 3 Trenches	13/12/1915	14/12/1915
War Diary	Albert	15/12/1915	23/12/1915
Heading	14th Brigade 32nd Division. 19th Battalion Lancashire Fusiliers January 1916 Appendices attached. Intelligence Summaries.		
Miscellaneous	To D.A.G. 3rd Echelon.	01/02/1916	01/02/1916
War Diary	Senlis	01/01/1916	09/01/1916
War Diary	Martinsart	10/01/1916	13/01/1916
War Diary	G 2 Subsector	14/01/1916	17/01/1916
War Diary	G 2 & Senlis	18/01/1916	18/01/1916
War Diary	Senlis	19/01/1916	25/01/1916
War Diary	Senlis & Authville	26/01/1916	26/01/1916
War Diary	Authville	27/01/1916	31/01/1916
Miscellaneous	Intelligence Report Jany. 14-15th.	14/01/1916	14/01/1916
Miscellaneous	19th Lanc. Fus. Daily Battalion Report.	15/01/1916	15/01/1916
Miscellaneous	Intelligence Report Jany. 15th. 16th.	15/01/1916	15/01/1916
Miscellaneous	Daily Situation Report 24 Hours 15-16 Jan. 1916	15/01/1916	15/01/1916
Miscellaneous	Intelligence Report Jany. 16. 17th.	16/01/1916	16/01/1916
Miscellaneous	19. Lanc. Fus. Daily Situation Report 24 Hours 16-17th Jan. 1916	16/01/1916	16/01/1916
Miscellaneous	Intelligence Report Jany 17. 18th.	17/01/1916	17/01/1916
Miscellaneous	19. Lanc. Fus. Daily Situation Report 24 Hours 17-18th Jany. 1916	17/01/1916	17/01/1916
Miscellaneous	14th Brigade. 32nd Division. 19th Battalion Lancashire Fusiliers February 1916 Appendices attached:- Intelligence Summaries.		
Miscellaneous	D.A.G. 3rd Echelon G.H.Q.	01/03/1915	01/03/1915
War Diary	Authville	01/02/1916	01/02/1916
War Diary	Trenches Sector. G 2.	02/02/1916	06/02/1916
War Diary	Senlis	07/02/1916	12/02/1916
War Diary	Montigny	13/02/1916	14/02/1916
War Diary	Montigny-Rainneville	15/02/1916	15/02/1916
War Diary	Rainneville	16/02/1916	27/02/1916

War Diary	Rainneville-Allonville	28/02/1916	28/02/1916
War Diary	Allonville-Albert	29/02/1916	29/02/1916
Miscellaneous	19th Lancs. Fus. Daily Situation Report. 24 Hours 1st. 2nd. Feby. 1916	01/02/1916	01/02/1916
Miscellaneous	Daily Situation Report 24 Hours. 2nd.-3rd. Feby. 1916	02/02/1916	02/02/1916
Miscellaneous	Situation Report 24 Hours 3rd-4th. Feb. 1916	03/02/1916	03/02/1916
Miscellaneous	Daily Situation Report 24 Hours 4th-5th. Feb. 1916	04/02/1916	04/02/1916
Heading	14th Brigade. 32nd Division. 19th Battalion Lancashire Fusiliers March 1916 Appendices attached. Daily Situation Reports.		
War Diary	Albert Subsector E 2	01/03/1916	01/03/1916
War Diary	Sub Sector E 2	02/03/1916	02/03/1916
War Diary	Sub Sector E 2 Albert	03/03/1916	03/03/1916
War Diary	Albert	04/03/1916	08/03/1916
War Diary	Albert-Sub Sector F 1	09/03/1916	09/03/1916
War Diary	Sub Sector FI	10/03/1916	14/03/1916
War Diary	Sub Sector F1-Millencourt	15/03/1916	15/03/1916
War Diary	Millencourt	16/03/1916	20/03/1916
War Diary	Millencourt Sub Sector F1	21/03/1916	21/03/1916
War Diary	F 1 Sub Sector	22/03/1916	25/03/1916
War Diary	Arras	26/03/1916	26/03/1916
War Diary	Sub Sector F1-Albert	27/03/1916	27/03/1916
War Diary	Albert Aveluy	28/03/1916	31/03/1916
Miscellaneous	Daily Situation Report 24 Hours 1-2nd March, 1916	01/03/1916	01/03/1916
Miscellaneous	Daily Situation Report 24 Hours 5th-6th Feb. 1916	05/02/1916	05/02/1916
Miscellaneous	Situation Report 24 Hours 9-10 March 1916	09/03/1916	09/03/1916
Miscellaneous	19th S.Bn. Lancashire Fusiliers. Situation Report 24 Hours 2/3rd March, 1916	02/03/1916	02/03/1916
Miscellaneous	Situation Report 24 Hours 10-11th March 1916 Sub-Sector F.1	10/03/1916	10/03/1916
Miscellaneous	Situation Report. 24 Hours 11-12th March, 1916	11/03/1916	11/03/1916
Miscellaneous	Situation Report. 24 Hours 12-13th March. 1916	12/03/1916	12/03/1916
Miscellaneous	Daily Situation Report. 24 Hours 13-14th March, 1916	13/03/1916	13/03/1916
Miscellaneous	Situation Report. F.1. Sub. Sector. 24 Hours 14-15th March, 1916	14/03/1916	14/03/1916
Miscellaneous	Situation Report. 24 Hours 21th-22nd March 1916 F.1. Sub-Sector.	21/03/1916	21/03/1916
Miscellaneous	Situation Report. 24 Hours 22nd-23rd March 1916 F.1. Sub-Sector.	22/03/1916	22/03/1916
Miscellaneous	Situation Report 24 Hours 4pm 23rd to 4pm 24th March 1916. Sub-Sector F.1	23/03/1916	23/03/1916
Miscellaneous	Situation Report 24 Hours 24th-25th March 1916. Sub-Sector F.1	24/03/1916	24/03/1916
Miscellaneous	Situation Report 24 Hours 25th-26th March 1916, F.1. Sub-Sector.	25/03/1916	25/03/1916
Miscellaneous	Situation Report 24 Hours 26th-27th March 1916 F.1. Sub-Sector.	26/03/1916	26/03/1916
Heading	14th Brigade. 32nd Division. 19th Battalion Lancashire Fusiliers April 1916 Appendices attached:- Battalion Operation Orders. Situation Reports		
War Diary	Albert Aveluy	01/04/1916	02/04/1916
War Diary	Albert-Authville Sub Sector	03/04/1916	03/04/1916
War Diary	Authville Sub Sector	04/04/1916	08/04/1916
War Diary	Authville Sub Sector Aveluy	09/04/1916	09/04/1916
War Diary	Aveluy	10/04/1916	10/04/1916
War Diary	Aveluy & Warloy	11/04/1916	11/04/1916

War Diary	Warloy	12/04/1916	30/04/1916
War Diary	War Diary 19 Lancashire Fus.		
Miscellaneous	Daily Situation Report Appendix I	03/04/1916	03/04/1916
Miscellaneous	Situation Report 4th-5th, April Sub-Sector F.G.I.	04/04/1916	04/04/1916
Miscellaneous	Situation Report. 24 Hours 5pm 5/4/16 To 5pm 6/4/16 Sub. Sector F.G.I.	05/04/1916	05/04/1916
Miscellaneous	Situation Report. 6th-7th April, 1916 Sub Sector F.G.I.	06/04/1916	06/04/1916
War Diary	Situation Report 7th To 8th April, 1916 Sub Sector F.G.I.	07/04/1916	07/04/1916
Miscellaneous	Situation Report 8th to 9th April, 1916 Sub Sector F.G.I.	08/04/1916	08/04/1916
Miscellaneous	Intelligence Report. April 3/4/16	03/04/1916	03/04/1916
Miscellaneous	Intelligence Report. April 4-5 Sub Sector F.G.I.	04/04/1916	04/04/1916
Miscellaneous	Intelligence Report April 6th/16	06/04/1916	06/04/1916
Miscellaneous	Intelligence Report April 7/4/16 Sub Sector F.G.I.	07/04/1916	07/04/1916
Miscellaneous	Intelligence Report April 7/16 5 Pm to 5 Pm	07/04/1916	07/04/1916
Miscellaneous			
Miscellaneous	A Form. Messages And Signals. App IV		
Miscellaneous	A Form. Messages And Signals.		
Miscellaneous	A Form. Messages And Signals. App V		
Miscellaneous	A Form. Messages And Signals.		
Diagram etc	Scale 1/5,000.		
Miscellaneous	14th Brigade. 32nd Division. 19th Battalion Lancashire Fusiliers May 1916		
War Diary	Rubempre	01/05/1916	04/05/1916
War Diary	Bouzincourt	05/05/1916	05/05/1916
War Diary	Bouzincourt-Authville Sub Sector	06/05/1916	06/05/1916
War Diary	Authville Sub Sector	07/05/1916	09/05/1916
War Diary	Authville Subsector-Aveluy	10/05/1916	10/05/1916
War Diary	Aveluy	11/05/1916	13/05/1916
War Diary	Aveluy Authville Sub Sector	14/05/1916	14/05/1916
War Diary	Authville Sub Sector	15/05/1916	18/05/1916
War Diary	Bouzincourt	18/05/1916	23/05/1916
War Diary	Bouzincourt-Senlis	24/05/1916	24/05/1916
War Diary	Senlis	25/05/1916	28/05/1916
War Diary	Senlis Contay	29/05/1916	29/05/1916
War Diary	Contay	30/05/1916	31/05/1916
Miscellaneous	Daily Situation Report. Appendix I	06/05/1916	06/05/1916
Miscellaneous	Daily Situation Report. 24 Lancs 7.5.16 To 8.5.16 Authville	07/05/1916	07/05/1916
Miscellaneous	Daily Situation Report 24 Hours 8th 9th May 1916 Authville Sub Sector.	08/05/1916	08/05/1916
Miscellaneous	Situation Report 24 Hours 9th. 10th May 1916, Authville Sub. Sector.	09/05/1916	09/05/1916
Miscellaneous	Situation Report. 9. pm 14.5.16 to 5.0pm 15.5.16 Authville Sub-Sector.	14/05/1916	14/05/1916
Miscellaneous	Situation Report. 24 Hours 15th-16th May 1916, Authville Sub-Sector.	15/05/1916	15/05/1916
Miscellaneous	Situation Report. 24 Hours 16th-17th May 1916, Authville Sub-Sector.	16/05/1916	16/05/1916
Miscellaneous	Situation Report 24 Hours 17th-18th May 1916 Authville Sub.-Sector.	17/05/1916	17/05/1916
Miscellaneous	A Form. Messages And Signals. Appendix II		
Miscellaneous	A Form. Messages And Signals.		
Miscellaneous	Daily Situation Report. 12 Midnight 6.5.16 to 5pm. 7.5.16 Authville Sub-Sector.	06/05/1916	06/05/1916

Miscellaneous	Intelligence Report. May 7th. 1916	07/05/1916	07/05/1916
Miscellaneous	Daily Situation Report. 24 Hours-7.5.16 to 8.5.16. Authville Sub-Sector.	07/05/1916	07/05/1916
Miscellaneous	Daily Situation Report. 24 Hours 8th-9th May 1916. Authville Sub-Sector.	08/05/1916	08/05/1916
Miscellaneous	Situation Report. 9Pm 14.5.16 to 5.0pm 15.5.16 Authville Sub-Sector	14/05/1916	14/05/1916
Miscellaneous	Situation Report. 24 Hours 15th-16th May 1916 Authville Sub-Sector.	15/05/1916	15/05/1916
Miscellaneous	Situation Report. 24 Hours 16th-17th May 1916 Authville Sub Sector.	16/05/1916	16/05/1916
Miscellaneous	Situation Report. 24 Hours 17th-18th May 1916 Authville Sub-Sector.	17/05/1916	17/05/1916
Heading	14th Brigade. 32nd Division. 1/19th Battalion Lancashire Fusiliers June 1916		
War Diary	Contay	01/06/1916	11/06/1916
War Diary	Contay-Warloy	12/06/1916	12/06/1916
War Diary	Warloy-Crucifix Corner Central Aveluy	13/06/1916	13/06/1916
War Diary	Crucifix Corner	14/06/1916	16/06/1916
War Diary	Authville Sub Sector	16/06/1916	19/06/1916
War Diary	Authville Sub Sector Crucifix Corner	20/06/1916	20/06/1916
War Diary	Crucifix Corner	21/06/1916	22/06/1916
War Diary	Crucifix Corner-Warloy	23/06/1916	24/06/1916
War Diary	Warloy	24/06/1916	26/06/1916
War Diary	Warloy-Billets Trenches Aveluy Wood	27/06/1916	27/06/1916
War Diary	Sheller Trenches Aveluy Wood-Senlis	28/06/1916	28/06/1916
War Diary	Senlis	29/06/1916	29/06/1916
War Diary	Senlis-Blackhorse Bridge	30/06/1916	30/06/1916
Heading	14th Bde. 32nd Div. 19th Battalion. Lancashire Fusiliers. July 1916		
Operation(al) Order(s)	14th Infantry Brigade Operation Order No. 54	19/07/1916	19/07/1916
Operation(al) Order(s)	14th Infantry Brigade Operation Order No. 55	20/07/1916	20/07/1916
Operation(al) Order(s)	14th Infantry Brigade Operation Order No. 56	24/07/1916	24/07/1916
Operation(al) Order(s)	14th Infantry Brigade Operation Order No. 57	28/07/1916	28/07/1916
Miscellaneous			
Miscellaneous	19th Lancashire Fus. War Diary-July 1916 Appendix I Bde. Operation Orders. 14th 96.		
Miscellaneous			
Miscellaneous	The Officer Commanding. 16th North'd Fus.		
Miscellaneous			
Miscellaneous	Messages And Signals.		
Miscellaneous			
Operation(al) Order(s)	96th Infantry Brigade Order No. 46	15/07/1916	15/07/1916
Miscellaneous	Work Report Night 16/9/16	16/09/1916	16/09/1916
Miscellaneous	Messages And Signals.	18/09/1916	18/09/1916
Miscellaneous		19/09/1916	19/09/1916
Miscellaneous		20/09/1916	20/09/1916
Miscellaneous		21/09/1916	21/09/1916
Miscellaneous		22/09/1916	22/09/1916
Miscellaneous			
Miscellaneous	C Form (Original). Messages And Signals.	23/09/1916	23/09/1916
Miscellaneous	C Form (Original). Messages And Signals.	24/09/1916	24/09/1916
Miscellaneous	Details Of Work On. 31-8-16	31/08/1916	31/08/1916
Miscellaneous	Details Of Work. On. 1-9-16	01/09/1916	01/09/1916
Miscellaneous	Details Of Work. On. 2.9.16	02/09/1916	02/09/1916
Miscellaneous	Details Of Work. On. 3.9.16	03/09/1916	03/09/1916

Miscellaneous	Details Of Work. On. 4-9-16	04/09/1916	04/09/1916
Miscellaneous	Details Of Work. On. 5-9-16	05/09/1916	05/09/1916
Miscellaneous	Details Of Work. On. 6-9-16	06/09/1916	06/09/1916
Miscellaneous	Details Of Work. On. 7-9-16	07/09/1916	07/09/1916
Miscellaneous	Details of Work. On. 9-9-16	09/09/1916	09/09/1916
Miscellaneous	Details of Work. On. 8/9/16	08/09/1916	08/09/1916
Miscellaneous	Details of Work. On. 10th	10/09/1916	10/09/1916
Miscellaneous	Details of Work. On. 11.9.16	11/09/1916	11/09/1916
Miscellaneous	Details of Work. On. 12-9-16	12/09/1916	12/09/1916
Miscellaneous	Details of Work. On. 13th.	13/09/1916	13/09/1916
Miscellaneous	Details of Work. On. 14th.	14/09/1916	14/09/1916
Miscellaneous	Details of Work. On. 15.9.16.	15/09/1916	15/09/1916
Miscellaneous	Details of Work. On. 16.9.16	16/09/1916	16/09/1916
Miscellaneous	Details of Work. On. 18-9-16	18/09/1916	18/09/1916
Miscellaneous	Details of Work. On. 19th/9/16	19/09/1916	19/09/1916
Miscellaneous	Details of Work. On. 20-9-16	20/09/1916	20/09/1916
Miscellaneous	Details of Work. On. 21th.	21/09/1916	21/09/1916
Miscellaneous	Details Of Work. On. 22nd.	22/09/1916	22/09/1916
Miscellaneous	Details of Work. On. 23rd.	23/09/1916	23/09/1916
Miscellaneous	Work Report For 5/6th. Sept.	05/09/1916	05/09/1916
Miscellaneous	Work Report For Night	04/09/1916	04/09/1916
Miscellaneous	To. Adjt 19 L.F. Work Report For 7th 8th Sept.	07/09/1916	07/09/1916
Miscellaneous	To. Adjt 19 L.F. Work Report For 8th/9th Sept.	08/09/1916	08/09/1916
Miscellaneous	To Adjt 19 L.F. Work Report For 10th 11th Sept.	10/09/1916	10/09/1916
Miscellaneous	To Adjt 19 L.F. Work Report For 11th/12th Sept.	11/09/1916	11/09/1916
Miscellaneous	To Adjt 19 L.F. Work Report For 13th/14th Sept.	13/09/1916	13/09/1916
Miscellaneous	Work Done By P & B Coy.	15/09/1916	15/09/1916
Heading	Appendix III G. 15/1 Work Reports		
Heading	Report On Operations 1st to 4th July		
Miscellaneous	Report on Operations 1st/4th July. 1916	01/07/1916	01/07/1916
Miscellaneous	Operations 1st/4th July 1916.	01/07/1916	01/07/1916
Miscellaneous	Report On Operations Carried Out By 19th Lancashire Fusiliers.	01/07/1916	01/07/1916
Miscellaneous	App. D		
Miscellaneous	Intelligence Report Operations of 1st to 3rd.		
Miscellaneous	Intelligence Report. July 1st-3rd 1916. Operations	01/07/1916	01/07/1916
Miscellaneous			
Miscellaneous	Intelligence Report. July 11th-14th Operations.	11/07/1916	11/07/1916
Miscellaneous	Report on fighting at ovillers 12th to 14th July 1916.	12/07/1916	12/07/1916
Miscellaneous	Report on The Fighting In Ovillers On The 12th.13th.14th. July 1916 By The 19th. Lancashire Fusiliers.	12/07/1916	12/07/1916
Miscellaneous			
Map			
War Diary	Thiepval Authville Wood	01/07/1916	03/07/1916
War Diary	Senlis	04/07/1916	04/07/1916
War Diary	Senlis-Forceville	05/07/1916	05/07/1916
War Diary	Forceville	06/07/1916	06/07/1916
War Diary	Forceville Bouzincourt	07/07/1916	07/07/1916
War Diary	Bouzincourt Donnet Post	08/07/1916	08/07/1916
War Diary	Donnet Post	09/07/1916	10/07/1916
War Diary	Donnet Post-Ovillers	11/07/1916	11/07/1916
War Diary	Ovillers	12/07/1916	14/07/1916
War Diary	Bouzincourt Warloy	15/07/1916	15/07/1916
War Diary	Warloy-Beauval	16/07/1916	16/07/1916
War Diary	Beauval-Le Souich	17/07/1916	17/07/1916

War Diary	Le Souich	18/07/1916	18/07/1916
War Diary	Le Souich Monts-On-Ternois	19/07/1916	19/07/1916
War Diary	Monts-En. Ternois-Monchy-Breton	20/07/1916	20/07/1916
War Diary	Monchy-Breton Cauchy-A-La. Tour	21/07/1916	21/07/1916
War Diary	Cauchy-A La. Tour.	22/07/1916	26/07/1916
War Diary	Houchin	26/07/1916	28/07/1916
War Diary	Houchin-Capelle	29/07/1916	29/07/1916
War Diary	Capelle	30/07/1916	31/07/1916
War Diary	Correction.	26/06/1916	26/06/1916
War Diary	14th Inf. Bde Operation Order No. 41	30/06/1916	30/06/1916
Operation(al) Order(s)	14th Infantry Brigade Operation Order No. 44	05/07/1916	05/07/1916
Operation(al) Order(s)	14th Infantry Brigade Operation Order No. 45	06/07/1916	06/07/1916
Miscellaneous			
Operation(al) Order(s)	14th Infantry Brigade Operation Order No. 46	08/07/1916	08/07/1916
Miscellaneous	14 Inf Bde Operation Order No. 47	11/07/1916	11/07/1916
Operation(al) Order(s)	14th Infantry Brigade Operation Order No. 48	14/07/1916	14/07/1916
Operation(al) Order(s)	14th Infantry Brigade Operation Order No. 53	18/07/1916	18/07/1916
Miscellaneous	Thiepval. Appendix "A".		
Miscellaneous	Particulars of Roads Behind The German Lines. From Information Obtained From Refugees. Appendix "A"		
Miscellaneous	Hostile Artillery Opposite 32nd Division Front. Appendix "A"		
Miscellaneous	Ferme De Mouquet. Appendix "A".		
Miscellaneous	Appendix "A" Rough Plan Of The Farm Du Mouquet		
Miscellaneous	The Officer Commanding 16th North'd Fus.	17/07/1916	17/07/1916
Miscellaneous	96th Infantry Brigade Order No. 47	17/07/1916	17/07/1916
Miscellaneous	14th Bde Operation Order No. 42	03/01/1916	03/01/1916
Miscellaneous	14th Inf Bde. Op. Order No. 43		
Miscellaneous			
Miscellaneous		02/07/1916	02/07/1916
Miscellaneous	A Form. Messages And Signals. App II		
Miscellaneous	A Form. Messages And Signals.		
Miscellaneous			
Miscellaneous	Messages And Signals.		
Miscellaneous			
Miscellaneous	Messages And Signals.		
Miscellaneous			
Miscellaneous	A Form. Messages And Signals.		
Miscellaneous	A Form. Messages And Signals.	03/07/1916	03/07/1916
Miscellaneous	A Form. Messages And Signals.		
Heading	A Coy B Coy C Coy G.H.Q.		
Miscellaneous	A Form. Messages And Signals.	06/07/1916	06/07/1916
Miscellaneous			
Map			
Miscellaneous			
Map		20/07/1916	20/07/1916
Map			
Map		28/07/1916	28/07/1916
Map			
Map	Messages And Signals.		
Heading	19 Lancashire Fus War Diary-July 1916 App III Reports On Infantry July 1-4 11-14		
Heading	19th Lancashire Fus. War Diary-July-1916 App. IV Bde. Operations Orders For Action Operation July 1-4 in Conformance With Forward Movement of 4th Area.		
Map	Officer Commanding 19th Lancashire Fusiliers.	26/06/1916	26/06/1916

Operation(al) Order(s)	14th Infantry Brigade Operation Order No. 37	22/06/1916	22/06/1916
Miscellaneous	Regimental Sector. Appendix "A"		
Map	Appendix B1. Time Table.		
Map	Appendix C. Carrying And Men Withdrawn From units for Certain duties.		
Map	Appendix. E List of Substitutes in case of Casualties.		
Map	Appendix F. Instructions Regarding Disposal of Prisoners of War And Of Collection Of Information From Prisoners, The Dead, And Captured Trenches.		
Map	Appendix I		
Map	Appendix F. Instructions For And Duties Of Brigade And Battalion Intelligence Officers.		
Map	Appendix C Signal Communications		
Miscellaneous	19th Lancashire Fus. War Diary-July-1916 App V. Battalion Operation Orders For Attack In Conformance With Forward Movement Of 4th Army.		
Miscellaneous	19th Lancashire Fusiliers. Operation Order No. 37	26/06/1916	26/06/1916
Miscellaneous	List Of Officers To Accompany Battn. Into Action. App. A.		
Miscellaneous	Officers & N.C.D. Left In Reserve.		
Miscellaneous	Appendix B. N.C.O. And Men Remaining Behind In Res		
Miscellaneous	Appendix "B" Time Table.		
Miscellaneous	App B		
Miscellaneous	Appendix C. Carrying Parties And Men Withdrawn From Coy For Certain Duties.		
Miscellaneous	19 Lancs Fusiliers.	24/06/1916	24/06/1916
Miscellaneous	B Group Trenches.		
Miscellaneous	B Group. Accomodation In Trenches.		
Miscellaneous	App. VI	04/07/1916	04/07/1916
Miscellaneous	Operations 8-14 July 1916 (Officer Accompanying Battalion In Action	08/07/1916	08/07/1916

(1)

WO95/2394

Nov '15 - July '16

19 Lancashire Fus

32ND DIVISION
14TH INFY BDE

19TH BN LANCS FUSILIERS

1915 NOV ~~JAN~~ - JLY 1916

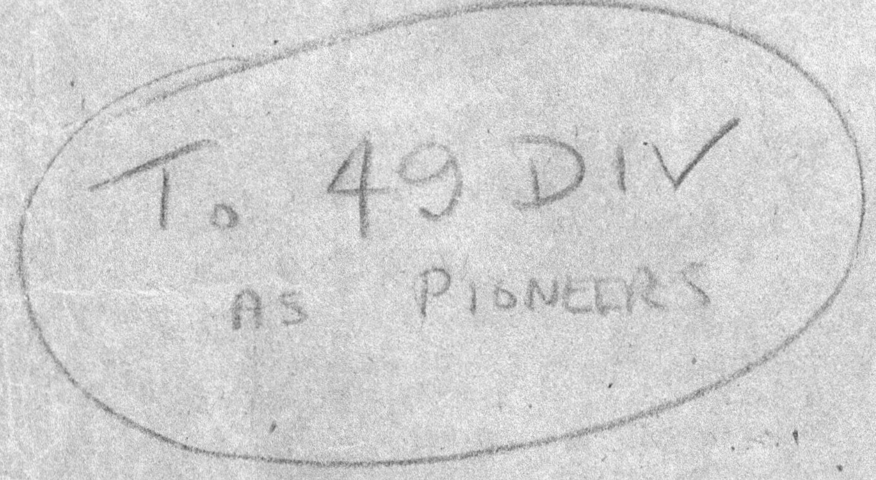

[illegible] was found to be unoccupied [illegible] top of crest, about [illegible] feet [illegible] [illegible] longitudinal [illegible] [illegible] about 150 yds. [illegible] both sides of the [illegible] firing positions have been [illegible] [illegible] being more than three feet [illegible] [illegible] firing [illegible] the enemy [illegible] possible.

Signal [illegible] two red flares [illegible] sent up from behind the German lines at 7.30 P.M.

[illegible]

Attached 32ND DIVISION
96TH INFY BDE

19TH BN LANCS FUS.

NOV - DEC 1915

32nd Division

19th Lancs: Fus:
vol I 96/32

Transferred to (95th = 14th Bde Dec 31st

121/7809

Nov. & Dec. 15

1.X.
6 sheets.

Instructions regarding War Diaries and Intelligence Summaries are contained in F. S. Regs., Part II. and the Staff Manual respectively. Title Pages will be prepared in manuscript.

WAR DIARY
or
~~INTELLIGENCE~~ SUMMARY
(Erase heading not required.)

Army Form C. 2118

19 Lancashire Fusiliers

Place	Nov. Date 1915	Hour	Summary of Events and Information	Remarks and references to Appendices
Codford	21st	4am	The battn started for Havre via Southhampton in three trains The passage was made during the night of the 21/22nd with lights out and escorted by a destroyer. TB	
Havre	22nd		Arrived at Havre at dawn - Battn disembarked at 8 am and marched up to the Rest camp, where tents were handed over to it. A Coy left by train & proceeded to COULONVILLERS TB	
HAVRE	23	6pm	The battn entrained and proceeded to PONT REMY thence the battn marched to NEUVILLE and went into billets - Rather a trying march, as the roads were very wet + the men were carrying a spare pair of boots and a blanket in addition to their usual equipment. TB	
NEUVILLE	24-26th		Remained in billets all day - Weather turned cold and frosty.	TB
FLEXICOURT	27th	7am	Marched off at 7 am arriving at our new billets at 2 pm - Weather very cold and frosty. Distance 17 miles.	TB
RAINNEVILLE	28th		Marched to new billeting area weather very cold and frosty Distance 18 miles.	TB
"	29th		Remained in billets - Weather very wet -	TB
ALBERT	30		Marched to our new fighting area - Were allotted billets - These were situated ~~about~~ ~~[illegible]~~ in the town about 3 miles in rear of front German trenches. The town was being bombarded intermittently.	TB

[illegible signature] Maj
14 L F

1875 Wt. W593/826 1,000,000 4/15 J.B.C. & A. A.D.S.S./Forms/C. 2118.

Instructions regarding War Diaries and Intelligence Summaries are contained in F. S. Regs., Part II. and the Staff Manual respectively. Title Pages will be prepared in manuscript.

WAR DIARY
or
~~INTELLIGENCE SUMMARY~~
(Erase heading not required.)

Army Form C. 2118

19 Lan Fus

Place	Date DEC	Hour	Summary of Events and Information	Remarks and references to Appendices
ALBERT	24		Two platoons from each Coy went into the trenches to be attached to 15 Lan Fus battn in E3. TB	
"	25		Two platoons from each Coy in trenches. One man wounded. " " " " " " ALBERT TB	
"	26		8 platoons in trenches. Two men wounded. TB Our guns bombarded enemy trenches heavily during the morning. Not a single shell sent back in reply. TB	
"	27		~~Relief of~~ 8 platoons in ALBERT relieved ~~by~~ 8 platoons in trenches TB	
SENLIS	28		Eight platoons out of trenches marched to SENLIS. Many men still bad with trench feet. Billets for men in barns with wooden bunks arranged in tiers. Men very comfortable, but no accomodation for officers as division billeted in same village. TB	
SENLIS	29		Eight platoons which were in trenches marched into SENLIS. Battn becomes divisional Reserve TB	
"	30		The battn continues training in billets. TB	
"	31		" " " " " " . and is transferred to 95th Brigade. TB	
			[signature] Lt Col Comdr. 19th L F	

1875 Wt. W593/826 1,000,000 4/15 J.B.C. & A. A.D.S.S./Forms/C. 2118.

Instructions regarding War Diaries and Intelligence Summaries are contained in F. S. Regs., Part II. and the Staff Manual respectively. Title Pages will be prepared in manuscript.

WAR DIARY
or
~~INTELLIGENCE SUMMARY~~
(Erase heading not required.)

Army Form C. 2118

19 Lan Frs

Place	1915 Date DEC	Hour	Summary of Events and Information	Remarks and references to Appendices
AILERT	1		~~Half~~ Half the officers and N.C.O's sent up to the trenches for instruction - weather wet.	
–	2		— — — —	
–	3		Platoons went into trenches 7th ESSEX and 8th NORFOLK'S for instruction weather wet and ~~cold~~ mild.	
–	4		Platoon training in trenches - weather mild but wet.	
–	5		— — — —	
–	6th		— — — —	
–	7		Companies went into trenches for company instruction - weather wet - trenches ditto	
–	8		— — — —	
–	9		— — — —	
–	10		— — — —	
Trenches E3	11		The battn went into the trenches and took over E3 sector from the 10th ESSEX Trenches in very bad condition - in many places waist deep in mud or water - Considerable amount of firing from German lines - 100 shells thrown into ALBERT. C Coy got bogged marching in from E2. A great many men had to be dug out but lost equipment - weather wet.	
	12th		Sniping and Artillery fire throughout the day. We replied effectively. The trenches were getting worse and worse. Communication almost impossible between trenches.	

1875 Wt. W593/826 1,000,000 4/15 J.B.C. & A. A.D.S.S./Forms/C. 2118.

Army Form C. 2118

Instructions regarding War Diaries and Intelligence Summaries are contained in F. S. Regs., Part II. and the Staff Manual respectively. Title Pages will be prepared in manuscript.

WAR DIARY

or

~~INTELLIGENCE SUMMARY~~

(Erase heading not required.)

19 Lan Fus

Place	Date 1915 DEC	Hour	Summary of Events and Information	Remarks and references to Appendices
E 3 Trenches	13		Usual firing continued on both sides - Germans sent a few whizbangs into our lines causing two casualties. Weather cold - Snow at night with hard frost.	IB
"	14		Firing continued - We had 2 casualties - A number of men going sick with trench feet - Weather frosty -	IB
Albert	15		We were relieved by the 16th Lanc. Fus. & marched back to town billets at Albert - 2 casualties besides numerous cases of trench feet -	IB
"	16		Working parties furnished for work on intermediate line.	IB
"	17		— — — —	IB
"	18		— — — —	IB
"	19		— — — — Our Artillery very active - all day, bombarding enemy trenches as a retaliation for the Germans blowing up a mine in our sector.	IB
"	20		Nearly whole battalion on working parties for intermediate line & on Bde fatigues	IB
"	21		Battn in Bde reserve - working parties & fatigues as before.	IB
	22		— — — —	IB
	23		— — — —	IB

1875 Wt. W593/826 1,000,000 4/15 J.B.C. & A. A.D.S.S./Forms/C. 2118.

14th Brigade

32nd Division.

<u>19th BATTALION</u>

<u>LANCASHIRE FUSILIERS</u>

<u>JANUARY 1 9 1 6</u>

Appendices attached:-

Intelligence Summaries.

To

D. A. G.

3rd. Echelon.

Attached is War Diary for the month of January in respect of the Battalion under my command.

1.2.16.

A. Rupert [illegible]
Lieut & Adjt.
for O. C.
19th Service Bn. L. F. 3rd Salford Bn.

Army Form C. 2118

Instructions regarding War Diaries and Intelligence Summaries are contained in F. S. Regs., Part II. and the Staff Manual respectively. Title Pages will be prepared in manuscript.

WAR DIARY
or
INTELLIGENCE SUMMARY
(Erase heading not required.)

Place	Date	Hour	Summary of Events and Information	Remarks and references to Appendices
	Jan 1916.			
SENLIS	1		Battn continues training in billets.	
	2		" " " "	
	3		"	
	4		" "	
	5		Battn transferred to 14 Bde 32 Div. {A mistake made – Battn did not transfer but the number of the Bde was changed from 95th to 14th	
	6.		Battn continued training in billets	
	7.		" " " " "	
	8.		" " " " "	
	9.		" " "	
MARTINSART	10		Battn marched from Senlis & went into billets in Martinsart at 4 pm. a detachment of one officer & 30 men hold McMahon's Post. Battn relieved 2 Rl. Inniskilling Fusiliers.	
"	11		Battn started training in billets MARTINSART.	
"	12		" continued " " " one company "A" went into AUTHUILLE to supply garrison for the village.	
"	13.		Battn continued training in Billets MARTINSART.	
G2 Subsector	14.		Battn relieved 15 H.L.I. in Subsector G.2 in front of the village of THIEPVAL, left of our line on the river ANCRE. Sector in which a cow is handed over as Trench Stores	

1875 Wt. W593/826 1,000,000 4/15 J.B.C. & A. A.D.S.S./Forms/C. 2118.

Instructions regarding War Diaries and Intelligence Summaries are contained in F. S. Regs., Part II. and the Staff Manual respectively. Title Pages will be prepared in manuscript.

WAR DIARY
or
INTELLIGENCE SUMMARY
(Erase heading not required.)

Army Form C. 2118

Place	Date	Hour	Summary of Events and Information	Remarks and references to Appendices
G.2 Subsection	14.		2/Manchesters on our right & the Hampshire Regt across the Ancre on our left. Trenches exceptionally good, & well drained.	
"	15		Quiet day except for nasty habit of the enemy, sending over "Sausages" into 'B' Coy trenches, no damage done. Patrols out at night but no exciting incidents.	
"	16.		Our own artillery were fairly active, but the enemy was silent. Sausages again. Two men wounded one accidentally. Another patrol but no encounter with the enemy.	
"	17.		Our field guns and howitzers quite active, enemy replied with shrapnel on to road behind. Otherwise very quiet. Mr. Barlow M.P. who raised this Battn visited the trenches.	
G2 & SENLIS	18.		Bn was relieved by 16. N.F. & marched back to Rest Billets Senlis (SENLIS). last company arrived at 11 p.m. Our tour in the trenches was easy as compared with previous tours, the excellent state of the trenches accounting for this.	
SENLIS	19		Battn spent the day cleaning up, kits equipment etc.	
"	20		" " " & kit inspections were held.	

1875 Wt. W593/826 1,000,000 4/15 J.B.C. & A. A.D.S.S./Forms/C. 2118.

Instructions regarding War Diaries and Intelligence Summaries are contained in F. S. Regs., Part II. and the Staff Manual respectively. Title Pages will be prepared in manuscript.

WAR DIARY
or
INTELLIGENCE SUMMARY
(Erase heading not required.)

Army Form C. 2118

Place	Date	Hour	Summary of Events and Information	Remarks and references to Appendices
SENLIS.	21		Bn started training – Two companies went out working, 2 companys had a gas demonstration; men walked through a room containing chlorine gas –	
SENLIS	22		Battn continued training in Billets – Route march –	
"	23		Sunday "Church Parades" and learning to put out the new "Hasty Apron Fence" was the work of the day – Training seriously hampered owing to working parties.	
"	24.		Inspection by the G.O.C. 14 Inf. Bde. Only A + C Coys present the other two companys were out on a working party –	
"	25		Two Companys B + D out on working party, other two companys continued training –	
SENLIS to AUTHUILLE	26.		Relieved the 16. N. Fus. in AUTHUILLE at 8.15. p.m. – 16 N.F. reported the village had been heavily shelled all day. Quiet when we arrived.	
AUTHUILLE	27		Kaisers birthday slight anxiety as to what the enemy might do. Our guns gave them a birthday present at 6 p.m. this necessitated the Battn taking refuge in dug outs – 400 men working all day –	
"	28		Large working parties – Quiet day until 6 p.m. when the enemy returned with thanks our birthday present of the 27th Result – 395 wagons of the	

1875 Wt. W593/826 1,000,000 4/15 J.B.C. & A. A.D.S.S./Forms/C. 2118.

Army Form C. 2118

Instructions regarding War Diaries and Intelligence Summaries are contained in F. S. Regs., Part II. and the Staff Manual respectively. Title Pages will be prepared in manuscript.

WAR DIARY
or
INTELLIGENCE SUMMARY
(Erase heading not required.)

Place	Date	Hour	Summary of Events and Information	Remarks and references to Appendices
AUTHUILLE	28		R.F.A. broke away, one horse killed, 2 men wounded. One of these waggons upset 'A' Coy rations which were fortunately retrieved later. Transport had lucky escape as they shelled AVELUY as it passed through. No casualties	
"	29.		Enemy bombarded our Trenches in G2 Subsector opposite their village of THIEPVAL, trenches and wire badly damaged, no further activity. Our men spent the day working in this Sector. (G2).	
"	30		Relief postponed, usual working parties.	
"	31.		~~Enemy~~ Bde report gas attack on D3 Sector 5 p.m. Heavy bombardment on the right. Usual large working parties. Weather much colder but fine.	

J M Graham Maj
Comd! 14th Lane Fus.

1875 Wt. W593/826 1,000,000 4/15 J.B.C. & A. A.D.S.S./Forms/C. 2118.

Intelligence Report.

Jany. 14 - 15th.

Subsector G.2.

General Activity. Enemy showed no signs of activity during the night no patrols or working parties were heard.

Enemy fired four shells between 10.45 p.m & 11 p.m. Shells burst behind sector. Flashes were reported to be seen in direction of St Pierre Divion & 18 counted between flash & report.

Burst of rapid rifle fire reported on left in direction of Subsector F1. at 8.45 pm

Patrols. Lt Nightingale 19th Lan Fus. went on patrol from Sap. XXVI

152 Maison Grise at 1.45 a.m. Reported no enemy to be seen. German sap head reported about 25 yds half right of Sap Head

A sentry was fired at by our snipers at point R.25 C6?.
He did not appear after second shot.
His hat appeared to be slate blue & similar to a "Glengarry".

James G. Whitehead
Lieut.

19th Batt. Lancs. Fus. 12. noon.

19th Lanc. Fus.

Daily Situation Report. 15.1.16.

Extremely quiet 24 hours. Night of 14th–15th quite uneventful except for a burst of rifle fire at 8.41 p.m. in direction of A.1. Sub-Sector.

Patrols.

2. Lieut. Nightingale went out from Sap XXVI "MAISON GRISE" at 1.45 am. – object: to thoroughly examine our own wire, and to investigate enemy sap half-right of XXVI Sap-head. No enemy patrol seen. Our wire needs repairing in parts but is quite safe. No sounds heard from enemy sap. This Officer was out for 1½ hours.

Artillery.

Enemy Artillery inactive. Our own artillery active on the left. A few howitzer shells fell into the enemy trench opposite CHATEAU THIEPVAL at 11.30 am. Damage seemed quite extensive. Enemy replied at 2.30 p.m. with a few whiz-bangs on support trenches behind 150 – 151, followed by several rifle-grenades. No damage.

Our Bombing-Officer fired two rifle-grenades at into supposed enemy M.G. emplacement at the "L" in THIEPVAL ROAD — Ref. map HAMEL 1/10000.

Trenches.

Very good condition. Slightly damaged in places, viz:– R. 25.a.5-1. Wire at this point badly needs repairing. Wire on the whole front G.2 Sector needs attention.

Working Parties

Working Party of 30 men of 15/H.L.I. cleared PAISLEY & ELGIN AVENUES. Two parties of 50 men & one of 25 men of the 1st Dorsets worked under R.E. on dug-outs & trench railway.

Materials most needed:– Trench boards.

[illegible]

20

To G.O.C. 14th Inf Bde

Annexed is Situation Report in respect of 24 hours 14th–15th inst.

15.1.16

A. Rupert Lunny 2 Lieut
5th R. Innis. Fus.
for Lieut. Col
Comdg 19th Lancs Fus.

Intelligence Report.

Jany. 15th. 16th.

Subsector. G.2. 12 noon.

Trench Mortars. Enemy's mortars threw bombs about 10 a.m. Position of mortar reported to be h25. a 82. in corner of wood.

Enemy threw bombs (6) in Trench 159. After first bomb had exploded a horn was heard. As the range was correct presumably this was a signal between an observer & the gun.

Patrol. Lt. J. G. Whitehead patrolled Trench 158 & 159. No activity of enemy was seen, or heard.

James G. Whitehead
Lieut.
19. Lanc. Fus.

Daily Situation Report.
24 hours 15th–16th Jan. 1916.

Fairly quiet 24 hours. No special activity on part of the enemy.

Patrols. Two patrols were sent out. One – under Lieut. J. G. Whitehead – with Sergt. Sharples & one man – object: to discover if enemy were on sunken road in front of THIEPVAL WOOD. Lieut. Whitehead went out from trench 159 & approached the road. Two rifle shots were then fired by the enemy, & he bore away to the right, following the line of the road, until fired on by machine gun from direction of cemetary – R. 25 b 7-8. Patrol then returned coming over parapet 158 trench. Patrol started 5.45 pm. returned 7.45 pm.

The other patrol – under Lieut. H. Musker – went out at 3.35 am. from trench 151. Object: to thoroughly examine our own wire. Going out they crossed & went some distance in front of our own wire. Here they encountered a low trip wire. They followed this along for some distance – retired because enemy repeatedly dropped Very lights quite close. They then proceeded to examine the wire & found from far side (1) a low line of rabbit wire (2) low barbed wire, mostly lying on the ground (3) line of concertina wire (4) a high line of rabbit wire – this close to our parapet. Patrol returned 6–0 am. Lieut. Musker took Pte Mulraney with him.

Artillery. Enemy fired 16 whiz-bangs at Section 150. All fell in rear of front line. No damage. This started at 12.30 pm. Our own artillery were active last night & at 11 pm. sent over 35 light shells into enemy lines in front of

ARTILLERY.

THIEPVAL CHATEAU. Single shells having been fired at same spot during to-day.

Six rounds of minenwerfer were fired by the enemy into trenches 156-157, destroying a newly made machine-gun emplacement. O. i/c trench-mortar thinks he has located position at cross-roads R. 25 a 5-8.

Our Bombing Officer fired several rifle-grenades at DIAMOND WOOD.

State of trenches:- Very good. Damage to trenches in 154, 156, 157 being repaired. BUCHANAN STREET, PAISLEY AVENUE, & ELGIN AVENUE have been cleaned, trench-boards being laid down in Buchanan Street. Parapet was improved 155. Latrine dug in 156.

Wire. Still poor, especially in front of 154 trench. Some wiring was done here last night, also in front of 162 and PETERHEAD. Working parties consisted of 40 men of 1st Dorsets, divided as follows:- 10 men Buchanan Street, 20 men Paisley Avenue, 10 men Elgin Avenue. Work on dug-outs & trench-railway has been kept back due to misunderstanding in orders of R.E. Officer.

M.G.O. reports position of enemy machine-gun at R. 25 b. 6/8.

Materials specially required:- Revetting material, posts for wire, & sand-bags.

A. Rupert [illegible]
2/Lt & Lt. [illegible]
Adj. 19 L.F.

Intelligence Report
Jany. 16. 1916

Subsector G.2. 12 noon

Activity. Enemy artillery very quiet. Enemy T.Mortar threw one bomb at M.Gun G. Alternate emplacement & partially destroyed it. This emplacement appears to be known to enemy as it has been very nearly hit on previous occasions.

Aeroplanes. 22 Allied Aeroplanes observed at 10.30. going NE from direction of G.1. Enemy opened heavy artillery fire. No aeroplane was observed to be hit. After passing over Thiepval aeroplanes turned W.

Lights.
At 5.30 p.m. a large flare in the sky was observed

This appeared to be several miles in rear of THIEPVAL & lasted for 2 or 3 seconds.

Observation

Enemy have observation post or M.Gun emplacement at point R 25 b 25. This appears to be a M.Gun emplacement as flashes were observed from this direction during the night.

M.Gun Emplacements observed at points R. 25 b 29. & R 25 b 21. (By telescope).

Enemy sniper post observed at point R. 25 c 62.

(Reported to Artillery)

M.Gun Emplacement reported at W part of N wall of THIEPVAL CHURCH 30 ft. from Ground.

Patrols.

Lt. J G [illegible] took out patrol from Sap 34. He reports no signs of recent work was seen on SUNKEN ROAD in direction of Hammerhead & Pethead Saps &

no signs of German patrols or working parties were seen or heard. M.Guns opened fire on from direction of Chalk at Sheepwal.

German dog was heard to be barking in Enemy's line.

Signals. Enemy appears to be using a very large flare which when it reaches the ground continues to burn for 2 or 3 seconds.

Working parties

Knocking was heard by sentry in enemy's line at point R 25 c 81.

James G. Whitehead
Lieut.

19th Lancs Fus.

19. Lanc. Fus.

Daily Situation Report
24 hours 16-17th Jan. 1916.

Quiet 24 hours.

PATROLS. Patrol, consisting of Lieut. H. J. C. Newman, 1 N.C.O. + two men, went out in front of 157 at 6.25 pm. Object: to ascertain whether the sunken road is used by enemy for any purposes. Lieut. Newman reports: "We went out by Sap 34 + took up a position on our side of the sunken road. We lay here for 80 minutes + neither saw nor heard enemy. We then patrolled along both towards HAMMERHEAD and PETERHEAD. – No result. We then crossed the road + proceeded for about 150 yards towards the enemy's lines. Moon was too bright to proceed further. – No signs of enemy here. The sunken road shows no sign of being used by the enemy, nor were any saps discovered."

ARTILLERY. Enemy artillery inactive. Several light shells fired into enemy trenches in front of CHATEAU THIEPVAL by our guns. Number of our howitzer shells fell into enemy trenches opposite Sub-Sector C.1. Good deal of damage done.

Machine Guns. Two enemy Machine Guns fired bursts in combination (1) situated (supposed) in the belfry tower of church at THIEPVAL. (2) situated somewhere in R.19 d 5.5. The one from the belfry fired three single shots, then opened up, along with the other, a converged traversing fire. An enemy machine gun was located in trenches opposite 154-155 – in the trees. Two of our guns engaged it, causing it to cease fire.

Enemy's trench mortars very active firing into trenches 151-152, 154, 155-156. New M.G. emplacement in 155 at point R 25 a 54 completely blown up. One man was wounded in 151. Trenches slightly damaged. These are being repaired. No retaliation on our part at all.

State of trenches: Good, being improved all along the line.

Wire: ~~[illegible]~~ Wiring done in front of 161-162, 154-153. Disused saps in front of 161 filled in & wired. Progress in wiring greatly hampered by lack of material.

General: Sound of a dog barking was heard from German lines opposite 158-157. Enemy now using brilliant rocket. This continues to burn on the ground for some seconds.

Sounds of Tapping heard opposite THIEPVAL POINT SOUTH and MAISON GRIS.

Materials needed: Sand-bags & wire-posts.

A. Rupert [illegible]

2. Lieut.

2. R. Innis. Fus.

Adjutant. 19th Lanc. Fus.

Intelligence Report.
Jany 17. 1916.

Subsector G.2. 12 noon.

Activity. General Activity very quiet.

Enemy fired rifle grenades on trenches 158 & 159 at 9.30 a.m with no result; also on point R25. c 4.5 in reply to ours. Some of our men reported wounded.

Enemy artillery fired on trench 159 at 6.30 p.m with no result.

Enemy: T.mortars fired two bombs on trench 159 at 6.30 p.m. No damage was done.

Note. Enemy ~~[illegible]~~ generally fire a number of rifle grenades & T.mortar Bombs on Trench 158 & 159 about stand to.

Patrols. 2/Lt. D. Wood took patrol out from HAMMERHEAD SAP to make general observation. He proceeded in direction of Cross roads. CRUIFIX - AUTUILLE & THIEPVAL. Reports enemys working parties were heard.

Note. Enemy have apparently put a large amount of new wire on left of Cross Roads & have also a very strong position commanding the valley as several M/Gun emplacements can be observed by Telescope.

Observation.

An observation post is to be clearly seen at point K25 b 11. (Just below left hand window of house in rear). It is covered in & could be used by a M/Gun. Two sentries can be clearly seen at a time. When fire was opened by our Snipers a lid was dropped over hole.

Patrols (b). A patrol under Lt Morris of 1 Sergeant & 3 men patrolled along trench 160, along MILL ROAD.

No signs of enemy's patrols or working parties were heard or seen. On enemy's side of ROAD signs of a track ~~made~~ by were seen & it appeared to have been recently patrolled. Patrol threw four grenades at enemy's wire to try to gain some information as to strength of enemy. Enemy did not fire a shot but replied with one ~~Ve~~ Flare.

James G. Whitehead
Lieut

19 Lancs Fus.

19. Lanc. Fus.

Daily Situation Report
24 hours 17-18th Jany. 1916.

Situation normal.

Patrols. Patrol under Lieut. W. M. Morris, consisting of a Sergt. & 3 men left PETERHEAD at 12.45 a.m. & returned at 2.15 a.m. Object: to ascertain strength of enemy wire; evidence of enemy patrols; position of enemy saps, if any.

Lieut. Morris reports:- "Visited the Mill Road & patrolled along it Northwards & also towards enemy trenches. No enemy seen, but it was obvious that the ground, especially near the road, had been patrolled. In order to discover the strength of the enemy holding the trench, some Mills bombs were thrown at the enemy's trench. These exploded, result - flare went up - but no rifle fire was opened. The enemy's wire is strong and an effective barrier.

Patrol under 2/Lieut. A. Wood, consisting of Sergt. & 1 private, left HAMMERHEAD at 6.30 p.m. & returned 8.30 p.m. Object: To investigate THIEPVAL ROAD and cross-roads R.25 a 8.4. 2/Lt. Wood reports:- "Enemy preparing defences on this road & also sapping. Bomb was thrown at this part & we returned."

Artillery. Not unusually active. Our artillery again shelled THIEPVAL, with some effect. Our howitzers fired several shells into enemy's trenches opposite 155-156. The enemy's reply is always with sausages & trench-mortars, which damage our trenches a good deal. These are especially active against 154. 155. 156. Early this morning the enemy sent some shrapnel into the ANCRE VALLEY, probably trying to sweep SPEYSIDE ROAD.

Trench Mortars. Our trench mortar between 158 & 159 fired several rounds for ranging. Enemy replied with rifle grenades.

Our Bombing Officer used the catapult from 154 trench but no effect could be noticed. Too fired rifle-grenades from MAISON GRIS. Enemy replying with the same sort of missile – wounding 4 men.

State of Trenches: Wet & slippery but not very bad. Greatest difficulty is bulging parapets & we are continually supporting these. Parts of damaged parapet being mended. Working parties all along the line clearing out mud.

Wire. Wiring done in front of 155 & 156 – 151 & disused trenches ~~round~~ between THIEPVAL POINT SOUTH and 154 wired & good deal of coiled wire pegged over trenches. Great deal of work yet needed.

Working Parties. Small parties wiring. Insufficiency of men for any big work to be undertaken.

Materials most needed: Sandbags & revetting material.

A. Rupert Morel 2. Lieut.
2. R. Innis. Fus.
Adjutant. 19. Lanc. Fus.

14th Brigade.

32nd Division.

19th BATTALION

LANCASHIRE FUSILIERS

FEBRUARY 1 9 1 6

Appendices attached :-

Intelligence Summaries.

SECRET

3.X.
6 sheets

D.A.G.
3rd Echelon
G.H.Q.

Attached is war diary of this Bn for the month of February.

A. Rupert Murray
Lt & Adj.
for OC 19 Lancs Fus

Army Form C. 2118

Instructions regarding War Diaries and Intelligence Summaries are contained in F. S. Regs., Part II. and the Staff Manual respectively. Title Pages will be prepared in manuscript.

WAR DIARY
or
INTELLIGENCE SUMMARY
(Erase heading not required.)

Place	Date	Hour	Summary of Events and Information	Remarks and references to Appendices
AUTHUILLE.	Feb. 1.		Men on fatigue in trenches till 1 p.m. Battalion proceeded to trenches at 5.30 p.m. & took over from the 15 H.L.I.	
Trenches Sector G2.	Feb. 2.		Batt busy repairing trenches & putting up new wire in front. Patrol, at night, had an exciting encounter with German patrol. Lieut. [illegible] attacked German patrol with grenades and pistol – German patrol [illegible] – Lieut. [illegible] slightly wounded in leg	
— do —	Feb 3.		Quiet day. Enemy put over several T. Mortar bombs into A. Coys trench one wounding seven men. Lt. Dixon took out a patrol which encountered & engaged a hostile patrol. Lt. Dixon was wounded & taken prisoner.	
do.	Feb 4.		Our artillery gave the enemy's trenches a hot time. Very feeble reply. Our patrols again active.	
do.	Feb 5.		Our artillery bombarded enemy trenches for about two hours. Enemy replied on AUTHUILLE & on rear line.	
do.	Feb 6.		Very quiet day. The battalion was relieved in the trenches by 16th Lancs Fus. at 9.30 p.m. & marched to SENLIS.	
SENLIS.	Feb 7		Battalion in rest billets. A & B Coys had baths. Cleaning of clothes & equipment.	

1875 Wt. W593/826 1,000,000 4/15 J.B.C. & A. A.D.S.S./Forms/C. 2118.

Army Form C. 2118

Instructions regarding War Diaries and Intelligence Summaries are contained in F. S. Regs., Part II. and the Staff Manual respectively. Title Pages will be prepared in manuscript.

WAR DIARY
or
INTELLIGENCE SUMMARY
(Erase heading not required.)

Place	Date	Hour	Summary of Events and Information	Remarks and references to Appendices
SENLIS.	Feb 8		½ Battalion on working party. C & D Coys carrying on with cleaning of clothes & equipment etc.	
"	Feb. 9.		Battalion busy having baths & cleaning clothes.	
"	Feb 10.		½ Battalion on working party. Remainder of the men washing their clothes.	
"	Feb 11		Very wet day. Battalion was inspected by Col. J H Graham.	
"	Feb. 12.		Battalion moved to new billeting area at MONTIGNY. for Brig. training.	
MONTIGNY	Feb 13.		Battn started training	
MONTIGNY	14		Battn continued training, ground for training very restricted & weather very bad.	
MONTIGNY -RAINNEVILLE	15.		Battn moved into Billets in RAINNEVILLE arrived at 4 15 p.m, in very bad weather. Billets fairly good, but village very dirty.	
RAINNEVILLE	16		Battn continued training.	
"	17		" " " but hampered by bad weather	
"	18.		Bde Route march proposed weather too bad so it was postponed, training in the men's billets, quite impossible to go outside.	

1875 Wt. W593/826 1,000,000 4/15 J.B.C. & A. A.D.S.S./Forms/C. 2118.

Instructions regarding War Diaries and Intelligence Summaries are contained in F. S. Regs., Part II. and the Staff Manual respectively. Title Pages will be prepared in manuscript.

WAR DIARY
or
INTELLIGENCE SUMMARY
(Erase heading not required.)

Army Form C. 2118

Place	Date	Hour	Summary of Events and Information	Remarks and references to Appendices
RAINNEVILLE	19.		Bde Route March - left RAINNEVILLE at 8.45 am and returned at 2.30 pm. Men march fairly well - 32 Div. G.O.C. ~~[illegible]~~ inspected us on the march.	
"	20.		Sunday set aside as a day of rest, church parade & football.	
"	21.		Continued training in billets	
"	22		" " "	
"	23		Battn Route March, very cold morning & signs of snow.	
"	24		Continued Training - Heavy fall of snow & very cold.	
"	25		Training held back on account of weather, N. East wind & snow all day. Roads impassable & traffic held up.	
"	26		All Coys working on roads clearing drifts, these were 5 to 6 foot deep in places. Brigade Cross Country Race postponed on account of weather	
	27		Sunday - Still freezing but prospects of a thaw - Brigade Cross Country Race run, very stiff course, 1st Dorset Regt won easily 15 H.L.I second, this Battn 3rd 2/Manchester Regt last, ~~the~~ our Battn did very well indeed, as they had had very little training.	

1875 Wt. W593/826 1,000,000 4/15 J.B.C. & A. A.D.S.S./Forms/C. 2118.

Instructions regarding War Diaries and Intelligence Summaries are contained in F. S. Regs., Part II. and the Staff Manual respectively. Title Pages will be prepared in manuscript.

WAR DIARY
or
INTELLIGENCE SUMMARY
(Erase heading not required.)

Army Form C. 2118

Place	Date	Hour	Summary of Events and Information	Remarks and references to Appendices
RAINNEVILLE – ALLONVILLE	28		14 Bde Tactical exercise with Skeleton Bn, very wet & damp under foot, arrived in RAINNEVILLE to find orders for move at once to ALLONVILLE 2 miles away – Battn arrived in Billets at 9-30 p.m.	
ALLONVILLE – ALBERT	29		After many counter orders from the Brigade Battn, moved to billets in ALBERT. Whole Battn arrived at 5 p.m. & is billetted in the Hospital. Our return to the vicinity of the Firing line is accompanied by a lively Artillery Cannonade. The Commanding Officer & 5 officers visited E 2 Subsection.	

[signature]

19th Lancs. Fus.

Daily Situation Report.

24 hours 1st–2nd May 1916.

Situation normal.

Patrols. Lieut. Newman was on listening post opposite R25 a 5.4 in a crater made by enemy's fire. A German patrol was heard reconnoitring towards Sap 40, evidently with intention of bombing sap. Lt. Newman crept out towards Sunken Road. Enemy threw a bomb, which failed to explode, on the road & opened fire with revolvers. Lieut. Newman threw a grenade which exploded & then emptied his revolver at enemy as they retreated. Enemy was [illegible].

Artillery. Not unusually active. From 12.15 to 1.30 pm enemy fired 30 How. shells in GEMELL ST. damaging trench mortar battery emplacement & partly burying gun. Our artillery very inactive. About 12 noon our light guns, firing from HAMEL side of River ANCRE, put about 20 shells in enemy's trenches opposite trench 159. Damage could not be ascertained as trenches are hidden.

Trench Mortars. Enemy fired 10 oil-cans into rear & communication trenches behind trench 154. No damage was done. Enemy sent over rifle-grenades into trench 155.

State of trenches. Good excepting trench 156, where great damage has been done by previous trench-mortar & artillery fire.

Working Parties. Good work has been done all day in trench 156 & along the whole line. Where wire has been damaged opposite trench 156 attempts were made to put up wire, but enemy machine gun forced our parties under cover — one Sergeant [illegible] Officer being hit.

Wire. Wire on extreme left & right is very good. In trenches occupied by two centre companies very thin indeed, owing to recent trench mortar & artillery bombardment.

Materials needed. Sand-bags, knife-rests, revetting material.

James G. [illegible] Lieut. for Lieut. & Adjt. 19th Lancs. Fus.

Daily Situation Report.

24 hours. 2nd – 3rd Feby 1916.

Situation Normal.

Patrols. 3 Patrols of 6 men each – including 2 bombers – went out from Point R25a 5.3. under direction of 2/Lieut. Dixon at 6.30 pm. to act as covering party & listening posts for working party on wire opposite Trench 156. They advanced to Sunken Road and reconnoitred immediately in front. They found no signs of enemy patrols & took up positions along road.

Lieut. Rosen & 1 Sgt. went out from PETERHEAD SAP at 9.0 pm to make general observation & act as covering party to working party on wire by PETERHEAD SAP. They patrolled Mill road opposite Trench 162 & found no sign of enemy. They took up position on road & returned by PETERHEAD SAP at 11 pm.

Cpl. Hayes & 2 bombers went out from Trench 154 at 3.45 am to act as covering party for working party on wire. They found no signs of enemy.

Patrol under Lt. Nightingale – consisting of 1 Sgt. & L'cpl. went out from Point R25c 3.3 to inspect our own wire. They found wire on extreme right to be very good. Part THIEPVAL POINT SOUTH wire was found to be badly damaged by enemy's fire. No signs of enemy patrol was seen but German wiring party was heard opposite Point 151.

Artillery. Enemy shelled PETERHEAD SAP and [illegible] in rear of Trench 162 with H.E. & whizz-bangs. Damage was done to wire & trenches. Our retaliation very slight. Enemy continued to search with H.E. along GEMMEL'S evidently attempting to find T.M. battery. Our artillery fired several salvoes about Cemetery & appeared to be registering.

Trench Mortars. Our batteries fired 2 T.M. & enemy replied with about 6 oil-cans. No apparent damage was done.

State of Trenches. Trenches very good. Good work has been done in trench 156 - by GEORGE ST. also in trench 162 & along whole Sub Section where needed. Dug-outs in rear of trench 154 are well under way.

Wire. Further damage was done to wire around PETERHEAD by enemy artillery. This & also the whole of the line has been repaired as much as possible, wiring parties being out the whole of the night. Opposite trench 156 we have constructed a fence of over 100 yards & hope to complete the other ground portion to-night.

Working Parties. Engaged on revetting & wiring along the whole line.

Materials. Sand bags, wire, revetting material & especially 5'6" wiring stakes.

(5'9) [signature]

Lieut. Col. [struck through]

Commanding 19th. Service Bn.

Lancashire Fusiliers. 3rd. Salford Bn.

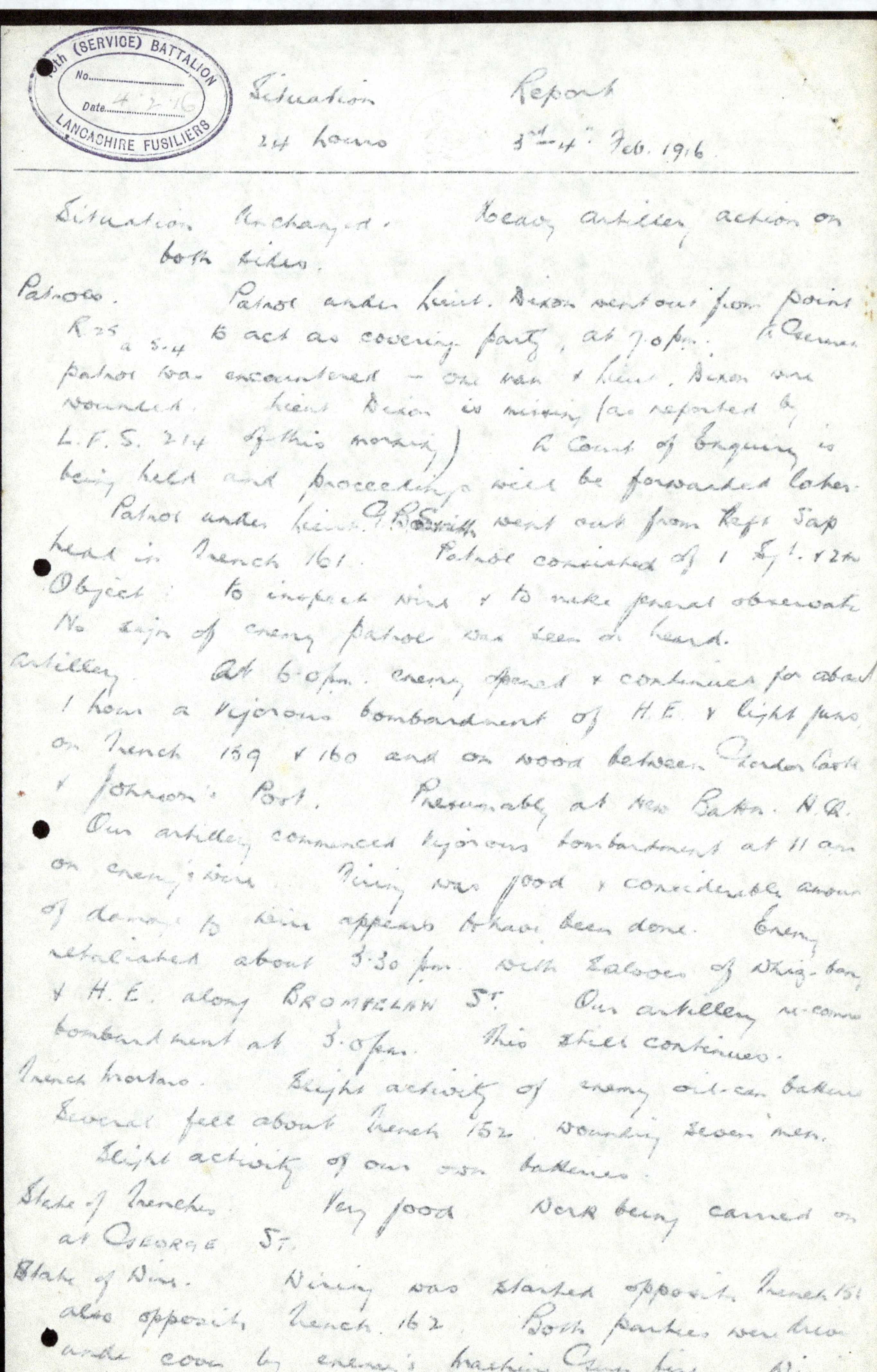

[illegible]th (SERVICE) BATTALION
No. ....
Date 4-2-16
LANCASHIRE FUSILIERS

Situation Report
24 hours 3rd–4th Feb. 1916.

Situation Unchanged. Heavy artillery action on both sides.

Patrols. Patrol under Lieut. Dixon went out from point R25 a 5.4 to act as covering party, at 7.0 pm. A German patrol was encountered – one man & Lieut. Dixon were wounded. Lieut Dixon is missing (as reported by L.F.S. 214 of this morning). A Court of Enquiry is being held and proceedings will be forwarded later.

Patrol under Lieut. G.B. Smith went out from Left Sap head in Trench 161. Patrol consisted of 1 Sgt. + 2 m
Object to inspect wire & to make general observatio
No sign of enemy patrol was seen or heard.

Artillery. At 6.0 pm. enemy opened & continued for about 1 hour a vigorous bombardment of H.E. & light guns on Trench 159 & 160 and on wood between Gordon Castle & Johnson's Post. Presumably at New Battn. H.Q.

Our artillery commenced vigorous bombardment at 11 am on enemy's wire. Firing was good & considerable amount of damage to wire appears to have been done. Enemy retaliated about 3.30 pm with salvoes of whiz-bang & H.E. along BROOMIELAW St. Our artillery re-commenced bombardment at 5.0 pm. This still continues.

Trench Mortars. Slight activity of enemy oil-can battery. Several fell about Trench 152 wounding seven men.

Slight activity of our own batteries.

State of Trenches. Very good. Work being carried on at GEORGE St.

State of Wire. Wiring was started opposite Trench 151 also opposite Trench 162. Both parties were drawn under cover by enemy's Machine Gun fire. Wiring party also sent out to repair wire opposite Trench 154.

This party also dispersed by Machine Gun fire.

Working Parties. Working parties of 15/H.L.I. were occupied on GEORGE St.

Materials most needed: Sandbags, Wiring Stakes 1½', Wick for Hurricane lamps, revetting material

James G. Whitehead
Lieut. for Lieut-Col.

Commanding 19th. Service Bn.
Lancashire Fusiliers. 3rd. Salford Bn.

Daily Situation Report

24 hours 4th–5th Feb. 1916.

Situation normal. Heavy artillery action on both sides.

Patrols. Patrol under C.S.M. Green, of 1 Sgt. & 2 men left PETERHEAD SAP at 11 pm & returned by PETERHEAD SAP 12.15 am. Object to make general observations along MILL ROAD. No signs of enemy were seen, but very frequent Very lights were put up by the enemy, with no firing.

2/Lieut. D. Wood and 1 N.C.O. went out from HAMMERHEAD SAP at 11.15 pm to bomb supposed ~~[illegible]~~ machine Gun emplacement East of cross roads – THIEPVAL ROAD and CRUCIFIX. Patrol threw six bombs into trench & retired. Enemy did not reply.

2/Lieut. W.R. Nightingale & 2 N.C.O's went out from Sap 25 at 11 pm & returned at 1.20 am. Object to ascertain if hedge which runs from SAUCHIE HALL ST. East was used by enemy. No sign of enemy was seen. Patrol proceeded through hedge to enemy's trenches, threw two bombs, & retired. Enemy sent up Very lights but did not open fire.

Artillery. Our artillery opened heavy bombardment at 10.50 am which lasted continuously until about 12.30 pm. Field guns & Heavies. Considerable damage appeared to be done to enemy's wire & trenches, guns sweeping the whole front of THIEPVAL. Enemy made feeble retaliation in the direction of AUTHUILLE.

Trench Mortars. Inaction.

State of Trenches. Trenches are rather muddy after last night's rain. No further damage has been done by enemy's fire.

State of Wire. No further damage has been done to wire by enemy's fire. Wiring was carried on undisturbed during the night.

Working Parties. Work of cleaning up trenches has been carried on where needed. Also on construction of new latrines.

Materials most needed. Sand-bags, revetting material. Small rifle-rests.

James G Whitehead
Lieut. for Lieut. Col.

14th Brigade.

32nd Division.

19th BATTALION

LANCASHIRE FUSILIERS

MARCH 1 9 1 6

Appendices attached:-

Daily Situation Reports.

Instructions regarding War Diaries and Intelligence Summaries are contained in F. S. Regs., Part II. and the Staff Manual respectively. Title Pages will be prepared in manuscript.

WAR DIARY
or
~~INTELLIGENCE SUMMARY~~
(Erase heading not required.)

Army Form C. 2118

Place	Date	Hour	Summary of Events and Information	Remarks and references to Appendices
	MARCH 1916			
ALBERT – SUBSECTOR E2	1		Battn relieved 6th RL BERKSHIRE REGT in Subsector E2, relief started at 8-30 a.m. & completed at 1-15 p.m.; due to only one communication trench. A & B Coy hold the front line, C Coy in Support, D Coy in Reserve. Subsector lies S.W of village of LA BOISSELLE – 15 HLI hold line on our right 2nd MANCHESTER Regt on our left. Trenches are muddy & uncomfortable	
SUBSECTOR E2	2		Quiet day – C & D Coys worked on trenches.	
SUBSECTOR E2 – ALBERT	3		Relieved by 2 K.O.Y.L.I of the 97 INF BDE, relief started at 4 pm completed at 9-30 p.m. Battn returned to Billets in ALBERT, last company arrived 12.30 p.m. Bn HQ in the WHITE CHATEAU.	
ALBERT	4.		All Coys on fatigue. Mining, carrying mining stores, clearing trenches in SUBSECTOR E3	
	5.		Billets, Fatigues	
	6		C & D Coys move to village of AVELUY – 14 Bde now holds SUBSECTORS E3 – F1.	
	7		ENEMY put a few shells into ALBERT one fell in the garden of the CHATEAU.	

1875 Wt. W593/826 1,000,000 4/15 J.B.C. & A. A.D.S.S./Forms/C. 2118.

Army Form C. 2118

Instructions regarding War Diaries and Intelligence Summaries are contained in F. S. Regs., Part II. and the Staff Manual respectively. Title Pages will be prepared in manuscript.

WAR DIARY
or
INTELLIGENCE SUMMARY
(Erase heading not required.)

Place	Date	Hour	Summary of Events and Information	Remarks and references to Appendices
	MARCH 1916			
ALBERT	8		In Billets. All Coys on fatigues.	
ALBERT – SUBSECTOR F1.	9		Battn relieved 15 H.L.I. in SUBSECTOR F1. Relief started 10 a.m. & completed 12-30 p.m. B, C & D Coys in the front line. A Coy in Reserve. 1/DORSET REGT on our Right. 2nd RL INNISKILLING FUS. on our left. Trenches lie in front of & W of village of OVILLERS la BOISSELLE. Front trenches rather poor.	
SUBSECTOR F1	10		B. Coy lines shelled with Enemy Howitzers, a dug out blown in causing the following casualties 2 Other Ranks killed & 2 wounded. Hard frost etc in greatly impeding work & causing the banks of trenches to fall in.	
	11.		Enemy bombarded with light shells the front of our SUBSECTOR starting at 11.30. C Coy lines received most attention, some 180 shells in all. But after our Artillery replied, the Enemy then switched on to the SUBSECTORS on our left, with shells of all calibre. No casualties were caused in our line.	

1875 Wt. W593/826 1,000,000 4/15 J.B.C. & A. A.D.S.S./Forms/C. 2118.

Army Form C. 2118

Instructions regarding War Diaries and Intelligence Summaries are contained in F. S. Regs., Part II. and the Staff Manual respectively. Title Pages will be prepared in manuscript.

WAR DIARY
or
INTELLIGENCE SUMMARY
(Erase heading not required.)

Place	Date	Hour	Summary of Events and Information	Remarks and references to Appendices
	MARCH	1916		
SUBSECTOR F1	12		Bombardment on our left was apparently the preparation for an hostile raid. 2 Patrols were sent out to gain information about NO MANS LAND no exciting event occurred.	
	13.		'A' Coy relieved 'B' Coy on the right of the SUBSECTOR. Lt GUILLAUME owing to shock & loss of memory left the trenches & was found wandering about the country.	
	14.		Two hostile aeroplanes crossed our lines & returned at about 9-30 pm. noise plainly heard but although it was a bright moonlight night these could not be seen.	
SUBSECTOR F1 - MILLENCOURT	15.		Battn relieved by 15 HLI relief completed at 9.15 pm. and Battn moved into DIVISIONAL RESERVE at MILLENCOURT.	
MILLENCOURT	16		In billets & all Coys cleaning up. 2/Lt STATHAM DORSET REGT atto this BATTN. went to hospital	
	17		In billets. Capt E W. LYON went to hospital suffering from acute Neuralgia.	
	18.		Some training done.	

1875 Wt. W593/826 1,000,000 4/15 J.B.C. & A. A.D.S.S./Forms/C. 2118.

Army Form C. 2118

Instructions regarding War Diaries and Intelligence Summaries are contained in F. S. Regs., Part II. and the Staff Manual respectively. Title Pages will be prepared in manuscript.

WAR DIARY
or
INTELLIGENCE SUMMARY
(Erase heading not required.)

Place	Date	Hour	Summary of Events and Information	Remarks and references to Appendices
	MARCH			
MILLENCOURT	19		Resting in Billets – SUNDAY.	
"	20		Continued Training.	
MILLENCOURT SUBSECTOR F1	21		Relieved 15 H.L.I. in SUBSECTOR F1. Relief started at 7 pm completed at 8.45 pm. A.B. & D Coys in the front line. 'C' Coy in Reserve. 1/DORSET REGT ~~Dorsets~~ on our right 16 LANCASHIRE FUS. on our left	
F1. SUBSECTOR	22		Quiet on both sides	
"	23		Heavy fall of snow. Usual few shells in the sector causing no damage	
	24		Quiet. Front line Coys worked at wiring. Reserve Coy in the communication trenches.	
	25		Quiet day. no operations	
	~~[illegible]~~		~~[illegible]~~	
[illegible]	26		No operations. Preparations made to support the 1 DORSET REGT on our Right in the RAID on 'Y. SAP' opposite SUBSECTOR E3 Raid to commence at 12.15 a.m. 27th	

1875 Wt. W593/826 1,000,000 4/15 J.B.C. & A. A.D.S.S./Forms/C. 2118.

Army Form C. 2118

Instructions regarding War Diaries and Intelligence Summaries are contained in F. S. Regs., Part II. and the Staff Manual respectively. Title Pages will be prepared in manuscript.

WAR DIARY
or
INTELLIGENCE SUMMARY

(Erase heading not required.)

Place	Date	Hour	Summary of Events and Information	Remarks and references to Appendices
SUBSECTOR F1 – ALBERT	27		12.27 am A mine was exploded on our Right. Our artillery immediately opened fire, on the FRONT of SUBSECTORS F1 E3. Enemy replied. Lewis guns & BDE MACHINE GUNS played on the enemy parapets. Casualties caused in the Battn by shell fire 4 men wounded. Our artillery ceased fire at 12.50 am & situation was normal at 2 a.m.	
			Battn was relieved by 15 H.L.I. relief completed at 9.45 pm & the Battn marched into BDE RESERVE. A & B Coy at AVELUY & C & D Coy in ALBERT. C.O. went on leave MAJOR H.G. HARRISON in command.	
ALBERT & AVELUY	28		All Coy employed on working parties. Continuous mining fatigue of 156 men in 2–8 hour shifts.	
	29.		Same as day before	
	30			
	31		31/3/16 H.G. Harrison Major Comm.dg 19th Lancashire Fusiliers	

1875 Wt. W593/826 1,000,000 4/15 J.B.C. & A. A.D.S.S./Forms/C. 2118.

Daily Situation Report.
24 hours 1-2nd March. 1916.

Situation normal. Quiet night except for enemy Machine Gun activity.

Patrols. No patrols. Two front line Coys each sent out one Officer & two men to examine our wire. Wire found to be weak generally but bad in front of Trench 119.

Artillery. Artillery reaches - See Intelligence report

State of Trenches. Better than can be expected after recent snow and frost. Work going on fixing up fire trenches and main communication trenches - Water and mud in front line & communication trenches over one foot deep in places.

Working Parties from Reserve & Support Coys - repairing and clearing up trenches where most needed.

Materials needed. Revetting materials, mud scoops, and Sand-bags.

A. Rupert Moxey
Lieut.
Adjutant.

Daily Situation Report

24 hours   5th–6th Feb. 1916.

Situation Normal.

Patrols. 2/Lieut. Whittles, 1 N.C.O. & 1 man went out from point R 25 c 3.9 at 1.55 am. & returned 2.50 am. Object: to reconnoitre edge of DIAMOND WOOD – pt. R 25 c 5.8 & to see if supposed Machine Gun emplacement was occupied by enemy. Very thick brushwood was found along edge of WOOD – No signs of enemy were heard.

Lieut. Musker & 2 N.C.O's went out from pt. R 25 a 4.5 at 2.15 am. & returned 4.30 am. Object: to reconnoitre SUNKEN ROAD & ground where Lt. Dixon was last seen. Sounds of enemy working was heard & patrol approached SUNKEN ROAD. Enemy appear to be digging along SUNKEN ROAD & an advanced covering party was seen. 1 N.C.O. was sent back to fire trench & our Machine Gun was laid on SUNKEN Rd. Patrol threw two bombs at enemy & retired. Enemy opened rifle fire from other side of SUNKEN ROAD. We then sent up a Very light & opened Machine Gun fire. All sounds of work then ceased.

Artillery. About 4.15 pm. enemy opened fire on JOHNSON POST & GORDON CASTLE, in retaliation to our morning Shrap. 40 or 50 shells were fired – H.E. & Shrapnel. No damage was done. Immediately afterwards batteries appeared to switch on to AUTHUILLE & salvoes were heard going in that direction. Occasional single shots were fired during this morning.

Trench Mortars. Occasional 'Oil-cans' have been fired during this morning. At about 5.15 pm. enemy commenced his usual practice of sending over 'Oil-cans' & rifle-grenades on trenches 157, 158 & 159. Damage was done to trenches in places

State of Trenches. Still slightly muddy after rain: although improvement is being carried on gradually. George St. is being rapidly improved.

State of Wire. No further damage has been done to wire, although in many places in the centre of the Sector it is decidedly weak. Our wiring parties were again working last night.

Working Parties. 15/H.L.I. have done good work on George St. & also on Trench 159.

Materials needed. Small knife rests are needed.

James Whitehead

Lieut. for Lt-Col.

Commanding 19th. Service Bn.
Lancashire Fusiliers, 3rd. Salford Bn.

Situation Report. 24 hours. 9–10th March 1916.

Situation normal – quiet 24 hours. Wind N.E.

Patrols. See Intelligence Report.

Artillery. Slight activity on both sides. Our artillery vigorously shelled OVILLIERS LA BOISELLE with H.E. and Shrapnel, yesterday afternoon.
Enemy fired several whiz-bangs opposite Trench 133. No damage done.

Trench Mortars. Inactive.

State of Trenches. Still in very bad condition, especially in front line. Working parties engaged pumping the day & night. Marked improvement apparent.

State of Wire. General condition good but very poor in places. Very weak opposite Trench 134. Wire being repaired with all speed.

Working Parties. Two platoons of 17th N.F. engaged repairing trench & parados in CONNISTON STREET. Parties of own reserve Coy. engaged repairing Trenches throughout sub. sector.

Materials most needed. Sandbags, trench boards, wiring posts. revetting material.

A Rupert Morley Lieut.
Adjutant for Lieut.-Col.
Comdg. 19th Lancs. Fus.

19th S. Bn Lancashire Fusiliers

Situation Report - 24 hours - 23rd March 1916

Situation normal quiet 24 hours. Wind S.W. and weather inclined to be wet.

Patrols - See Intelligence Report

Artillery inactive on both sides. We sent over a few light shells this am. Enemy replied with 10 [illegible] on to the Support trench. Usual Trench Mortars & Rifle grenade exchanges.

State of Trenches - improving. Work was done on clearing Fishmongers St, Drummond St, Kirkgate Avenue, Chief St, Arbroath St, Thames Tunnel, New C.O.'s dug out. No wiring was done but this needs attention.

Materials - Trench Boards, Sand Bags, Nine Straps, Posts for wiring.

Lieut & Adjt.
for Lieut Col.
Comdg 19th Lancashire Fusrs

Situation Report.

24 hours 10–11th March 1916.

Sub-Sector F.1.

Situation normal at present.

Patrols. None sent out.

Artillery. Very active on both sides. Enemy shelled trenches 131, 132 & 133 with Hows. at about 4.50 pm. About 50 shells fell, damaging trenches slightly. One dug-out was knocked in, killing 2 men & wounding two.

6.15 pm. Our own field guns opened fire by mistake in response to two red lights sent up by enemy.

10.30 pm. Asked artillery for S.O.S. test. Batteries fired 10 shells within one minute of order leaving Orderly Room. About 20 minutes afterwards enemy opened fire on trenches 131–133 & MITCHELL ST. with field guns, in salvoes of four. About 150 shells came over. Our own field guns replied on enemy trenches in front of F.1. Sub-Sector. Enemy then opened heavy fire on the left, probably left of F.2. & G.1. Sub-Sectors, with howitzers & field guns. Our own artillery replied.

Fire slackened at about midnight.

Hostile shelling did some damage to trenches 131, 132, 133, & MITCHELL ST. – not considerable.

Telephone communication with left Coy. was interrupted.

During the bombardment enemy How. shells were heard going in the direction of ALBERT & AVELUY.

11-0 am. About 10 light shells from enemy field guns fell into trench 133 & MITCHELL ST.

Noon – 3 pm. Intermittent enemy shelling into same area. Our guns have not replied.

Enemy are using flares, possibly attempting to

discover our artillery signals. About Nine red and green flares were sent up at 7 pm. 10° in front of Trench 133 - No activity observed.

Sentries reported other red flares in front of this Sector at about 10 am.

State of Trenches. Still very bad and wet. Trenches 131, 132, 133, & MITCHELL ST. damaged by hostile fire. The thaw is causing the sides of the trenches to fall in.

Trench 135 very poor and open to view of enemy on left flank. All available men worked during the night & afternoon clearing & improving, but the number available is quite insufficient.

State of Wire. Poor. Party wired in front of Trench 134 between 8 pm. & 11 pm. but bombardment interfered with working parties. Party going out to-night.

Working Parties. Men of Reserve Coy. engaged in THORSBY ST. LANCASTER AV. & Sap in Trench 135 & in building new cook house. R.E. working on dug-out at DONNET POST. Coys. in front line clearing, revetting & laying down trench boards.

Materials needed. Trench Boards, wiring posts, revetting materials. Also pumps, in good order.

A Rupert Huxley [illegible]

Lieut & Adjt.
for Lieut-Col

Commanding 19th. Service Bn.
Lancashire Fusiliers.

Situation Report.

24 hours 11–12th March, 1916.

Situation Normal. Quiet 24 hours.

Patrols. Please see Intelligence Report.

Artillery. Inactive on both sides.

10.5 am. Enemy put two salvoes of light shells near LOWER DONNET. Single shots have been fired by the enemy intermittently into trenches where work was going on. No damage done.

3.30 pm. Our field guns fired about 20 shots into Trench (X.7.b.9/9 – X.7.b.9/6) where enemy working party was heard hammering on iron. – hammering ceased.

Since then artillery have fired single shots intermittently.

A few rifle grenades came over into Trench 136 at "Stand to" this morning. No damage done.

State of Trenches. Improving with the weather but the thaw is causing banks to fall in.

Working Parties. R.E. working on C.O's new dug-out. Men of Reserve Coy. working on LANCASTER Av., THURSBY St. JOHN O GAUNT ST., new COOKHOUSE & two saps in Trench 136. Coys. in front line cleaning and improving trenches. Trenches 135 and 136 cleared, deepened & trench boards laid down, & overhead cover improved. Damage done to MITCHELL ST. & GRANGE ST. repaired. Good weather has allowed more work to be done, but number of men available is too small to shew great improvement.

State of Wire. Parties strengthened about 60 yards of Hasty Apron Fence in front of NEW TRENCH. Wiring also done in front of Trench 135. Wire still needs strengthening.

Materials needed. Wiring stakes 3'6", Trench boards, revetting material, Sand bags.

A Rupert Murray Lieut. & Adjt.
for Lieut. Col. Comdt. 19th B.

Situation Report
24 hours 12-13th March 1916.

Situation Normal. Quiet 24 hours.

Patrols. See Intelligence Report. Names of Officer & N.C.O. – 2/Lieut. C.A. STIEBEL & Sgt. PRESTWICH. Sgt. Prestwich was unfortunately wounded & the patrol was unable to discover any valuable information.

Artillery. Enemy fired four whiz-bangs into trench B2. Enemy also tried to locate one of our Field Batteries behind this sector. No other activity.

Our artillery action.

8.30 am. Field Guns fired four rounds at trench (X.7.b. 9/9 – X.7.b. 9/6.) where enemy were heard working.

12 noon – 2 pm. Field Battery fired 200 shells, cutting wire in front of enemy trenches (X.7b.9/6 – X.7b.9¾/5b). The wire was completely cut.

An intermittent fire has been & is being kept up by Field Guns on enemy trenches opposite this sector.

State of Trenches. Improving with good weather but still need a great deal of attention. LONGRIDGE St. has to be cleared & made serviceable.

Working Parties. Parties of Reserve Coy. engaged in cleaning up & laying trench boards in LANCASTER Av. JOHN O' GAUNT ST. 1 N.C.O. & 10 men working on new cookhouse. 4 N.C.O.s & 20 men on saps in trenches B5 & B6. Coys. in front line continue to improve their trenches. No. B5 cleared, trench boards laid down, parapet & parados built up, & overhead cover improved.

BARROW ST. pumped clear of water.

State of Wire – Needs much improvement. Wiring done in front of Trench 135. More wiring to be done to-night.

Materials Needed – Wiring Stakes. Trench boards.

A. Rupert [illegible] / Lieut. & Adjt.
for Lieut. Col.

Commanding 19th. Service Bn.
Lancashire Fusiliers.

Daily Situation Report

24 hours 13th - 14th March 1916.

Situation normal. Quiet 24 hours.

Patrols. See Intelligence Report.

Artillery. Enemy heavily shelled batteries behind this sector, & endeavoured to put pom-pom anti-aircraft gun out of action. No activity on part of our artillery.

Four red & 1 green flares were sent up by enemy opposite this sector at 8 pm. yesterday.

State of Trenches. Much improved & quite dry in places. Front line trenches require organised working parties in order to sand-bag — revet the parapet & parados, & also relay trench-boards.

Working Parties. Work has been continued on LANCASTER AV. & JOHN O GAUNT ST., saps in trenches 135 & 136, & on new cook-house.

Coys. worked on their front line trenches, & Centre Coy. improved fire-step in GRANGE ST. & BARROW ST.

State of Wire. Wiring was done along whole front last night. Bright moonlight greatly interfered with work until early morning. Wire still requires a great deal of attention before it becomes an impassable barrier to the enemy.

Materials Needed. Screw Posts, trench ladders, & cross-handles.

[illegible] Lieut. & Adjt.

for Lieut. Col.

Commanding 18th Service Bn.

Lancashire Fusiliers.

Situation Report. F.1. Sub-Sector.
24 hours. 14th–15th March 1916.

Situation normal. Quiet 24 hours.

Patrols. See Intelligence Report.

Artillery. Inaction on both sides.
2 pm. Enemy sent over a few light shells below DONNET POST, due to men walking outside trench.
No further activity on either side.
Enemy put several rifle-grenades into Trench 135 and over Trench 134, which is some distance from enemy away.
Our own rifle-grenades are useless at this range.

State of Trenches. Improving, but work still needed.

Working Parties. Work carried on in same trenches as yesterday. About 110 men of reserve Coy. employed. Coys. in front line at work on their trenches.
Party of 30 cleared & deepened LONGRIDGE ST.
Two platoons of 17th Northumberland Fusiliers at work in CONISTON ST.

State of Wire. More wire put out last night, but wire still needs great attention.

Materials Needed. Wiring Stakes & Trench ladders.

A. Rupert [illegible]

Lieut. & Adjt.
for Lieut. Col.
Comdg. 19th Lancs. Fus.

Situation Report.

24 hours 21st - 22nd March 1916.

F.1. Sub-Sector.

Situation normal. Quiet 24 hours.

Patrols. Nil.

Artillery - Activity nil on both sides until 2 p.m. When wire-cutting operations commenced against enemy wire opposite trenches at X.8.C.2040. 100 shrapnel and 20 H.E. were fired.

During observation of above, enemy sniped our observation post with "pip-squeaks".

State of trenches. Improved. Fort fire trench in very bad condition, especially on the left where whole trench needs ~~rebuilding, i.e.~~ revetting & making & fire-steps remade.

Working Parties. One platoon of 17th Northumberland Fusiliers at work constructing fire-bays in CONISTON ST.

Party of 4 N.C.O's & 24 men of reserve Coy. working on Sap X.7.9.

Parties clearing St. Vincent Street and Pendle Hill Street.

State of Wire. Still very bad, and in places non-existent. This will be attended to to-night.

Materials urgently needed. Wiring stakes, 12 box periscopes to complete look-outs. Wood material for knife-rests, trench-boards, revetting stakes - iron.

A. Rupert ... [illegible]
Lieut. & Adjt.
for Lieut.-Col.
Comdg. 19th Lancs. Fus.

Situation Report
24 hrs. 22nd – 23rd March, 1916.

F.1. Sub-Sector.

Situation normal. Rain during afternoon and Night of 22–23rd March, 1916. Wind – E.

Patrols. 2/Lieut. Hurley & one other rank went out from X.7.2 at 7.30 pm. Patrol went forward 200 yds. then turned half-right & struck Sunken Road about X.7.d 50/35, returned via road, to our own wire, went along this towards starting point X.7.3. Patrol returned at 9.0 pm.

Object of Patrol was to discover any copper wire. None was found.

Covering party for parties wiring in front of X.7.8 also patrolled with similar object (to find copper wire) but discovered Nothing.

Artillery. Inactive.

4 pm. Four whiz-bangs fell about X.7.5 & at 7.30 pm another whiz-bang fell at X.7.7. No damage was done.

2.30 pm to-day. Enemy fired two whiz-bangs at the fire trench end of RIVINGTON ST. and four between X.7.5 – X.7.4. No damage done.

Our Field guns cutting wire at point in front of enemy line – X.8.c 05/65. Still firing. F.O.O. proposes to use between 100 & 150 rounds.

Enemy using rifle grenades against X.7.6 – X.7.5. No casualties nor damage.

State of Trenches. Not improved by recent rain.

Working Parties. Parties clearing JOHN O'GAUNT ST. & RIVINGTON ST. Saps between X.7.9 – X.7.7.

LONGRIDGE ST. being cleared and work done on new cook house.

R.E. at work on new bomb-store & dug-out at [illegible] POST.

Front line coys. working on their sections of Trench, revetting, clearing & sand-bagging.

State of Wire. Portion wired in front of X.7.9, X.7.8., X.7.6 & X.7.3. last night.

Although the higher wire is broken & looks weak, there is a great deal of loose & trip wire.

Materials needed. Screw posts, sand-bags, & 6' x 3'6" iron posts for revetting.

A. Rupert Moxey Lieut.
Adjutant.

Situation Report
24 hours 4 pm 23rd to 4 pm 24th March 1916.
Sub-Sector P.1.

Situation normal. All quiet on front of this sub-sector during last 24 hours. Very heavy fall of snow during early morning. Wind - S-S.W.

Patrols. No patrols sent out.
Whilst wiring parties were out their covering parties searched for enemy copper wire. Nothing discovered.

Artillery. Inactive.
Our artillery continued wire-cutting operations opposite point X.13.9 until about 4.30pm yesterday.
About 4-5 pm enemy dropped a few whiz-bangs in vicinity of point X.7.5. No damage done.
Four rifle grenades fell into our wire opposite point X.7.5 between 8.45 pm and 9.0 pm.

Sniping. Enemy displays considerable activity with rifle & machine gun from direction of OVILLIERS-LA BOISELLE.

State of Trenches. Poor. It is expected that work of cleaning trenches will be greatly impaired by present weather conditions.

Working Parties. As yesterday.
Party of 100 men of 2nd/10th Manchester Regiment at work on OVILLERS POST.

State of Wire. Improving. More wiring done during Night.

Materials urgently needed.

Iron screw stakes for wiring.

6' & 3'6" iron stakes for revetting.

Lieut. & Adjt.
for Lieut-Col
Comndg. 19th Lancs. Fus.

Situation Report
24 hours 24th – 25th March 1916.

Sub-Sector. F.1.

Situation normal. Quiet 24 hours. Wind – S.W.

Patrols. None sent out.

Artillery. Inaction on both sides on this Front.
10 pm Enemy fired 3 whiz-bangs into Point X.7.10.
8-0 am Whiz bang dropped near DONNET POST.
2-30 pm A few light shells fell at Junction of CONISTON ST. and JOHN O' GAUNT ST. No damage done.
5 rifle grenades fell about Point X.7.6 No damage done.

State of Trenches. Improved since yesterday. Gradually drying up.

Working Parties. Usual parties continued work on JOHN O' GAUNT ST., LONGRIDGE ST., Saps. LANCASTER AV., CONISTON ST.
Coys. in front line cleaning up trenches & laying down sump boards.
Overhead Cover erected in X.7.7.8.

State of Wire. Some improvement in state of wire. Party wired in front of X.7.4-5 from 9.30pm.

Materials needed. Screw posts, Iron Stakes for revetting, & material for Raise rests.

A Kippet Murray Lieut. & Adjt.
for Lieut-Col.
Comndg. 19th Lancs Fus.

Situation Report
24 hours 25th to 26th March, 1916.
F. 1 Sub-Sector.

Situation Normal. Wind - S - S.W.

Patrols: Patrol consisting of 2/Lieut. E.C.E. CHAMBERS and Pte Howarth went out from point X.13.9 at 10 pm. After walking along the South side of the Sunken road for about 30 yds. they turned on to the road but found nothing; owing to enemy sniping along the road they turned off the road and advanced along side of same for about 100 yards, when patrol turned onto the road again but did not see or hear any signs of the enemy. Patrol then returned along South side of the road and entered advanced trench at point X.13.9 at 11.15 pm.

(2). Patrol consisting of 2/Lieut. C.A. STIEBEL and Pte Clarke went out from Sap in X.7.6 at 10.30 pm. and returned at 11.30 pm. No enemy patrol was encountered, seen or heard.

Artillery. No special activity.

Enemy fired about 12 light shells into X13.9 and WHALLEY ST. Slight damage done, but has now been repaired.

Also, a few whiz-bangs fell into X.7.3, X.7.5 X.7.9 & X.7.10. Damage done has been repaired.

Hostile rifle grenades fell [illegible] near to Coy. H.Q. in CARTMELL ST. and in front of X.7.5.

State of Trenches. No improvement. Rain has hindered work considerably.

Working Parties. As yesterday. Work of cleaning up trenches continued.

Men have been kept busy in front & communication trenches pumping & making new sump-holes.

(1).

State of Wire. No work done on this.

Three parties sent out at 7.30 pm. in front of X7. 4-5 but were unable to do any work owing to hostile machine-gun fire.

Materials needed. Iron screw posts.

A. Rupert [illegible]
Lieut. & Adjt.
for Lieut. Col.
Comdg. 19th Lancs Fus.

Situation Report
24 hours 26th – 27th March 1916
F.1. Sub-Sector.

Situation normal. Wind – S.S.W. Rain

1. Patrols. None sent out

2. Artillery. Quiet on both sides until 12.19 am when mine was exploded in Sub Sector E.3

Immediately after explosion our artillery opened fire behind enemy lines at La Boisselle and Ovillers. Enemy replied mainly on Sub-Sector E.3 but some light shells ~~[illegible]~~ along our line slightly damaging our wire and trenches and causing four slight casualties. Our artillery quieted down at 12.50 am, enemy continued until about 1.45 am. At 2.0 am all was quiet again.

x 11 am Enemy fired one whiz-bang at DONNET POST.

2 pm A few light shells fell into Trench X.13.8.

x 12 am Our 8" howitzers shelled LA BOISELLE intermittently.

4.10 pm Enemy fired two salvoes in direction of New Cook House, Trench Railway Valley, X7.9. No damage done.

3 Trench Mortars Two 3" Stokes T.M. were placed in WALTNEY ST and ESTWAITE ST. respectively yesterday. These fired about 60 rounds into enemy wire and trenches opposite X7. 7-8 during bombardment.

Miscellaneous Dummy figures were put out in front of X7.5 & X7.4. Some difficulty was experienced in getting these out in front of X7.4, as enemy played machine guns along the front. During the bombardment these figures drew a good deal of machine gun fire, and even some artillery.

Enemy appeared to be rather anxious during the

early part of the Night, numerous flares being sent up and much machine gun firing. Anxiety was further increased by fire of our own machine guns at about 12 midnight; enemy replied with heavy machine gun fire & sent up very lights continuously.

State of Trenches. Bad. Some drying up yesterday afternoon but rain to-day is hinder any improvement.

Working Parties. Usual working parties cleaning trenches, laying trump boards & mending these. Pumping and making new sump pits.

Damage done to front line by shell fire has been repaired. Work continued on new cook-house.

State of Wire. Slightly damaged by enemy artillery in front of X7.4-5 and X7.9-10.

No work was done on wire last night.

A Rupert [illegible]

Lieut. & Adjt.
for Major,
Comndg. 19th Lancs. Fus.

14th Brigade.

32nd Division.

19th BATTALION

LANCASHIRE FUSILIERS

APRIL 1 9 1 6

Appendices attached:-

Battalion Operation Orders.

Situation Reports.

Sheet 1

Instructions regarding War Diaries and Intelligence Summaries are contained in F. S. Regs., Part II. and the Staff Manual respectively. Title Pages will be prepared in manuscript.

WAR DIARY
or
INTELLIGENCE SUMMARY
(Erase heading not required.)

Army Form C. 2118

19th LANCASHIRE FUS.

Place	Date	Hour	Summary of Events and Information 1916	Remarks and references to Appendices
ALBERT & AVELUY	APRIL 1.		Bn in Bde Reserve A & B Coys ALBERT, C & D Coys detached at AVELUY – Draft of 1 officer (2Lt I. JONES) and 13 other ranks arrived –	
	2.		In Bde Reserve & finding working parties.	
ALBERT – AUTHUILLE SUBSECTOR	3		Bn relieved 16 N.F in AUTHUILLE SUBSECTOR commencing at 7 p.m. 'C' Coy RIGHT FRONT, D Coy LEFT FRONT, B Coy in SUPPORT, A Coy in Shelters at CRUCIFIX CORNER – A Battn of 70th Bde on our RIGHT, 1/DORSET REGT on our LEFT – TRENCHES lie S.W of village of THIEPVAL. See Bde Operation orders App II	
AUTHUILLE SUBSECTOR	4		Quiet day, no operations	
	5			
	6.		Bn Readjustment of FRONT held by Bde. Bn took over another 500 yds of TRENCH and 'B' Coy moved in on the LEFT. D Coy holding CENTRE A Coy moved up into SUPPORT. Bn now holds line from MERSEY ST to KILMUN ST See APPENDIX III	FOR DETAIL SEE DAILY SITUATION REPORT ATTD. APP I
	8.			
AUTHUILLE SUBSECTOR & AVELUY.	9		Bn relieved by 2nd MANCHESTER REGT and proceeded to BILLETS in AVELUY where working parties of about 550 men had to be supplied – One other rank wounded – Bde Operation order attached (See APP II)	

1875 Wt. W593/826 1,000,000 4/15 J.B.C. & A. A.D.S.S./Forms/C. 2118.

Sheet 2

Army Form C. 2118

Instructions regarding War Diaries and Intelligence Summaries are contained in F. S. Regs., Part II. and the Staff Manual respectively. Title Pages will be prepared in manuscript.

WAR DIARY
or
INTELLIGENCE SUMMARY

(Erase heading not required.)

Place	Date APRIL	Hour	Summary of Events and Information	Remarks and references to Appendices
AVELUY	10		Bn in Bde SUPPORT – Fatigues again – Enemy shelled village – 3 other ranks wounded	
AVELUY & WARLOY	11.		Bn relieved by XI BORDER REGT (97 BDE), relief commenced at 10.45 pm. Bn clear of AVELUY by 11-30 pm. and moved to BILLETS in WARLOY, all in by 2-30 a.m. 12th inst. See APP II for Bde operation orders ~~and App E for Battn Op Orders~~	Cops of Bn
WARLOY.	12		In BILLETS cleaning up.	
	13.		Training commenced.	
	14		Training in Billets	
	15.		Continued training in billets – 2Lt STIEBEL sprained or broke his ankle and went to hospital	
	16.		SUNDAY – CHURCH PARADES only.	
	17.		Continued training in billets, 2Lt WOOD and 2 other ranks wounded while at Bomb Practice – 2Lt WOOD's ~~[illegible]~~ right hand was blown off. This officer no doubt saved several lives by attempting to throw away a badly thrown bomb.	
	18.		Continued training – Capt HEYWOOD rejoined Battn.	
	19.		" " 2 other ranks accidentally wounded.	

Army Form C. 2118

Sheet 3

Instructions regarding War Diaries and Intelligence Summaries are contained in F. S. Regs., Part II. and the Staff Manual respectively. Title Pages will be prepared in manuscript.

WAR DIARY
or
INTELLIGENCE SUMMARY
(Erase heading not required.)

Place	Date	Hour	Summary of Events and Information	Remarks and references to Appendices
	APRIL			
WARLOY	20		Battn continued training in Billets – Fighting kit adopted – Haversack in place of pack and water proof sheet securely attached to the belt below Haversack.	
	22		Training in Billets	
	23.		Battn moved to RUBEMPRE via CONTAY. HERISSART – and took over billets from 96th Inf Bde (2 Rl Inniskilling Fus) – Area known as DIVISIONAL TRAINING AREA See Bde op. order App II. Battn op order App V	
	24.		Battn started training – Lt EVANS joined Battn –	
	25.		Training in Billets	
	26		do –	
	27		Divisional Tactical Exercise. Consisted of attacking & capturing the 1st and 2nd line system of trenches – 14 Bde in DIVISIONAL RESERVE – Extremely warm day as men wore Steel Helmets they were rather done at the finish – Bde. Bn operation orders attached App IV	
	28		Flammenwerfer Display near CONTAY – about 6 officers & 20 other ranks attended	
	29		Training continued – Flammenwerfer display again whole Bn attended. 2/Lt CARTMELL and 2/Lt SHIELS joined Bn from G.H.Q CADET SCHOOL	
	30		SUNDAY. No WORK –	

J.M. Graham [signature]
Lt Col
Commanding 19th Service Bn.
Lancashire Fusiliers.

1875 Wt. W593/826 1,000,000 4/15 J.B.C. & A. A.D.S.S./Forms/C. 2118.

WAR DIARY
19 LANCASHIRE FUS.

APPENDICES to WAR DIARY

APP I - Daily Situation Report & Intelligence Reports of Battn while in front line trenches

APP II - Bde Operation Orders

APP III - Readjustment of line held by 14 Bde

APP IV - Bde and Battn Operation Orders for Divisional Tactical Scheme 27th April

APP V - Battn operation order for move from CONTAY - RUBEMPRE

Daily Situation Report APPENDIX I

24 hours 5 pm 3/4/16 to 5 pm 4/4/16.

Sub-Sector F G 1.

Situation Normal Wind – North.

1. Patrols: None sent out.

2. Artillery. 10.45 am Enemy fired about twenty 15 cm. shells behind X1.7. No damage was done.

1 pm Enemy commenced to put over Shrapnel near COOK-HOUSE in TRENCH RAILWAY VALLEY. These came over by single shots with about 2 minutes interval until 3 pm. Enemy then increased his range and shells went over CRUCIFIX CORNER to AVELUY.

3.30 pm In reply to our Trench Mortars enemy put over about twenty whiz-bangs in direction of this mortar.

Occasional whiz-bangs fell intermittently around WOOD POST during the day.

3. Trench Mortars. Enemy Trench mortars very active this morning, & blew in part of fire trench in X1.8.

In retaliation at 3.30 pm light Trench mortars put over some forty rounds into enemy front line along with about eleven rounds from heavy T.M.

Some damage is presumed as one bomb fell on part of enemy line where work was doing.

4. State of Trenches. Dry but likely to be muddy and wet in bad weather. Parapets rather crumbly all along the line & need attention. Communication trenches

need cleaning and sump boards put down.

Working Parties. Men in front line cleaning up and doing minor repairs to their part of trench. Filling sandbags preparation to building up the parapet during the night.

State of Wire. No wiring done during the night. This needs attention, especially in front of X1.8. Wiring parties are going out to-night.

Materials Needed. Screw posts. Iron Stakes 6 ft. & 3' 6" for revetting. Timber for latrines.

(s'd) A.R.M.

Lieut. & Adjt.

for Major.

Comndg. 19th Lancers. Fane's Horse.

Situation Report
4th – 5th April
Sub-Sector F.G.1.

Situation normal. Very quiet day. Wind – N.

1. Patrols. See Intelligence Report.

2. Artillery. 10·50 am Our Field guns put about 10 shells into enemy trench at Point X1·a·6/8 and did some damage.
3·30 pm Field guns again sent over few shells into enemy trenches at Point X1·a·7/7.
In reply to latter, enemy sent over about 20 whiz-bangs into and around WOOD POST

3. Trench Mortars. Inaction on both sides.

4. State of Trenches. Dry. Sandbagging is giving way in many places and causing the parapets to bulge and fall in.

5. Working Parties. 1 N.C.O. and 20 men at work on Lyon Street, clearing and deepening and laying Trench boards.
1 N.C.O. + 6 men engaged on new latrine at WOOD POST.
Support Coy. carrying meals to firing line.
Parapet built up in places and part of trench knocked in by enemy trench mortar repaired.

6. State of Wire. Wire put out in front of X1·7 and X1·5. Our wire is moderately strong a good deal of loose wire lying about.

Materials needed. Timber for latrines; revetting stakes gratings half gratings for fire-steps.

[signature illegible] for Major Commdg 17. L.F.

Situation Report.

24 hours 5 pm 5/4/16 to 5 pm 6/4/16.

Sub-Sector F.G.1.

Situation Normal. Wind N.E.

1. Patrols. See Intelligence Report.

2. Artillery. Inactive on both sides. Our field guns put a few shells into enemy's front line possibly for ranging purposes.

3. Trench Mortars. Our Trench Mortars fired 10 rounds at party working in enemy trench at X1. b. 2/8. These fell within 10 yards of party and work ceased. Enemy replied with with 6 oil cans, which all fell about 30 yds short of our trenches.

4 State of Trenches. No great improvement since yesterday. – Still quite good and dry.

5. Working Parties. 1 N.C.O. and 15 men at work on LIME STREET. Damage done by hostile fire to this was repaired. 2 Refuse pits were dug behind X1. 7-6. Parapet repaired in places in the front line. New Latrines in X1-5 and at WOOD POST. not quite completed.

6. State of Wire – Improved. Wire put out in front of X1. 7. 5-4.

7. Materials Required. Trench Boards.

A Rupert Winney[illegible]

[illegible] Adjt

for Major.

Comdg. 19 Lancs. Fusiliers

Situation Report

6th – 7th April 1916 5 pm to 5 pm

Sub Sector F.G.1.

Situation unchanged.

1. Patrols. None sent out.

2. Artillery. Enemy artillery active.

Between 7 pm & 8 pm heavy bombardment on the left in direction of HAMEL. Heavy shells probably 15 cm passed over this Sub Sector to HAMEL from direction of CONTALMAISON.

Two salvoes of 3 light shells fell at DUMP, TRENCH RAILWAY in AUTHUILLE WOOD at 12.15 am and at 2.45 am.

Between 11.30 am & 12.30 pm enemy sent over about 30 or 40 15 C.M. shells, which fell around Coy. H.Q. in AINTREE ST., somewhat damaging this trench. Enemy were probably searching for T.M. Battery.

2 pm Enemy fired a few 77 mm shells into AUTHUILLE WOOD by TRENCH RAILWAY DUMP. One railway truck damaged. Enemy then kept up single shots at this same place, no further damage.

Our guns fired a few light shells in enemy trench at point X1 6 2/8, where working party was again seen.

3. Trench Mortar. Fired four rounds at about 8 pm. A great column of earth went up & it is presumed that shots fell into enemy trench. Bombing Officer fired about 25 Rifle grenades at working party of point 41 – good results.

State of Trenches. Sticky owing to light rain last night

Working Parties. 1 N.C.O. and 15 men in MOUNT EAGLE ST. and LIME ST. deepening and laying down trench boards.

1 N.C.O. & 10 men worked all night in Trench X1-6 reclaiming broken in part of trench. A similar party on all day.

About 20 men working on WOOD POST defences, adjusting old loop holed trenches, left by the French, and building up parapet.

1 N.C.O. & 6 men clearing up and relaying trench-boards in ROCK ST.

Party of 10 men making wire balls.

State of Wire. Wiring done in front of X1-5 and N 6-1-2. Wire balls to be put out to night.

Materials needed. Wiring stakes, barbed wire, sandbags, revetting stakes - iron.

[illegible] Lieut. & Adjt.
for Lieut-Col.
Comdg. 19. Lancs. Fus.

Situation Report

7 to 8 April 1916 5 pm to 5 pm

Sub Sector F.G.1

Situation normal Quiet 24 hours.

1. Patrols. 2/Lieut. N. Whitten went out last night but it was too light to get near to enemy line. All appeared to be quiet.

2. Artillery. No special activity. Enemy continues to put occasional shots (77mm) near DUMP on TRENCH RAILWAY.

In reply to 2 Trench Mortar Bombs, enemy fired about 25 77mm shells near to Coy H.Q. in DAVAAR STREET. Our guns did not reply.

Our own Field guns have been firing into the enemy lines in front of this sector. As most of these shells are going over into 2nd line no observation could be obtained from our lines.

3. Trench Mortars. 14/2 T.M. Battery sent over two shells into enemy line opposite R.31.1. Groans were heard when these exploded in the enemy trench.

4. Trenches. Their good, improving a lot on the left. One can now easily walk along the front of the whole sub-sector.

5. Working Party. Work of deepening trenches & laying trenchboards continued in MONTEAGLE & LIME ST.

Latrines at WOOD POST completed.

Party making wire balls.

Work being done in front line building up and revetting parapet, relaying trenchboards.

6. Wiring. State of wire slightly improved. Wiring done in front of R. 31-1 & Q. 36-2, also in front of Q. 36.1 – N. 6-1 & 1.5.

7. Materials needed. Barbed wire, revetting stakes

[illegible]

Lieut. & Adjt.
for Lieut. Col.
Comdg. 1st Lancs. Fus.

Situation Report
8th – 9th April 1916.   5 pm to 5 pm.
Sub-Sector F G 1.

Situation normal. Very quiet 24 hours.

1. Patrols. See Intelligence Report.

2. Artillery. Inactive on both sides. Enemy fired a few 77 mm shells over N.E. end of AUTHUILLE.

3. Trench Mortars. No activity on either side. Enemy put a few rifle grenades into R. 31-1, wounding one man.

4. State of Trenches. Still very dry; much improved on the Left.

5. Working Parties. Coys. in front line improving trenches generally; sandbagging and revetting parapet and parados. Sandbag barricade completed at WOOD POST.
Latrines dug in X1. 7-5. These have been boarded over according to instructions.

6. Wiring. All along the line – X1-6. W. 6-2. R. 36-1 R3-1. Parties worked until 8.30 am as mist still hung over the valleys.

7. Materials Needed. Barbed wire, French wire, plain wire and revetting stakes iron 3 ft. 6 ins.

A R ... [illegible]
Lieut. & Adjt.
for Lieut.-Col.
Comndg. 19th Lancs. Fus.

Intelligence Report.

April 3/4/16.

Subsector X.1. — 5 P.M. to 5 P.M.

<u>Operations.</u> Very quiet during the night. [illegible] enemy trenches with a few [illegible] shells opposite [illegible] St. At 10.45 A.M. enemy replied with a few shells towards CRUCIFIX CORNER.

At 10.15 A.M. we sent over 10 small mortar bombs at a working party located in the German front line opposite [illegible] St with good effect. Enemy replied with a number of aerial torpedoes along our front line. One aerial torpedo blew in our trench at point X.1.8. No other damage done. We replied with five footballs & some Shrapnel Shells.

At 11-25 A.M. enemy artillery fired about twenty 15 cm shells at our trenches about point X.1.7 doing little damage.

<u>Intelligence.</u> Nothing to report.

<u>Patrols.</u> No patrols were sent out

last night.

General. Enemy sent up plenty of flares during the night. No [illegible] were observed during the night.

19th Lancs Fus   [illegible] Hood 2nd Lieut

Intelligence Report
April 4-5 [illegible]

Sub-Sector E.4.1.

Operations – No special artillery activity.

Our own Field guns fired about 15 shells into enemy trench at point X1.a 63/87. A great deal of chalk and earth was thrown into the air.

In reply to our Field guns sending shells into X1.a 7/7 (?) enemy sent over about 30 whizz bangs round Hoop Post.

Intelligence – Enemy appeared busy in their own trenches at about point X1.b.31/87; sounds of hammering and digging were heard. This point was fired on by our Lewis guns but work did not cease.

Patrol. 2/Lt. Shield (?) and 2 other ranks went out from trench X1.b. Some difficulty was experienced in getting through our own wire.

Patrol went out about 100 yds.

& the enemy was on the alert & kept sending up flares & kept up a continuous machine gun fire.
Patrol did not get near enough to see enemy wire.

<u>General.</u> From the inactivity of enemy artillery during to-day it is possible that a relief is being carried out.

L Hood 2/Lieut.
Intelligence Officer
1/9 Lancs Fus.

Intelligence Report

[illegible]

[illegible] [illegible]

[illegible] [illegible] [illegible]

[illegible] [illegible] [illegible] [illegible] [illegible] [illegible] [illegible]

[illegible] [illegible] [illegible] [illegible]

[illegible] [illegible] [illegible] [illegible] [illegible] from the [illegible]

[illegible] [illegible] [illegible] [illegible] front

[illegible]

[illegible] [illegible] [illegible] [illegible] they returned at [illegible]

General Nothing to report.

Lt. Hood 2nd Lieut.

14th Jan ... Intelligence Officer.

Intelligence report.

April 7/16

5 PM to 5 PM

Sub-Sector F. G1

Operations. Artillery bombardment by both sides in direction of HAMEL 10 to 9 PM to 9.15 PM. [illegible] between 7.0 PM + 7.45 PM enemy fired shells over this sector which dropped in the vicinity of AUTHUILLE VILLAGE

Our rifle grenadiers [illegible] a German working party about point X.1.5 at 8.35 PM [illegible] [illegible] to ground [illegible] shells [illegible] point where the enemy [illegible] working on their [illegible] work [illegible]

At stand to this morning enemy dropped rifle grenades on our front line without doing any damage. We [illegible] the [illegible] grenades on their front line.

Intelligence Enemy were [illegible] on their front line [illegible] opposite X.1.6 & X.1.5 at 8.35 PM + 9.0 PM [illegible]

A German [illegible] opposite X.1.5 supposed to be on the end of [illegible] at the latter was [illegible]

Patrols No patrols were sent out during the night

General Red + green rockets were sent up in the direction of THIEPVAL WOOD during the artillery bombardment on the left of this sector

E. Wood 2nd Lt
19th Lancers Fus Intelligence Officer

Remarks [illegible] eight 15cm shells [illegible] about [illegible] St. doing a small amount of damage to the trench 11 [illegible]

Intelligence Report

[illegible] 8th [illegible] 5PM [illegible]

[illegible] Operations [illegible] hospital [illegible] heavy [illegible].

[illegible] PM [illegible] guns [illegible] [illegible] shells on enemy's trench opposite [illegible] G. [illegible] were heard [illegible] enemy's trench

[illegible] artillery dropped twenty five [illegible] shells in the vicinity of [illegible] between [illegible] AM & [illegible] AM doing little damage [illegible] from [illegible] shells & a few rifle grenades were sent over the [illegible] point W.62

[illegible] trench at G.31.1

[illegible] considerable [illegible] G.31.1 slightly damaging the trench in places

Intelligence: Enemy were opposite [illegible] chiefly [illegible] tied together in [illegible] were seen to enter a trench at the

7th [illegible] at 10-30 A.M. [illegible]

Patrols night — No patrols were sent out last night

General — Enemy did not send up [illegible] from this sector last night

19th Lancs Fus

F. Wood 2/Lt
Intelligence Officer

N.B. Wiring was carried out along the part of this Sub-Sector last night the covering parties doing patrol duty

"A" Form. Army Form C. 2121.

MESSAGES AND SIGNALS. No. of Message

Prefix ... Code ... m.	Words	Charge	This message is on a/c of:	Recd. at ... m.
Office of Origin and Service Instructions.	Sent		... Service.	Date
	At ... m.			From
	To			
	By		(Signature of "Franking Officer.")	By

APP IV

TO

Copy. No 1.

Sender's Number.	Day of Month	In reply to Number	AAA
SCD. 501.	26.		

Operation Order No. 26 (a) AAA.

· 32nd Divisional Tactical Exercise.

1). Battalion will parade as strong as possible at JUNCTION (in RUBEMPRE) of MIRVAUX - PIERREGOT ROAD in the order · SIGNALLERS A'B'C'D Coys at 8·0 a.m. Tomorrow · 27· & will march via CROSS ROAD · T. 27·d.1 BEAUCOURT - MONTIGNY - BEHENCOURT - to COPSE C.19.c 9/1 and will be in position by 10.15 a.m.

2. On arrival at COPSE, Coys will send 1 runner each to Battn. HQ - Battn. HQ. to send two runners to Bde HQ.

3). Battalion will wear fighting kit & carry haversack rations & water bottles (filled). Only 100 rounds SAA per man will be carried, remainder to be handed in

From

Place (1).

Time

The above may be forwarded as now corrected. (Z)

Censor. Signature of Addressor or person authorised to telegraph in his name.

* This line should be erased if not required.

(688-9) --McC. & Co. Ltd., London.-- W 14142/641. 225,000 4/15. Forms C 2121/10.

"A" Form.

Army Form C. 2121.

MESSAGES AND SIGNALS.

No. of Message ....

Prefix ....Code............m.	Words	Charge	This message is on a/c of:	Recd. at..............m.
Office of Origin and Service Instructions.	Sent		......................Service.	Date ....
	At..............m.			From ....
	To			
	By		(Signature of "Franking Officer.")	By ....

TO (2).

Sender's Number.	Day of Month.	In reply to Number.	AAA
* S.C.D. 501.	26.		

return AAA. Dismounted Officers will wear same kit as the men – O.C. Coys. will make sure that all ranks are dressed alike & that waterproof sheets are securely fastened. Magazines & rifles to be empty AAA.

(3) Lewis Guns will accompany Battalion & be used as a Coy. weapon. Transport Sergeant to make arrangements for limbers to carry these AAA.

(4) Sergt.-Cook to arrange for breakfasts at 6.45 am. AAA Cookers will leave RUBEMPRE at 10 am. & follow the same route to BEHENCOURT – from thence along the BAIZEUX ROAD to the first CROSS-ROADS (C.16.a) where they will wait until needed – Cookers will NOT move along the ROAD if any pending

From

Place

Time

(cont'd)

The above may be forwarded as now corrected. (Z)

Censor. Signature of Addressor or person authorised to telegraph in his name.

* This line should be erased if not required.

225,000. W 14042—M 44. H. W. & V., Ld. 12.15.

"A" Form. Army Form C. 2121.

MESSAGES AND SIGNALS. No. of Message

Prefix Code m. | Words | Charge | This message is on a/c of: | Recd. at m.

Office of Origin and Service Instructions. | Sent At m. To By | Service. (Signature of "Franking Officer.") | Date From By

TO (5).

Sender's Number.	Day of Month	In reply to Number	AAA
56D. 501.	26.		

are going on in that area AAA

C.Q.M.S. will accompany each cooker AAA

Water carts will NOT accompany the Battalion AAA

(5) 2/Lieut. Whittles is detailed as Liaison Officer (mounted) & will report to MAJOR BIRDWOOD at CROSS ROAD - C. 16.a. - at ZERO TIME.

(6) Drummers will accompany Battn. & on arrival at rendezvous will leave one man in charge of instruments & remainder rejoin Coy.

(7) Grooms of mounted Officers will accompany the Battalion (without fighting kit) & will make arrangements for a feed for horses.

From

Place (Cont'd).

Time

The above may be forwarded as now corrected. (Z)

Censor. Signature of Addressor or person authorised to telegraph in his name.

* This line should be erased if not required.

(688-9) --McC. & Co. Ltd., London.-- W 14142/641. 225,000 4/15. Forms C 2121/10.

"A" Form.
MESSAGES AND SIGNALS.

Army Form
No. of Mes

Prefix .... Code .... m. | Words | Charge | This message is on a/c of: | Recd. at

Office of Origin and Service Instructions.

Sent
At ....m.
To ....
By ....

..........Service.
(Signature of "Franking Officer.")

Date ....
From ....
By ....

TO (4).

Sender's Number.	Day of Month.	In reply to Number.	AAA
* S.C.D. 501	26.		

(8). Attention of Officers concerned is called to para. 11 of 14. Inf. Bde. S.G. 151/1 published this afternoon.

From SCINDE.
Place
Time 11.10 pm.

A Rupert Lucas

The above may be forwarded as now corrected. (Z)

Censor. Signature of Addressor or person authorised to telegraph in his name. [signature]

* This line should be erased if not required.

225,000. W 14042—M 44. H. W & V., Ld. 12.15.

"A" Form.

Army Form C. 2121.

MESSAGES AND SIGNALS.

No. of Message..........

Prefix.............Code.............m.	Words	Charge	This message is on a/c of:	Recd. at...........m.
Office of Origin and Service Instructions.	Sent		..........Service.	Date..........
	At..........m.		ARS	From..........
	To..........			
	By..........		(Signature of "Franking Officer.")	By..........

TO { O.C. Coy.

COPY No.

Sender's Number.	Day of Month.	In reply to Number.	AAA
* S.C.D. 341	22		

Operation Order No. 25 AAA.

Battalion will move into the CONTAY AREA for training to-morrow 23rd inst AAA

(A) Battalion will parade at Brewery W. end of WARLOY at 10.20 am & will march in the order 'B' 'D' 'C' 'A' Coys. via CONTAY – HERISSART – to RUBEMPRE, and there take over billets vacated by 2nd Rl. INNIS. FUS – for which purpose billeting party of 1 Officer per Coy. and H.Q. and 1 N.C.O. per platoon, Signals & Transport will parade Battn. HQ WARLOY at 7.30 am AAA. Each Coy. will take over billets of the corresponding Coy. of the outgoing Battalion AAA.

From

Place

Time

(1).

The above may be forwarded as now corrected. (Z)

Censor. Signature of Addressor or person authorised to telegraph in his name.

* This line should be erased if not required.

225,000. W 14042—M 44. H. W & V., Ld. 12.15.

"A" Form. Army Form C. 2121.

MESSAGES AND SIGNALS.

No. of Message

Prefix ... Code ... m. Words Charge

Office of Origin and Service Instructions.

Sent At ... m. To ... By ...

This message is on a/c of: ... Service. (Signature of "Franking Officer.")

Recd. at ... m. Date ... From ... By ...

TO (2)

Sender's Number.	Day of Month.	In reply to Number.	AAA
* S.C.D. 341	27		

(b) Waterproof capes will be carried or (if wet) worn on the person, & not handed in to Q.M. AAA

Blankets will be at Q.M. Stores at 7.30 am AAA

Officers Kits at 8.30 am AAA.

(c) T.O. will make arrangements to convey Officers mess stuff, which must be clear of WARLOY by 9.30 am. AAA.

(d) DINNERS – Sergt-Cook will make arrangements to have them ready ½ hour after arrival in billets. AAA.

(e) Lieut. H. A. Smith will remain behind to hand over billets to incoming Battn. & will obtain receipt as to their cleanliness AAA. O.C. Coys. will see that billets are left clean & well

From

Place

Time

(2)

The above may be forwarded as now corrected. (Z)

Censor. Signature of Addressor or person authorised to telegraph in his name.

* This line should be erased if not required.

225,000. W 14042—M 44. H. W & V., Ld. 12.15.

"A" Form. Army Form C. 2121.

MESSAGES AND SIGNALS. No. of Message ....

Prefix .... Code .... m. | Words | Charge | This message is on a/c of: .... Service. | Recd. at .... m.

Office of Origin and Service Instructions. | Sent At .... m. To .... By .... | (Signature of "Franking Officer.") | Date .... From .... By ....

TO (3)

Sender's Number.	Day of Month.	In reply to Number.	AAA
* S.C.D. 341	22		

render certificate to this effect to Orderly Room before departure AAA.
(f) Rations will be delivered at RUBEMPRE to-morrow by supply wagons AAA.

ACKNOWLEDGE

From SCINDE.
Place
Time 5.30 pm.

The above may be forwarded as now corrected. (Z) A. [illegible] Lieut. & Adjt.

Censor. Signature of Addressor or person authorised to telegraph in his name.

* This line should be erased if not required.

225,000. W 14042—M 44. H. W & V., Ld. 12.15.

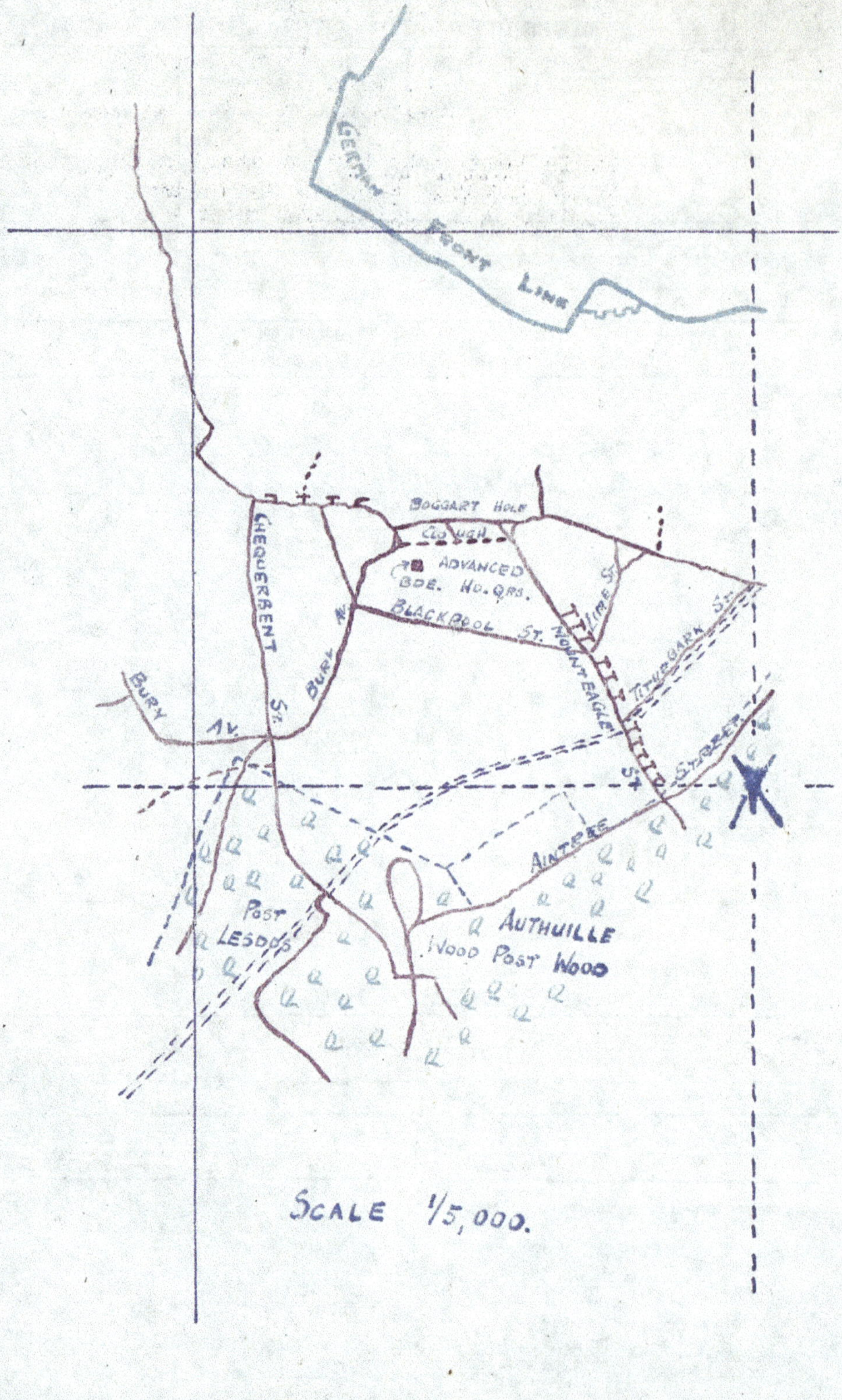

GERMAN FRONT LINE

BOGGART HOLE CLOUGH

ADVANCED BDE. HQ. QRS.

CHEQUERBENT ST.

BURY AV.

BURY AV.

BLACKPOOL ST.

LIME ST.

MOUNT EAGLE ST.

TITHEBARN ST.

AINTREE STREET

POST LESDOS

AUTHUILLE WOOD POST

WOOD

SCALE 1/5,000.

14th Brigade.

32nd Division.

19th BATTALION

LANCASHIRE FUSILIERS

M A Y 1 9 1 6

Appendices attached:-

Daily Situation Reports.

Instructions regarding War Diaries and Intelligence Summaries are contained in F. S. Regs., Part II. and the Staff Manual respectively. Title Pages will be prepared in manuscript.

WAR DIARY or ~~INTELLIGENCE~~ SUMMARY

(Erase heading not required.)

XXXII

Army Form C. 2118

19th Lan: Fus
Vol 6

Place	Date	Hour	Summary of Events and Information	Remarks and references to Appendices
RUBEMPRE	May 1-5.16		Bn in training area CONTAY AREA and took part in 32ND DIVISIONAL TACTICAL EXERCISE.	
"	2.		Training continued.	
"	3.		Training continued and and during the afternoon "Regt. Sports" were held. 'A' Coy obtained most points 'B' Coy 2nd. 'D' Coy 3rd. 'C' Coy 4th.	
"	4.		Repeated 32ND DIVL TACTICAL EXERCISE under G.O.C. Brigade.	
RUBEMPRE – BOUZINCOURT	5		Battn moved to BOUZINCOURT and took over billets of 17. H.L.I. 97 BDE. Very close weather and men experienced much difficulty on the march. G.O.C's 32nd Div and 14 BDE inspected the Battn on the march. Bn left RUBEMPRE 8.30 a.m. halted for 2¼ hours between CONTAY – WARLOY and arrived BOUZINCOURT at 3.30 p.m. See Bde and Bn Operation Orders App II. Lt Col J.M.A. GRAHAM to hospital.	
BOUZINCOURT – AUTHUILLE SUBSECTOR	6		Battn relieved 2. RL INNISKILLING. FUS in AUTHUILLE SUBSECTOR. Battn left BOUZINCOURT 8.45 p.m. Battn of 25th INF BDE on our right. 1st DORSET REGT on our left. For disposition of Battn see Bn operation orders App. II	6.X. 86 sheet
AUTHUILLE SUBSECTOR	7.		Enemy active with T.M. against the left of our line, trenches much damaged, casualties 1 man killed 5 men wounded. At 11 p.m. ENEMY opened up heavy bombardment no information up to time of writing.	See SITUATION REPORTS App I

1875 Wt. W593/826 1,000,000 4/15 J.B.C. & A. A.D.S.S./Forms/C. 2118.

Army Form C. 2118

Instructions regarding War Diaries and Intelligence Summaries are contained in F. S. Regs., Part II. and the Staff Manual respectively. Title Pages will be prepared in manuscript.

WAR DIARY
or
~~INTELLIGENCE SUMMARY~~
(Erase heading not required.)

Place	Date MAY	Hour	Summary of Events and Information	Remarks and references to Appendices
AUTHUILLE SUBSECTOR	8		Bombardment started at 11 pm on the 7th continued until 12.30 a.m. Enemy carried out raid on part of line held by 1st DORSETS. For details see Daily Situation Report. 2Lt Cartwell died of wounds. 'B' Coy suffered so severely that this Coy had to be relieved by 'C' Coy.	See Sit. Reports App I
"	9.		Quiet day. Worked hard on damaged trenches.	
AUTHUILLE SUBSECTOR - AVELUY	10		Battn relieved by 2nd MANCHESTER REGT and moved into BDE RESERVE - AVELUY and CRUCIFIX CORNER. For dispositions see Bn Operation orders App II. Relief was completed by 10 pm and Battn in billets & dugouts by 11.00 pm. Capt R.W. LEWIS RAMC. evacuated sick and Lt J.M. WISHART reported for duty.	
AVELUY.	11.		Battn supplied 440 men for fatigues.	
"	12		Do. - Lt Col. J.M.A. GRAHAM. D.S.O rejoined Battn from Hd Qrs.	
"	13		Do.	
AVELUY AUTHUILLE SUB-SECTOR	14		Fatigues up till 1 pm. Bn relieved 2 MANCHESTER REGT in AUTHUILLE SUBSECTOR. For disposition of Bn see Bn operation orders App II. 2. W. YORKSHIRE REGT 23rd BDE on our right. 1 DORSET REGT on our left.	

1875 Wt. W593/826 1,000,000 4/15 J.B.C. & A. A.D.S.S./Forms/C. 2118.

Army Form C. 2118.

WAR DIARY
or
~~INTELLIGENCE SUMMARY~~
(Erase heading not required.)

Instructions regarding War Diaries and Intelligence Summaries are contained in F. S. Regs., Part II. and the Staff Manual respectively. Title Pages will be prepared in manuscript.

Place	Date MAY	Hour	Summary of Events and Information	Remarks and references to Appendices
AUTHUILLE SUBSECTOR	15.		Lt R.C. MASTERMAN – 2Lt E.D. ASHTON – 2Lt R.L. GEORGE joined from 13th Bn LANCS FUS.	
			2 SCOTS. RIF. relieved 2 W. YORKS on our right	See
"	16			Sit. Reports
"	17			App I
AUTHUILLE SUBSECTOR – BOUZINCOURT	18		Battn was relieved by 11. BORDER REGT 97 BDE. – Relief completed 12.30 and Battn arrived in BOUZINCOURT at 2 a.m. – See Battn & Bde operation orders App II	
BOUZINCOURT	19.		In huts – Found large fatigue parties. 2Lt A.N. DUSSEE joined from 4th Bn LANCS FUS.	
"	20.		Lt G.G. BOWEN LANCS FUS joined his own Battn (2nd). C Coy moved to AVELUY see op. orders	
"	21		In huts.	
"	22		do	
"	23		do 2Lt S.G.N. SHAW joined from 13th Battn LANCS FUS	
BOUZINCOURT – SENLIS.	24		2 MANCHESTER REGT relieved Battn in BOUZINCOURT & Battn moved to SENLIS taking over billets from 15 H.L.I. See operation orders App II 2Lts. G.H. DYKES – H.C. YOUNG joined from 13th LANCS FUS	
SENLIS	25.		Training in Billets	
"	26		do	
"	27		do	

Instructions regarding War Diaries and Intelligence Summaries are contained in F. S. Regs., Part II. and the Staff Manual respectively. Title Pages will be prepared in manuscript.

WAR DIARY
or
~~INTELLIGENCE~~ SUMMARY

(Erase heading not required.)

Army Form C. 2118.

Place	Date	Hour	Summary of Events and Information	Remarks and references to Appendices
	MAY			
SENLIS.	28		Training in Billets	
SENLIS – CONTAY	29		Bn moved into CONTAY AREA for training. See operation orders. App II.	
CONTAY.	30		Battn training.	
"	31.		Training in Billets.	

[illegible] Lt Col
Comdg 19th Lan Fus

2449 Wt. W14957/M90 750,000 1/16 J.B.C. & A. Forms/C.2118/12.

APPENDIX I.

Daily Intelligence Report

12 Midnight 6.5.16 to 5 pm 7.5.16.

AUTHUILLE Sub-Sector.

Situation normal. Weather dull

1. Patrols. None sent out.

2. Artillery. Enemy artillery inactive.
At 9.0am three rounds of 7.7 c.m. fell near CAMPBELL POST. A few 7.7 c.m shells fell on the Right of Trench X1.5 and round WOOD POST. No serious damage done.
2 pm. Our artillery replied to activity of hostile Trench Mortars. About 30 4.5 How. shells were sent over at about point R.31.c 5/6

3. Trench Mortars. Between 12.30 and 2 pm enemy used heavy Trench Mortars against Trench R.31.1. Damage was done to front line, especially near head of STAFFA St. where trench was completely blown in. This hostile activity resulted in five casualties.

4. State of Trenches. Have been severely treated by hostile artillery, especially on the Left.

5. Working Parties. Coys. in front line worked on Trenches, after dinner filling sandbags & doing minor repairs. Work of building up parapet to be carried out to-night.
Reserve Coy. 1 N.C.O. & 20 men working on X1.5.
1 N.C.O & 20 men on R.31.2.1.

6. State of Wire. Very weak & in places completely broken. Work to be done on this to-night.

7. Materials Needed. Sand bags, Knife rests, barbed wire, Screw stakes, revetting stakes.

Lieut. & Adjt.
for Major

Daily Situation Report.

24 hours [illegible] 5-2-16 to 6-2-16

[illegible]

Situation normal. Weather dull.

1 Patrols. At 9.30 pm patrol of 2/Lt Healey and 6 other Ranks left Trench at [illegible] opposite LIME STREET. Object to recover body of a soldier of 15th Lancs Fusiliers which was some 10 yds in front of our wire. This was successfully carried out and body returned at 10 pm. [illegible] Sent an escort of enemy [illegible] Telephone wire.

At 1.30 pm patrol under 2/Lt Cartwright and 30 other Ranks left trench [illegible]. German working parties were observed returning [illegible]. Party returned and Lewis guns were turned on in the direction of working parties. Party came in at 9.[illegible] pm.

2 Artillery. Enemy [illegible] from the usual has been active with his guns against R 31.1.2 & 1.3.

2.30 pm 1 Howitzer shell fell at the head of STRAFA STREET killing 1 man wounding 3 other.

3.0 pm About 30 Shrapnel over R31.2 junction of DAVAAR Av & DURHAM Av.

9.00 About 12 H.E. 77 mm into [illegible]. No damage was done.

Our artillery [illegible] on enemy lines opposite. Our [illegible] against R 31.1/2 [illegible] Trench [illegible] Enemy [illegible]. About 15 rounds were fired.

11.0 pm Enemy opened fire on left of sector with Artillery (Heavy chiefly) heavy and light Howitzers and Minenwerfer. This fire extended over the THIEPVAL Sector. At same time bombardment was heard to the North of RIVER ANCRE.

(Continued)

(2)

the bombardment was not [illegible] [illegible] [illegible] [illegible] [illegible] a heavy [illegible] [illegible] [illegible] [illegible] and [illegible] [illegible] fire.

Our field guns opened on a right [illegible] 11.15 pm. Later (about 3 mins) 4.5 Hows were turned on. Enemy bombardment was now [illegible] chiefly on [illegible] SECTOR. At 11.25 enemy [illegible] sending up numerous coloured flares and [illegible] coloured rockets. These latter were sent up from [illegible] [illegible] [illegible] [illegible] [illegible]. No apparent sequence could be detected in the enemy's use of these various flares which seemed to be sent up indiscriminately all along the front. At 11.35 [illegible] [illegible] from left Company [illegible] [illegible] [illegible] [illegible] and forward. At 12.10 am enemy fire slackened [illegible] [illegible] [illegible] [illegible] [illegible] until 12.30 am after which the situation became practically normal. Trenches R.31 1.2 was seriously damaged and heavy casualties were sustained by the company holding this part of line. 1 officer and 7 other ranks killed, 14 OR wounded.

2.30 am Enemy opened [illegible] [illegible] fire in reply from Hows & shrapnel fire. Situation was normal at 3.30 am and has remained unchanged.

3. Trench Mortars. As stated above enemy used these with effect during the bombardment. R31.1.2 trench suffered from these which were [illegible] [illegible].

Rifle grenades were also used during bombardment.

Our T Mortars in this sector did not reply.

4. State of Trenches. Considerably [illegible] damaged on the left. All yesterday's work has been destroyed. [illegible] ST & R.1.3 have also suffered.

(Continued)

(3)

5. Working Parties. 7.30 – 11 p.m. 3.30 – 8.30 p.m. and 9.0 a.m. – 12 noon
1 Officer, 2 N.C.O.s and 30 men of Reserve Coy. at work on R.31 – 1.2 – STAFFA STREET.
1 Officer + 43 men of H.L.I. at work on new trench WG 2.1 from 9 – 10.30 p.m.
Men in front line employed repairing trenches and filling sand bags.

6. State of Wire. Damaged slightly opposite X1-5-6, seriously on the left R.1. 1.2.
5 coils put out in front of WG 2.1 also some in front of R.1.

7. Material needed.
Wire, screw pickets, revetting material

A. Rupert [illegible]
Lieut. & Adjutant
for Major
Comdg 1/9 Lancashire Fus.

Battn Intelligence Report

In line [illegible] 17 – 18 Nov 1916

[illegible] SECTOR

Weather normal [illegible]

1 **Patrols** Have been out last evening [illegible] parties for men being searched for any sign of hostile [illegible]

2 **Artillery** Inactive on both sides. About 12 minutes fire directed behind front line [illegible] At 12.45 pm [illegible] CONCESSION POST.

3 **Trench Mortars** No activity on either side.

4 **Enemy Attitude** [illegible] quiet but [illegible] are [illegible] as [illegible] can be [illegible] by [illegible] the line.

5 **Working Parties** Busy on front line filling sand bags, clearing and rebuilding trenches back from line and communication, overhead cover and fire step improved in [illegible] but this trench still needs widening and [illegible]

[illegible] still working on [illegible]

6 **[illegible]** All week. More wire [illegible] put out last night in front of [illegible] line was strengthened in places by [illegible] and tying loose wire to posts.

7 **[illegible]** [illegible] and [illegible] material.

[illegible]
for Major
Comdg 17 [illegible]

Situation Report.

24 hours 9th – 10th May 1916.

AUTHUILLE SUB: SECTOR.

Situation Normal. weather fine.

1. Patrols. None sent out but covering parties to men wiring moved about 'No man's land', no sign of enemy was seen and no telephone were found. At 10.30 pm enemy wiring party in front of R.31.2 was dispersed by Lewis gun fire.

2. Artillery. At 2.45 pm. enemy sent over two 7.7 m H.E at CAMPBELL POST. Enemy artillery quiet. Our own Field Guns have kept up an intermittent fire on enemy trenches opposite this sector, apparently ranging. From 12 mid day to 1.45 pm our Howitzers fired on enemy trenches opposite R.31-1.2, also X1.4.5. At 2.30 pm. our 8" Hows. began shelling enemy trenches at R.31 a, c and up to time of writing this report, shelling still continues. Damage can not be estimated.

3. Trench Mortars. Quiet on both sides. Some rifle grenades were sent over into R31.1.2 & X1.4.5.

4. State of Trenches. Not improved by rain yesterday. Some good work has been done in R31.1.2.

5. Working parties. Coys. employed clearing and rebuilding firing line. Two parties of Manchester Regt worked from 7.45 to 1 am. The fire trench is much improved.

6. Wire. Improving, wire put up in front of R.31.1.2 X1.4.5 & strengthened in weak spots.

7. Materials needed. Screw posts.

Lieut & Adjutant
for Major

Commanding 19th Service Bn,
Lancashire Fusiliers.

Situation Report.

9. pm. 14.5.16 to 5.0 pm 15.5.16.

AUTHUILLE SUB-SECTOR.

Situation NORMAL : weather inclined to be wet.

1. Patrols. None sent out.

2. Artillery. Enemy artillery have had periods of activity. Between 11 & 11.15 pm. enemy opened barrage with Whiz-bangs on trench X1.4. There was also some heavy Machine Gun fire. Our artillery replied and enemy's fire quietened at 11.15. During night whiz bangs also fell in R31.1, Staffa Street. Little damage was done. 10.30 am 4 Whiz-bangs fell in HAIGH ST. At 11.30 am. 12 whiz-bangs fell behind R31.2. We replied with Rifle Grenades and Light Trench Mortars. *

3. Trench Mortars. Enemy used Trench Mortars against X1.4 between 11 & 11.15 pm. We replied with 15 2" T.Ms. Occasional trench Mortars fell on R.31.1-2. At 10.40 pm 2 Trench Mortars fell behind W.6.2. Little damage was done. Great many Rifle Grenades sent on X1.4 & R31.1.2 during day.

4. State of Trenches. Poor, due to rain and severe treatment by enemy. X1.4 damaged by activity last night. Also parts of AINTREE and MOUNTEAGLE Streets.

5. Working Parties. Coys. in front line working on trenches repairing damage done.

6. State of wire. Still very poor. A great deal of work is needed on this. Not much wiring was done owing to relief.

7. Materials required. Screw Posts, Sump Board, Revetting Stakes. (Iron)

* Our 4.5" Hows. shelled enemy trenches opposite trench R31.1. between 3.30 and 4.15 pm. Enemy retaliated by shelling trench R31.1-2. at same time with Whiz-bangs.

A Knapp Lt [illegible]

Situation Report.

24 hours 15th - 16th May 1916.
AUTHUILLE SUB-SECTOR.

1. Patrols. 2 Lieut. A.B. SMITH and 3 O.R. went out from trench R1.7 at 9.30 pm, patrolled along hedge for about 100 yds, turned left and went along front of trench W61.2. Party returned at 12.30 am. No sign of enemy patrol or fine telephone wire. Transport was heard behind enemy's lines about point R.32.c.

Patrol under Sgt Smith and 3 other Ranks left trench R31.1 at 10.5 pm, and went toward enemy's lines in order to hear if enemy was working on wire. No working party heard and it was too light to approach very close. Party returned at 11.30 pm.

2. Artillery. Enemy Artillery quiet. Occasional whiz-bangs along the left of sector. Between 9.30 & 10.30 enemy sent over about 30 10.5 cm. shells, apparently registering on our 2nd line and Bn. H.Q.rs at CAMPBELL POST. No damage done. Our artillery active after mid-day. During the afternoon Howitzers shelled enemy's trenches in R.31. Our field guns also fired about the same part of line. Aeroplanes were apparently working in conjunction with artillery.

3. Trench Mortars. No special activity. Usual occasional oil cans near STAFFA ST. Trench slightly damaged. Our light Trench Mortars sent over a few bombs into enemy lines opposite R31.1 with good effect.

4. State of Trenches. Improvement retarded by inclement weather, but today's sun has done much towards helping our working parties.

5. Working Parties. During the afternoon, all men off duty in the front line have been working in trenches, cleaning and revetting.

(Continued.)

(2).

Working Parties (continued) 1 N.C.O. and 20 men of Reserve Coy. at work in R.31.1-2. 1 N.C.O. and 12 men at work in X1.4-5.

[illegible]. Wire. Improving slowly. The moon was rather too bright for work on the left. About 7 Coils put out in front of W.6.1. X.1.7, making a fairly effective barrier.

7. Materials required. Screw Stakes, Revetting Stakes (wire)

A Rupert [illegible]
Lieut & Adjutant
for Lieut. Col.
Comdg 19th Lancas. Fusiliers

Situation Report.

24 hours 16th - 17th May 1916.
AUTHUILLE SUB-SECTOR.

1. Patrols. None sent out owing to moon light.
2. Artillery. Enemy artillery active. Attention has been confined to the left of the subsector, and it is probable that guns are ranging on our lines of trenches.
At 11.10 pm. 8 shrapnel shells burst over HOUGH ST.
At 4 am 12 10.5 cm. shells fell, - 1 behind STAFFA ST and the remainder behind DURHAM ST. No damage done.
9.30 am. 6 10.5 cm. shells fell behind DURHAM ST and 1 by CAMPBELL POST.
10.0 am. Whizbangs in X1.4, killing 1 man and wounding 1, also further damaging trenches.
11.0 am 3 10.5 cm. shells at CAMPBELL POST also whizbangs in R31.1.2
5 pm. 5 10.5 cm. shells at CAMPBELL POST.
At 4.0 pm our field guns shelled enemy trenches in R.31.
3. Trench Mortars. Inactive on both sides.
4 State of Trenches. Much improved and more work is being done than was possible during the wet weather. From X1.4 to X1.6 the line is dangerously exposed to hostile Machine gun fire. Trench needs deepening and overhead traverses put up. - Enemy are no doubt observing our movements in this part of the line ~~[illegible]~~ thus causing many casualties.
Open track from head of Trench Railway to WOOD POST is searched by M.G. fire and casualties have been caused. It is suggested that a sand bag parapet be built for protection.
5. Working Parties. Coys in front line repairing damage. The following parties from Reserve Coy:
1 N.C.O + 12 men at work in X1.5.
1 N.C.O. + 20 men at work in X1.4.
1 N.C.O + 20 men at work in R31.1.2.

(Continued)

(2).

6. State of Wire. No improvement as no parties went out owing to moonlight. 1 Party tried 3 times and were driven in by hostile machine gun fire.

7. Material Required: Iron Stakes and Screwing Stakes [illegible]

8. General. Between 9.45 and 11 pm, an aeroplane, presumably British, patrolled the lines.

At 2.45 am. 5 Rockets were sent up in accordance with 14th Bde SG. 104.

A Rupert [illegible] Lieut. Adjutant
for Lieut. Col.
Comdg. 19th Lancs. Fusrs.

Situation Report.

24 hours 17th – 18th May 1916.
AUTHUILLE SUB-SECTOR.

1. Patrols. None sent out during the night, moon was rather too light.

2. Artillery. Artillery has been moderately active on both sides during the whole period under review.
12.25 am Enemy opened rapid bombardment with 10.5 cm Hows, Field guns, and Trench Mortars against Trench R.1.4 and new trench from BURY AVENUE. Firing lasted 5 minutes. Damage was done to trenches but no casualties. Our artillery replied with Field Guns as there was no heavy artillery available.
At 6 am a few 10.5 cm howitzers fell behind STAFFA ST and DURHAM ST.
9.30 am About 13 10.5 cm Hows. behind DURHAM ST and to left of CAMPBELL POST.
12.30 About 20 Shrapnel and H.E. at junction of OBAN AVENUE and HOUGH ST. Our artillery fired 30 rounds 4.5 in retaliation.
Between 11 and 12.30 pm our 4.5 Howitzers sent over about 20 rounds into R.31.c.d.
Our Field Guns have [illegible] retaliation for Trench Mortars and oil cans.

3. Trench Mortars. Enemy active.
3.30 pm about 12 rounds behind STAFFA ST.
The attention of the enemy has been attracted by the throwing up of sand bags containing earth from RUSSIAN SAP.
From 9 am salvoes of oil cans have come over along the whole front. Very little damage done.
Our 2" Mortars fired 12 rounds in retaliation to the bombardment by enemy.
Enemy T.M. battery located about R.31.c.4.2 also R.31.a [illegible]

(continued)

4. State of Trenches. Intervening K1-4-5 again damaged but work is being carried on

5. Working Parties. Usual work by coys in the line. Reserve Coy. supplied

1 N.C.O and 40 men in R31-1-2

1 N.C.O and 20 - in K1-4-5.

6. State of Wire: No great improvement yet, - Moonlight interfering with work. Party worked in front of R31.1 for 2 hours but were eventually driven in. While this party was out a German patrol was observed going towards the THIEPVAL SECTOR - Lewis gun fire was opened.

7. Materials required

Revetting Stakes (iron), Barbed wire, screw Stakes

Sd. [illegible] Lieut adjt
for Lieut Col.
Comdg 19 Lancashire Fus.

"A" Form. Army Form C. 2121

MESSAGES AND SIGNALS.

No. of Message

APPENDIX II

Prefix ... Code ... m.	Words	Charge	This message is on a/c of:	Recd. at ... m.
Office of Origin and Service Instructions.	Sent		... Service.	Date
	At ... m.			From
	To			
	By		(Signature of "Franking Officer.")	By

TO O.C. Coy

COPY No 1

Sender's Number.	Day of Month	In reply to Number	
* SCD 537	10		AAA

Operation Order 28 AAA

Ref Maps 1/40,000 ALBERT and 1/10,000 OVILLERS and BEAUMONT AAA.

(1). The Bn will be relieved in subsector by 2/Manchester Regt to day. AAA

(2) 1 guide per platoon and Lewis gun Sect. to be at CRUCIFIX CORNER by 7.50 pm, there to meet platoons of 2/Manchester Regt and lead them forward to the line AAA

(3). On relief A & B Coys. will take over dug outs at CRUCIFIX CORNER. B Coy will supply garrison for AVELUY BRIDGE HEAD defences AAA C & D Coys will take over billets of Manchr Regt in AVELUY.

From
Place
Time

(1)

The above may be forwarded as now corrected. (Z)

Censor. Signature of Addressor or person authorised to telegraph in his name.

* This line should be erased if not required.

(988-9) —McC. & Co. Ltd., London.— W 14142/611. 225,000. 4/15. Forms C 2121/10.

"A" Form.

Army Form C. 2121

MESSAGES AND SIGNALS.

No. of Message

Prefix ... Code ... m.	Words	Charge	This message is on a/c of:	Recd. at ... m.
Office of Origin and Service Instructions.	Sent		... Service.	Date
	At ... m.			From
	To			
	By		(Signature of "Franking Officer.")	By

TO (2)

Sender's Number.	Day of Month	In reply to Number	AAA
* SCD 534.	10		

D Coy. will detail 100 men for AVELUY Keeps No 1 and 2. C Coy will relieve guards at present furnished by 2/Manchr. Regt. AAA

(4) For the purpose of taking over dug outs & billets Lieut. H.A. SMITH and 1 N.C.O. per platoon will proceed to CRUCIFIX CORNER and AVELUY by 4.30 pm. AAA.

(5) Q.M. to arrange for Officers Kits, Rations and Cooking in accordance with above disposition.

Also for 1 limber and Mess cart to proceed via ALBERT to arrive RATION DUMP AUTHUILLE by 6.30 pm. for Officers Kit & Mess Stuffs.

Field Kitchens will be sent to

From

Place (Continued)

Time

The above may be forwarded as now corrected. (Z)

Censor. Signature of Addressor or person authorised to telegraph in his name

* This line should be erased if not required.

(688-9) —McC. & Co. Ltd., London.— W 14149/1141. 225,000. 4/15. Forms C 2121/10.

"A" Form.

Army Form C. 2121.

MESSAGES AND SIGNALS.

No. of Message

Prefix Code m.	Words	Charge	This message is on a/c of:	Recd. at m.
Office of Origin and Service Instructions.	Sent		Service.	Date
	At m.			From
	To			
	By		(Signature of "Franking Officer.")	By

TO (3)

Sender's Number.	Day of Month	In reply to Number	
* SCD 537.	10.		AAA

Coy. Ration Dumps where they will collect Dixies and return - A+B coys to dugouts CRUCIFIX CORNER, C+D coys to AVELUY.

All Transport to be clear of CRUCIFIX CORNER by 9·30 pm. AAA.

C+D coys Trench kits to be at usual Ration Dump in AUTHUILLE by 6 30 pm. A+B coys to make arrangem^ts for kits etc. to be taken down by Trench Railway to CRUCIFIX CORNER AAA.

(6) Arrival in Billets + Dugouts to be reported immediately. AAA.

C coy will leave trenches by DAVAAR AVENUE.

ACKNOWLEDGE!

From SCINDE

Place -

Time 11 30 am

The above may be forwarded as now corrected. (Z) [signature] Lieut + Adjt.

Censor. Signature of Addressor or person authorised to telegraph in his name.

* This line should be erased if not required.

(088-9) —McC. & Co. Ltd., London.— W 14142/641. 225,000. 4/15. Forms C 2121/10.

"A" Form. Army Form

MESSAGES AND SIGNALS.

No. of Message

Prefix Code m. | Words | Charge | This message is on a/c of: Service. | Recd. at m.

Office of Origin and Service Instructions.

Sent At m. To By

(Signature of "Franking Officer.")

Date From By

TO Head Quarters Mess Copy No.

Sender's Number.	Day of Month	In reply to Number	AAA
* SCD 30	13		

Operation Order 29 AAA Ref Map 1/40000 ALBERT TO,000 OVILLERS and BEAUMONT

1 Bn will relieve 2/MANCHESTER REGT in AUTHUILLE Sub sector on the night of 14/15 May AAA.

(2) Platoons and Lewis gun guides of 2/MRs will meet ingoing platoons Lewis guns at CRUCIFIX CORNER at 8 pm AAA

(3) A Coy will hold right of the line and will leave CRUCIFIX CORNER at 8 pm AAA

(4) B Coy will hold centre of line and will leave CRUCIFIX CORNER at 8.20 pm AAA.

(5) C Coy will hold left of line and will leave AVELUY at 7.50 pm AAA.

(6) "D" Coy will be in reserve 2 platoons at WOOD POST 2 platoons in TOBERMORY ST and

From

Place (1)

Time

The above may be forwarded as now corrected. (Z)

Censor. Signature of Addressor or person authorised to telegraph in his name.

* This line should be erased if not required.

(4198) Wt. W14042—M44. 300000 Pads. 12/15. Sir J. C. & S.

"A" Form

Army Form C. 2121

MESSAGES AND SIGNALS.

No. of Message

Prefix ... Code ... m. Office of Origin and Service Instructions.	Words	Charge	This message is on a/c of: ... Service.	Recd. at ... m.
	Sent			Date
	At ... m.			From
	To			
	By		(Signature of "Franking Officer.")	By

TO

Sender's Number.	Day of Month	In reply to Number	
* SCD 30	13		AAA

will leave AVELUY at 8.30 pm AAA

(2) Cooking arrangements as last time AAA

No transport forward AVELUY before 10.30 pm AAA

(3) A coy. will make arrangements to have Officers trench kits and Mess Stuff taken up by TRENCH RAILWAY AAA

B coy will have trench kits at CRUCIFIX CORNER C & D coys at CHURCH AVELUY by 7.30 pm where they will be collected by Transport.

(4) a. Usual returns for trench stores to be rendered in duplicate to Orderly Room by 8 am 15.5.16.

(5) Relief complete to be reported in code which will be issued.

NOTE! COYS WILL PROCEED BY PLATOONS WITH 5 MINS INTERVAL ... ACKNOWLEDGE!!

From SCINDE			
Place			
Time 3.30 pm			[illegible signature]

The above may be forwarded as now corrected.

(Z)

Censor.

Signature of Addressor or person authorised to telegraph in his name.

* This line should be erased if not required.

(4198) Wt. W14042—M44. 300000 Pads. 12/15. Sir J. C. & S.

"A" Form. Army Form C. 2121.

MESSAGES AND SIGNALS.

No. of Message ....

Prefix .... Code .... m.	Words	Charge	This message is on a/c of:	Recd. at .... m.
Office of Origin and Service Instructions.	Sent		.... Service.	Date ....
	At .... m.			From ....
	To			
	By		(Signature of "Franking Officer.")	By ....

TO O.R. Copy No 1

Sender's Number.	Day of Month.	In reply to Number.	AAA
* S.C.D. 114A	17		

Operation Orders No 30 Ref Map 1/40000 ALBERT

1 Battn will be relieved by 11th BORDER REGT on the night of 18/19th MAY and on relief will move into DIVISIONAL RESERVE – BOUZINCOURT and will be prepared to move at 1 hours notice AAA.

2 (A). Platoons and Lewis Gun guides will be at CRUCIFIX CORNER at 9.30 p.m. there to meet corresponding units and lead them forward into the line AAA.

(B) On relief Coys will march by platoons etc. at 200 yards interval via AVELUY – CROSS ROADS W.16b 8/3 to BOUZINCOURT there to take over billets vacated by 11th BORDER REGT AAA. For this purpose billetting party of 1 NCO per platoon and H.Q. Qrs will rendezvous Bn Hd Qrs at 2 pm 18th May and will march under 2Lt Whittles to BOUZINCOURT VIA ALBERT AAA

From

Place (1)

Time

The above may be forwarded as now corrected. (Z)

Censor. Signature of Addressor or person authorised to telegraph in his name.

* This line should be erased if not required.

225,000. W 14042—M 44. H. W. & V., Ld. 12/15.

"A" Form.

MESSAGES AND SIGNALS.

Army Form C. .

No. of Message ....

Prefix ....Code............m. Office of Origin and Service Instructions.	Words	Charge	This message is on a/c of: ....Service. (Signature of "Franking Officer.")	Recd. at ....m.
	Sent			Date
	At ....m.			From
	To			By
	By			

TO (2)

Sender's Number.	Day of Month.	In reply to Number.	
*			AAA

(C) Officers TRENCH KITS and Mess Baskets and Coy cooking materials to be at respective Coy dumps by 7.30 pm. These to be collected by Transport which will be arranged accordingly. Add No TRANSPORT to leave WEST BARRIER AVELUY until 10.30 pm.

(D) On relief C Coy will leave trenches by DAVAAR AV AAA

(E) Arrival in Billets to be reported at once.

List of Trench Stores handed over to incoming Battn and distribution of S.A.A left in trenches to be rendered to Orderly Room by 9 am. 19th May.

(F) No smoking allowed on AVELUY-BOUZINCOURT ROAD.

From BEHAR

Place

Time

The above may be forwarded as now corrected.

(Z) A Rupert [illegible] Lieut & Adjutant

Censor.

Signature of Addressor or person authorised to telegraph in his name.

* This line should be erased if not required.

5,000. W 14042—M 44. H. W. & V., Ld. 12/15.

"A" Form. Army Form C. 2121.

MESSAGES AND SIGNALS. No. of Message.

Prefix ... Code ... m.	Words	Charge	This message is on a/c of:	Recd. at ... m.
Office of Origin and Service Instructions.	Sent At ... m. To ... By ...		... Service. (Signature of "Franking Officer.")	Date ... From ... By ...

TO — Coy. — Coy. — No. 3

Sender's Number.	Day of Month	In reply to Number	AAA
* B.H.R. 767.	20.		

Operation Order No. 30 (a) AAA.

(a) "C" Coy. will move to billets at AVELUY this day, leaving BOUZINCOURT at 3·0 pm & proceeding to AVELUY via NORTHUMBERLAND AVENUE and new pioneer road AAA.

(b) Billeting Party of 1 Officer & 4 N.C.O's of "C" Coy. will report to Town Major, AVELUY by 3·0 pm. AAA.

(c) Q.M. will arrange Transport (details later) which will proceed to AVELUY via ALBERT. AAA.

(d). "C" Coy. will continue to furnish daily the fatigue party found by them to-day AAA. "C" Coy. will also arrange to take charge of 50 picks & 50 shovels left daily by fatigue party of "A" Coy.

From
Place (1).
Time

The above may be forwarded as now corrected. (Z)

Censor. Signature of Addressor or person authorised to telegraph in his name.

* This line should be erased if not required.

(4.98) Wt. W4.042—M44. 300000 Pads. 12/15. Sir J. C. & S.

"A" Form. Army Form C. 2121.

MESSAGES AND SIGNALS.

No. of Message

Prefix ... Code ... m.	Words	Charge	This message is on a/c of:	Recd. at ... m.
Office of Origin and Service Instructions.	Sent		... Service.	Date
	At ... m.			From
	To			By
	By		(Signature of "Franking Officer.")	

TO (2).

Sender's Number.	Day of Month	In reply to Number	
* B.A.R. 767	30		AAA

(a). O.C. 'C' Coy. will use Signal Officer at AVELUY CHATEAU as Report Centre AAA.

Arrivals in billets will be reported as soon as possible & Casualty Wire will be sent daily at usual hours.

From BEHAR.

Place

Time 6.50 am.

The above may be forwarded as now corrected. (Z) [illegible] Lieut. & Adjutant.

Censor. Signature of Addressor or person authorised to telegraph in his name.

* This line should be erased if not required.

(1.98) Wt. W3.042—M44. 300000 Pads. 12/15. Sir J. C. & S.

"A" Form.

Army Form C. 21[illegible]

MESSAGES AND SIGNALS.

Prefix .... Code .... m. | Words | Charge

No. of Message ....

Office of Origin and Service Instructions.

Sent
At .... m.
To ....
By ....

This message is on a/c of:
.... Service.
(Signature of "Franking Officer.")

Recd. at .... m.
Date ....
From ....
By ....

TO — Own Copy. Copy No

Sender's Number. * BHA. 187 | Day of Month 23. | In reply to Number | AAA

Operation Order No 31 AAA.
Ref. Map 1/40,000 ALBERT AAA

1. The Battalion will move to billets in SENLIS on the evening of the 24th May and take over accommodation as now occupied by 15/H.L.I. AAA.

2. 2nd Manchester Regt. will take over billets in BOUZINCOURT + AVELUY now occupied by this Batn. AAA.

3. Billeting Party of 1 N.C.O. per Platoon Signallers, H.Q. + Transport under Lieut. HEWITT will parade Bn HQ at 2 pm. + proceed to SENLIS for the purpose of taking over billets vacated by 15/H.L.I. AAA

4. (a) Three Coys. in BOUZINCOURT

From
Place
Time

(1)

The above may be forwarded as now corrected.

(Z)

Censor.

Signature of Addressor or person authorised to telegraph in his name.

* This line should be erased if not required.

(688-9) —McC. & Co. Ltd., London.— W 14142/641. 225,000. 4/15. Forms C 2121/16.

"A" Form. Army Form C. 2121.

MESSAGES AND SIGNALS.

No. of Message

Prefix ... Code ... m.	Words	Charge	This message is on a/c of:	Recd. at ... m.
Office of Origin and Service Instructions.	Sent		... Service.	Date
	At ... m.			From
	To			
	By		(Signature of "Franking Officer.")	By

TO (2).

Sender's Number.	Day of Month	In reply to Number	
* BHR. 187.	23.		AAA

will move off as relieved by Coys. of 2nd Manchester Regt. and will march via CROSS ROADS V.12.C. to SENLIS AAA.
(b) 'B' Coy. will not leave AVELUY until 8-30 pm. if then relieved by 2nd Manchester Regt. will proceed to SENLIS via AVELUY - BOUZINCOURT ROAD & CROSS ROADS V.12.C. AAA.
5 (a). Officers kit to be Q.M. Stores by 12 noon AAA.
(b) Waterproof capes of 3 Coys. in BOUZINCOURT to be in Q.M. Stores by 10 am. Those of 'C' Coy. to be stacked at Coy. HQ. AVELUY by 8 am.
(c). One limber will be allotted to each Coy for mess baskets etc.

From (contd 4).
Place
Time

The above may be forwarded as now corrected. (Z)

Censor. Signature of Addressor or person authorised to telegraph in his name.

* This line should be erased if not required.

(6S8-9) —McC. & Co. Ltd., London.— W 14142/641. 225,000. 4/15. Forms C 2121/10.

"A" Form. Army Form C. 2121.

MESSAGES AND SIGNALS.

No. of Message______

Prefix* ...... Code ...... m.	Words	Charge	This message is on a/c of:	Recd. at ...... m.
Office of Origin and Service Instructions.	Sent		...... Service.	Date
	At ...... m.			From
	To			
	By		(Signature of "Franking Officer.")	By

TO (3).

Sender's Number.	Day of Month	In reply to Number	
* BHR. 187.	23.		AAA

6. Working parties will be found as usual.

7. (a). O.C. Coys. will be held personally responsible that their huts & surrounding ground are left scrupulously clean, and will render to the Adjutant a certificate to this effect AAA

(b). Arrivals in billets as [illegible] to be reported at once. AAA

ACKNOWLEDGE.

From BENAR.

Place

Time 4.10 pm

A R [illegible] Lieut.

Adjutant.

The above may be forwarded as now corrected. (Z)

...... Censor. Signature of Addressor or person authorised to telegraph in his name.

* This line should be erased if not required.

(688-9) —McC. & Co. Ltd., London.— W 14142/641. 225,000. 4/15. Forms C 2121/13.

"A" Form.

Army Form C. 2121.

MESSAGES AND SIGNALS.

No. of Message

....Code......m. and Service Instructions.	Words	Charge	This message is on a/c of:	Recd. at......m.
	Sent		......Service.	Date
	At......m.			From
	To			
	By		(Signature of "Franking Officer.")	By

TO Own Coy. — COPY - No. 1 -

Sender's Number.	Day of Month	In reply to Number	AAA
* B.H.R. 223	28		

Operation Order No. 32 AAA.

Ref. map 1/40000. ALBERT. AAA.

1. Battalion will move into TRAINING AREA to-morrow, 29th inst. & be billeted in CONTAY.

(a) Battalion will parade at Battn. HQ at 5.30 pm in ~~[illegible]~~ full marching order & will march in the order SIGNALLERS D. C. B. A. Coys. via WARLOY to CONTAY & there take over billets vacated by 15th LANCS. FUS. for which purpose billeting party of 1 N.C.O. per platoon SIGNALLERS, H.Q., & TRANSPORT under 2/Lieut. W.R. NIGHTINGALE will parade Battn. HQ. at 1.30 pm & proceed to CONTAY. AAA.

From

Place

Time (1)

The above may be forwarded as now corrected. (Z)

Censor. Signature of Addressor or person authorised to telegraph in his name.

* This line should be erased if not required.

(4193) Wt. W14042—M14. 300000 Pads. 12/15 Sir J. C. & S

(2)

"A" Form. Army Form C. 2121

MESSAGES AND SIGNALS.

No. of Message

Prefix Code m.	Words	Charge	This message is on a/c of:	Recd. at m.
Office of Origin and Service Instructions.	Sent		Service.	Date
	At m.			From
	To			
	By		(Signature of "Franking Officer.")	By

TO (2).

Sender's Number.	Day of Month	In reply to Number	
* BHR. 223.	28.		AAA

(b). Waterproof capes will be rolled in bundles of ten clearly marked & stacked at Q.M. Stores by 8 am. AAA Officers' valises will be at Q.M. Stores by 8.30 am. AAA
(c) Teas will be at 4.15 pm. and Sergt cook will arrange for teas on arrival in billets about 8.30 pm. AAA
(d) T.O. will make arrangements for Transport of Officers mess baskets etc. & Orderly room boxes. AAA.
(e) Billets vacated by this Battalion will be taken over by 2nd R. Innis. Fus. AAA.
(f). Strict march discipline must be observed AAA.
(g.) All billets must be left scrupulously clean & O.C. Coys. will render certificate to this office before leaving. AAA.

From
Place— BEHAR.
Time 9.50 pm

The above may be forwarded as now corrected. (Z) [signature] Lieut. & Adjutant.

Censor. Signature of Addressor or person authorised to telegraph in his name.

* This line should be erased if not required.

(4198) Wt. W14042—M14. 300000 Pads. 12/15 Sir J. C. & S

Daily Situation Report.

12 Midnight 6.5.16 to 5 pm 7.5.16.

AUTHUILLE SUB-SECTOR.

Situation normal. Weather dull.

1. Patrols. None sent out.

2. Artillery. Enemy artillery inactive.

At 9-0am Nine rounds of 7.7 C.M. fell near CAMPBELL POST. A few 7.7 C.M. shells fell on the Right of Trench X1.5 and round WOOD POST. No serious damage done.

2 pm Our artillery replied to activity of hostile Trench Mortars. About 30 4.5 How. Shells were sent over at about point R.31.C 5/6.

3. Trench Mortars. Between 12.30 and 2 pm enemy used heavy Trench Mortars against Trench R.31.1. Damage was done to front line, especially near head of STAFFA St. where trench was completely blown in. This hostile activity resulted in five casualties.

4. State of Trenches. Have been severely treated by hostile artillery, especially on the Left.

5. Working Parties. Coys. in front line worked on trenches; after dinner, filling sandbags & doing minor repairs. Work of building up parapet to be carried out to-night.

Reserve Coy:- 1 N.C.O. & 20 men working on X1.5.

1 N.C.O & 20 men on R.31.2.1.

6. State of Wire. Very weak & in places completely broken. Work to be done on this to-night.

7. Materials Needed. Sand-bags, Knife rests, barbed wire, screw stakes, revetting stakes.

A. Rupert Lewis

Lieut. & Adjt.

for Major.

Commanding 19th. Service Bn.

Lancashire Fusiliers.

Intelligence Report.

May 7th 1916.

AUTHUILLE Sub-Sector. 12 Midnight to 12 Noon.

Operations. Very quiet. At 9.30 a.m. Nine 77 mm. Shells fell round CAMPBELL POST. 1 Shell into Trench R.31.1. At 5.30 a.m. an oil-can fell behind Trench R.31.2.

Intelligence. Nothing to report.

Patrols. None sent out.

General. Enemy very quiet on front of this Sub-Sector & it is possible that a relief was being carried out. Further proof of this, is that at 'Stand to' this morning much shouting was heard in the enemy trenches as though men were being called to their proper places.

A. Rupert Moxey
Lieut. & Adjt.
for Intelligence Offr.
19th Lancs. Fus.

Daily Situation Report.

24 hours - 7.5.16 to 8.5.16.

AUTHUILLE SUB-SECTOR.

Situation Normal. Weather dull.

1. Patrols. At 9.20 pm. patrol of 2/Lt. Huxley and 6 other Ranks left Trench X1.5 opposite LIME STREET, - object to recover body of a soldier of 15th Lancs. Fusrs. which was some 70 yds. in front of our wire. This was successfully carried out and party returned at 10 pm. Party saw no sign of enemy or any Telephone wire.

At 8.30 pm. patrol under 2/Lt. Cartwright, - and 30 other Ranks left trench W6.1. German working party was observed repairing wire. Party returned and Lewis guns were turned on in this direction, - working ceased. Party came in at 9.15 pm.

2. Artillery. Enemy apart from the raid has been active with his guns against R31-1-2, X1-5
2.30 pm. 1 Howitzer shell fell at the head of STAFFA STREET killing 1 man & wounding 3 others.
5.0 pm. About 30 Shrapnell over R31-2 & junction of DAVAAR AV & DURHAM AV.
9.20 About 12 H.E. 77 mm into trench X1.5. Some damage was done.

Our artillery replied suitably with HE & Shrapnell on enemy's lines opposite. Our 4.5 hows. were turned on against Pt. R31C 6/8 to try to knock out Enemy T. Mortar. About 15 rounds were fired.

11.0 pm. Enemy opened fire on left of sector with Artillery (Hows. chiefly) heavy and light Mortars and Minnenwerfer. His fire extended over the THIEPVAL Sector, at same time bombardment was opened to the North of RIVER ANCRE.

Cvl

(Continued!).

This bombardment was not at first treated seriously, and in view of further operations, artillery support was not immediately asked for.
Our Field guns opened up on night lines at 11.15 pm, later (about 3 mins.) 4.5 Hows. were turned on. Enemy bombardment was now intense specially over THIEPVAL SECTOR. At 11.25 enemy started sending up numerous coloured flares and orange coloured rockets. These latter were sent up from point in Enemy trench opposite TRENCH W.6.2. No apparent sequence could be detected in the enemys use of these rockets & flares which seemed to be sent up indiscriminately all along the front. At 11.35 communication to our left Company was broken and runners were sent forward. At 12.15 am. enemy fire slackened, our artillery kept up slow barage until 1.0 am, after which hour, situation became temporally normal. Trenches R31. 1.2 were seriously damaged and heavy casualties were sustained by the company holding this part of line. 1 Officer and 7 Other Ranks Killed - 24 O.R. wounded.

2.30 am. Enemy opened whiz bang fire in reply to our Hows. & Shrapnel fire. Situation was normal at 3.30 and has remained unchanged.

3. Trench Mortars. As stated above enemy used these with effect during the bombardment. R31 - 1.2 trench suffers from these which came over intermittently. Rifle grenades were also used during bombardment. Our T. Mortars in this sector did not reply.

4. State of Trenches Considerably more damaged on the left. All yesterdays work has been destroyed. STAFFA ST & X1.5 have also suffered.

(Continued).

5. Working Parties. 7.30 – 11 pm. 3.30 – 8.30 am and 9.0 am – 12 noon
1 Officer, 2 N.C.O's and 30 men of Reserve Coy. at work on R.31 – 1.2., STAFFA STREET.
1 Officer + 43 men of H.L.I. at work on New trench W6.2.1 from 9 – 10.50 pm
Men in front line employed repairing trenches and filling sand bags.

6. State of Wire. Damaged slightly opposite X1 – 5 – 6, seriously on the left R31. 1.2.
5 Coils put out in front of W6.2.1, also some in front of R31.1

7. Materials needed.
Wire, screw posts, revetting material

A. Rupert Moon
Lieut + Adjutant
for Major.
Comdg 19th Lancashire Fus[rs].

Daily Situation Report.

24 hours 8th - 9th May 1916.

AUTHUILLE SUB-SECTOR.

Situation normal. weather wet.

1. Patrols. None sent out but covering parties for new wiring searched for any sign of telephone wire.

2 Artillery. - Inactive on both sides. About 12 midnight a few shrapnel fell behind front line R 31.2.
At 12.45 p.m. 3 77mm over CAMPBELL POST.

3. Trench Mortars - No activity on either side.

4. State of Trenches. - Improving slowly but more men are needed to work in them than can be supplied by Bn. holding the line.

5. Working Parties - Coys in front line filling sand bags, clearing and rebuilding trenches, both front line and communication, - overhead cover and fire step improved in X1. 5-4, but this trench still needs deepening and revetting.
Party under R.E. working in DURHAM ST.

6 State of Wire - Still weak. More wire was put out last night in front of R.31 1-2, W62 X1-5. Wire was repaired in places by joining and tying loose ends to posts.

7. Material needed - Wire, screw posts, and revetting material.

A. Rupert Morris[?]

Lieut. Adjutant.
for Major.
Comdg 19th Lancs. Fusiliers.

Col.

Situation Report.

9 pm 14.5.16 to 6.0 pm 15.5.16.

AUTHUILLE SUB-SECTOR.

Situation NORMAL · weather inclined to be wet.

1. Patrols. None sent out.

2. Artillery. Enemy artillery have had periods of activity. Between 11 + 11.15 pm enemy opened barrage with Whiz-bangs on trench X1.4. There was also some heavy Machine Gun fire. Our artillery replied and enemy's fire quietened at 11.15. During night whiz bangs also fell in R31.1, Staffa Street. Little damage was done. 10.30 am 4 Whiz-bangs fell in HAUGH ST. At 11.30 am 12 whiz-bangs fell behind R31.2. We replied with Rifle Grenades and Light Trench Mortars.

×

3. Trench Mortars. Enemy used Trench Mortars against X1.4 between 11 + 11.15 pm. We replied with 15 2" T.Ms. Occasional Trench Mortars fell on R.31.1.2. At 10.40 pm 2 Trench Mortars fell behind W.6.2. Little damage was done. Great many Rifle Grenades sent on X1.4 + R31.1.2 during day.

4. State of Trenches. Poor, due to rain and severe treatment by enemy. X1.4 damaged by activity last night. Also parts of AINTREE and MOUNTEAGLE Streets.

5. Working Parties. Coys. in front line working on trenches repairing damage done.

6. State of wire. Still very poor. A great deal of work is needed on this. Not much wiring was done owing to relief.

7. Materials required. Screw Posts; Sump Boards, Revetting Stakes. (Iron)

× Our 4.5" Hows. shelled enemy trenches opposite trench R.31.1 between 3.30 and 4.15 pm. Enemy retaliated by shelling trench R31.1-2- at same time, with Whiz-bangs.

A H[illegible]
Lieut. + Adjutant
For Lieut. Col.

Situation Report

24 hours 15th - 16th May 1916.

AUTHUILLE SUB-SECTOR.

1. Patrols. Lieut. G.B. SMITH and 3 O.R. went out from trench X1.7 at 9.30 pm, & patrolled along hedge for about 100 yds, turned left and went along front of trench W612. Party returned at 12.30 am. No sign of enemy patrol or fine telephone wire. Transport was heard behind enemy's lines about point R.32.c.

Patrol under Sgt Smith and 3 other Ranks left trench R.31.1 at 10.5 pm. and went toward enemy's lines in order to hear if enemy was working on wire. No working party heard and it was too light to approach very close. Party returned at 11.30 pm.

2. Artillery. Enemy Artillery quiet. - Occasional whiz-bangs along the left of sector. Between 9.30 & 10.30 enemy sent over about 30 10.5 cm. shells, apparently registering on our 2nd line and Bn. HQrs at CAMPBELL POST. No damage done. Our artillery active after mid-day. During the afternoon Howitzers shelled enemy's trenches in R.31. Our Field guns also fired on about the same part of line. Aeroplanes were apparently working in conjunction with artillery.

3. Trench Mortars. No special activity. Usual occasional oil cans near STAFFA ST. Trench slightly damaged. Our light Trench Mortars sent over a few bombs into enemy lines opposite R31.1 with good effect.

4. State of Trenches. Improvement retarded by inclement weather, but today's sun has done much towards helping our working parties.

5. Working Parties. During the afternoon, all men off duty in the front line have been working in trenches, clearing and revetting.

(Continued.)

(2).

Working Parties (continued). 1 NCO and 20 men of Reserve Coy at work in R 31.1-2. 1 NCO and 12 men at work in X1.4-5.

6. Wire. Improving slowly. The moon was rather too bright for work on the left. About 7 coils put out in front of W61 X17, making a fairly effective barrier.

7. Materials required. Screw Stakes, Revetting Stakes (iron)

A. Rupert Lorne [?]
Lieut & Adjutant
for Lieut Col.
Comdg 19th Lancas. Fusiliers

Situation Report.

24 hours 16th - 17th May 1916

AUTHUILLE SUB-SECTOR.

1. Patrols None sent out owing to moon light
2. Artillery. Enemy artillery active. Attention has been confined to the left of the subsector, and it is probable that guns are ranging on our lines of trenches
At 11-10 pm 8 shrapnel shells burst over HOUGH ST.
At 4 am. 12 10·5 cm shells fell, 1 behind STAFFA ST and the remainder behind DURHAM ST. No damage done
9 30 am 6 10·5 cm. shells fell behind DURHAM ST and 1 by CAMPBELL POST.
10·0 am Whizbangs in X1·4, killing 1 man and wounding 1, also further damaging trenches.
11·0 am 3 10·5 cm. shells at CAMPBELL POST also Whiz bangs in R31·1·2.
3 pm. 5 10·5 cm shells at CAMPBELL POST.
At 4·0 pm our Field guns shelled enemy trenches in R.31.
3. Trench Mortars. Inactive on both sides.
4 State of Trenches Much improved and more work is being done than was possible during the wet weather. From X1·4 to X1·6 the line is dangerously exposed to hostile Machine gun fire. Trench needs deepening and overhead traverses put up. Enemy are no doubt observing our movements in this part of the line thus causing many casualties.
Open track from head of Trench Railway to WOOD POST is searched by MG fire and casualties have been caused. It is suggested that a sand bag parapet be built for protection.
5. Working Parties. Coys in front line repairing damage. The following parties from Reserve Coy:-
1 NCO + 12 men at work in X1·5.
1 NCO. + 20 men at work in X1·4.
1 NCO + 20 men at work in R31·1·2.

(Continued!).

(2).

6 Slate of wire. No improvement as no parties went out owing to moonlight. 1 Party tried 3 times and were driven in by hostile machine gun fire.

7 Material required: Screw Stakes and Revetting Stakes (nil)

8 General. Between 9.45 and 11 pm, an aeroplane, presumably British patrolled the lines.
At 2.45 am. 6 Rockets were sent up in accordance with 14th Bde SG. 104.

A Rupert [illegible] Lieut. Adjutant
for Lieut. Col.
Comdg. 19th Lancs. Fusrs.

Situation Report.

24 hours 17th - 18th May 1916.

AUTHUILLE SUB-SECTOR.

1. Patrols. None sent out during the night, moon was rather too light.

2. Artillery Artillery has been moderately active on both sides during the whole period under review.

12.25 am. Enemy opened rapid bombardment with 10.5 cm Hows., Field guns, and Trench Mortars against Trench X1-4 and new trench from BURY AVENUE. Firing lasted 5 minutes. - Damage was done to trenches but no casualties. Our artillery replied with Field Guns, - there was no heavy artillery available.

At 6 am a few 10.5 cm Howitzers fell behind STAFFA ST and DURHAM, ST.

8.30 am About 15 10.5 cm Hows. behind DURHAM ST. and to left of CAMPBELL POST

12.30 About 20 Shrapnel and H.E. at junction of OBAN AVENUE and HOUGH ST. Our artillery fired 20 rounds 4.5 in retaliation.

Between 11 and 12.30 pm our 4.5 Howitzers sent over about 20 rounds into R31 c.d.

Our Field Guns have attempted retaliation for Trench Mortars and Oil cans.

3. Trench Mortars. - Enemy active.

5.30 pm. about 12 rounds behind SANDA ST. the attention of the enemy has been attracted by the throwing up of sand bags containing earth from RUSSIAN SAP.

From 9. am. salvoes of oil cans have come over along the whole front. Very little damage done.

Our 2" Mortars fired 10 rounds in retaliation to 12.15 am strafe by enemy.

Enemy T.M. batteries located about R31.c 6/2. also R31 a 5.5/15.

(Continued!)

4. State of Trenches. Improving X1.4.5 again damaged but work is being carried on.

5. Working Parties. Usual work by coys in the line. Reserve Coy. supplied

1 N.C.O. and 20 men in R31.1.2

1 N.C.O. and 20 - in X1.4.5.

6. State of wire. No great improvement yet, - Moonlight interferes with work. Party worked in front of R31.1 for 2 hours but were eventually driven in. While this party was out a German patrol was observed going towards the THIEPVAL SECTOR. - Lewis Gun fire was opened.

7. Materials required.

Revetting Stakes (iron), Barbed wire, wiring Stakes

A. Rupert Hussey Lieut & Adjt.
for Lieut Col.
Comdg. 19th Lancashire Fus.rs

14th Brigade.

32nd Division.

1/19th BATTALION

LANCASHIRE FUSILIERS

JUNE 1916;

Instructions regarding War Diaries and Intelligence Summaries are contained in F. S. Regs., Part II. and the Staff Manual respectively. Title Pages will be prepared in manuscript.

WAR DIARY
or
~~INTELLIGENCE SUMMARY~~
(Erase heading not required.)

XXXII

19 LANCASHIRE FUS.

Army Form C. 2118

JUNE 1916. Vol 7

Place	Date (JUNE)	Hour	Summary of Events and Information	Remarks and references to Appendices
CONTAY.	1		Battn training in DIVL TRAINING AREA.	
	2–8		Battn continued training	
	9.		14 Bde Assault at Arms. Bn did well and was 2nd in Bde. (on points).	
	10–11		Continued training ~~in~~ area	
CONTAY–WARLOY	12.		Battn attended 32ND DIVISION TACTICAL EXERCISE and on completion moved to WARLOY where billets were taken over from 17 H.L.I. Op. orders att. APP. I & II	
WARLOY–CRUCIFIX CORNER (near) AVELUY	13		Battn relieved 16th Bn LANCASHIRE FUS at CRUCIFIX CORNER. (DUGOUTS built in to the bank) Op. order attached APP. I & II. Lt COL J.M.A. GRAHAM D.S.O. went on leave an Bn was commanded by MAJOR J. AMBROSE-SMITH.	
CRUCIFIX CORNER	14–15		Battn found large working parties both night and day.	
CRUCIFIX CORNER–AUTHUILLE SUB. SECTOR	16.		Battn continued working parties and relieved 2 MANCHESTER REGT in AUTHUILLE SUBSECTOR, relief began 9.30 pm and completed at 3.30 am 17th June. Delay in relief caused by Battn finding night working parties up to 1 am.	

7.X. 3 sheets

1875 Wt. W593/826 1,000,000 4/15 J.B.C. & A. A.D.S.S./Forms/C. 2118.

Instructions regarding War Diaries and Intelligence Summaries are contained in F. S. Regs., Part II. and the Staff Manual respectively. Title Pages will be prepared in manuscript.

WAR DIARY
or
~~INTELLIGENCE SUMMARY~~
(Erase heading not required.)

No 2

JUNE.

15th LANCS FUS.

Army Form C. 2118

Place	Date	Hour	Summary of Events and Information	Remarks and references to Appendices
AUTHUILLE SUBSECTOR	17 18 19		Bn in Trenches. Situation and Intelligence reports attached App. III	
AUTHUILLE SUBSECTOR. CRUCIFIX CORNER	20.		Battn was relieved in Subsector by 2 MANCHESTER REGT. relief completed at 3.45 a.m (due to continuing working parties during the relief)	
CRUCIFIX CORNER	21 22		Battn found large working parties.	
CRUCIFIX CORNER - ~~[illegible]~~ WARLOY.	23.		Battn relieved by 2. K.O.Y.L.I. and moved to billets in ~~[illegible]~~ WARLOY relief completed at 12.5 a.m. 24th June. Op. Orders att. App. I + II	
WARLOY	24 25 26		Battn in Billets in WARLOY and preparations for "operations of Fourth Army" were made. Battn was addressed with other Battns of the Bde by the G.O.C. 32nd Div. on 26th June. G.O.C. 14th Inf Bde also addressed the Battn. Preliminary Bombardment of German Trenches in preparation for the attack in the front of the 4th Army. began on 24th and continued until the 30th	
WARLOY. Shelter Trenches AVELUY WOOD	27		Battn moved to Shelter Trenches AVELUY WOOD. Exact locality - W 10 b 10/60 Ref Map 1/20000 TRENCH MAP 57 D SE. This is preliminary move conforming with plan of attack of 32nd Div. ~~At about 3 am heavy rain began to fall and [illegible] continued until 8.30 am, from this time showers were experienced and at~~	Op Order App I II

1875 Wt. W593/826 1,000,000 4/15 J.B.C. & A. A.D.S.S./Forms/C. 2118.

Instructions regarding War Diaries and Intelligence Summaries are contained in F. S. Regs., Part II. and the Staff Manual respectively. Title Pages will be prepared in manuscript.

WAR DIARY
or
INTELLIGENCE SUMMARY
(Erase heading not required.)

No 3. Army Form C. 2118

JUNE 19th LANC. FUS

Place	Date	Hour	Summary of Events and Information	Remarks and references to Appendices
Shelter Trenches AVELUY WOOD - SENLIS	28		At 3 am rain began to fall and continued until about 8.30 am after this showers fell during the day. The ground became sodden at 7.30 pm orders were received that operations were cancelled and Battn withdrew to billets in SENLIS. The men were wet & muddy and would have been useless for scrapping. Battn arrived in SENLIS 2 a.m 29th June.	
SENLIS.	29		Battn remained in billets cleaned up & refitted.	
SENLIS - BLACK HORSE BRIDGE	30		Battn moved to shelters BLACK HORSE BRIDGE at W edge of village of AUTHUILLE, this move was made to conform with plan of operation of 32nd Div. Battn arrived at the above ~~[illegible]~~ shelters at 2 a.m. on 1st July	

30/6/16.

[signature] Lt Col
Comdg 19th Lan Fus

1875 Wt. W593/826 1,000,000 4/15 J.B.C. & A. A.D.S.S./Forms/C. 2118.

14th Bde.
32nd Div.

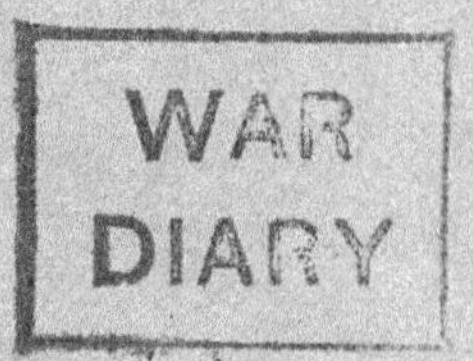

19th BATTALION.

LANCASHIRE FUSILIERS.

JULY 1916

Apps I to VI. Reports on Operations :-

1st to 4th.
12th to 14th July 1916.

Intelligence report during operations.
Sketch Maps.
Operation Orders.
Composition of staff.

SECRET. Copy no. 8..

14th INFANTRY BRIGADE OPERATION ORDER no. 54.

MAP REFERENCE LENS Sheet 1/100,000. 19th July, 1916.

1. The Brigade will move to-morrow to the area MONCHY BRETON - ORLENCOURT - OSTREVILLE - MARQUAY. Route - TERNAS - LIGNY ST. FLOCHEL - MARQUAY.

2. The Brigade will be clear of MONTS-EN-TERNOIS by 9.30 a.m. and will pass the starting point, road junction 1 mile N. of CHURCH at MONTS-EN-TERNOIS, as follows :-

Brigade Headquarters............9.0 a.m.
19th Lan. Fus....................9.5 a.m.
14th Bde. T.M.Batty.)
14th Bde. M.G.Coy.)............9.10 a.m.
15th H.L.I.......................9.15 a.m.
1st Dorset Regt.................9.20 a.m.
2nd Manchester Regt.............9.25 a.m.
90th Field Ambulance............9.30 a.m.

3. Transport will accompany units.

4. Dress marching order with caps.

5. Billeting parties will meet the Staff Captain at the CHURCH, MARQUAY, at 9.0 a.m.

6. Units will obtain Brigade time from Brigade Headquarters at 7.0 a.m. daily till further orders.

7. Arrival in billets will be reported to Brigade Headquarters which will close at MONCHEUX at 8.30 a.m. and open at the same hour at MONCHY BRETON.

8. A C K N O W L E D G E .

[signature] Captain,
Bde. Major, 14th Infantry Brigade.

Issued at 3.15 p.m.

Copies to:-

No. 1 War Diary No. 1
2 War Diary No. 2
3 G. O. C.
4 File.
5 32nd Division
6 1st Dorset Regt.
7 2nd Manchester Regt.
8 19th Lan. Fus.
9 15th H. L. I.
10 14th Bde. M.G.Coy.
11 14th Bde. T.M.Batty.
12 2/Coy. 32/Divl. Train.
13 96th Inf. Bde.
14 97th Inf. Bde.
15 Signals 14/Inf. Bde.
16 90th Fd. Ambulance.
17 A.D.M.S. 32/Div.
18 Town Major MARQUAY.
19 Staff Captain.

SECRET. Copy No..8......

14th INFANTRY BRIGADE OPERATION ORDER No.55.

MAP REFERENCE - Sheet LENS No.11, and HAZEBROUCK No.5a
Scale - 1/100,000.

20th JULY 1916.

1. The Brigade will move tomorrow to the area RAIMBERT - CAUCHY-A - LA-TOUR- FLORINGHEM.
Route - VALHUON - PERNES.

2. The Brigade will be clear of road junction ¼ mile W. of P in PERNES by noon, and will pass the starting point road junction E. of Church, VALHUON, as follows,-

Bde. Headquarters	9. 0 a.m.
1st Dorset Regiment	9. 5 a.m.
15th H.L.I.	9.10 a.m.
2nd Manchester Regiment	9.15 a.m.
14th Bde.M.G.Coy	9.20 a.m.
19th Lancashire Fusiliers	9.25 a.m.
14th Bde.T.M.Battery	9.30 a.m.
90th Field Ambulance	9.35 a.m.

No Unit, except 1st Dorset Regiment, 19th Lancashire Fusiliers, and 14th T.M.Battery, will use the MONCHY-BRETON - VALHUON Road when proceeding to the starting point.

3. Transport will accompany Units.

4. Dress - Marching order.

5. Billeting parties will meet the Staff Captain at the Church, FLORINGHEM at 9 a.m.

6. Arrival in Billets will be reported to Bde. Headquarters which will close at MONCHY-BRETON at 8.30 a.m., and open at the same hour at RAIMBERT.

7. Acknowledge.

Captain,
Bde. Major, 14th Infantry Brigade.

Issued at 6.30 p.m.
Copies to,-

1. War Diary No.1
2. War Diary No.2.
3. G. O. C.
4. File.
5. 32nd Division 'G'.
6. 1st Dorset Regt.
7. 2nd Manchester Regt.
8. 19th Lanc. Fus.
9. 15th H.L.I.
10. 14th Bde.M.G.Coy
11. 14th Bde.T.M.Battery
12. No.2 Coy 32nd Div.Train.
13. 96th Inf.Bde.
14. 97th Inf.Bde.
15. Signals 14th Inf.Bde.
16. 90th Field Ambulance
17. A.D.M.S. 32nd Division
18. Staff Captain.

SECRET. Copy No. 8..

14th INFANTRY BRIGADE OPERATION ORDER No.56.

Map Reference. Sheet 36 B. 1/40,000. 24th July 1916.

1. The Brigade will march to the area RUITZ, HOUCHIN, HAILLICOURT on 26th July, by the following route:-
AUCHEL - MARLES LES MINES - PLACE a BRUAY.

2. The Brigade will be clear of MARLES LES MINES by 11 a.m. and will pass the starting point road junction C.21.b.42.30 as follows :-

Bde. Headquarters....................9.5 a.m.
2nd Manchester Regt..................9.10 a.m.
15th H. L. I.........................9.15 a.m.
19th Lan. Fus........................9.20 a.m.
1st Dorset Regt......................9.25 a.m.
14th T.M.Batty.)
14th M.G.Coy.)......................9.30 a.m.

3. Transport with units.

4. Dress - Marching order.

5. Billeting parties will meet the Staff Captain at the CHURCH, HAILLICOURT at 11 a.m.

6. Arrival in billets will be reported to Bde. Headquarters which will close at 9 a.m. in RAIMBERT and open at RUITZ at the same hour.

7. ACKNOWLEDGE.

[signature]
Captain,
for Bde. Major, 14th Infantry Brigade.

Issued at 4 p.m.

Copies to :-

No.1 War Diary No.1	10 14/Bde. M.G.Coy.
2 War Diary No.2	11 14/Bde. T.M.Batty.
3 G. O. C.	12 Signals 14/Inf. Bde.
4 File.	13 90/Fd. Ambulance.
5 32/Division.'G'.	14 A.D.M.S. 32/Div.
6 1/Dorset Regt.	15 3/Coy. 32/Div. Train.
7 2/Manchester Regt.	16 96/Inf. Bde.
8 19/Lan. Fus.	17 97/Inf. Bde.
9 15/H. L. I.	Staff Captain.

SECRET. Copy No. 8.

14th INFANTRY BRIGADE OPERATION ORDER No.57.

REF: MAP Sheet 36 B 1/40,000. 28/7/16.

1. The 14th Infantry Brigade (less 2/Manchester Regt., 15/H. L. I. and ½ 14/Bde. M.G.Coy.) will move to ANNEZIN on 29th July.

Route via. K.16.a.2.8. - K.10.b.2.9. - K.4.a.5.8. - E.28.c.08. - E.22.c.5.9. - E.10.d.4.3. - E.9.b.8.7.

The Brigade will pass the starting point K.16.a.2 8.as follows :-

Bde. Headquarters..............9.30 a.m.
19/Lan. Fus....................9.32 a.m.
1/Dorset Regt..................9.37 a.m.
14/Bde.M.G.Coy.................9.42 a.m.
14/Bde.T.M.Batty...............9.45 a.m.

Transport will accompany Units.

Billeting parties will meet the Staff Captain at the CHURCH, ANNEZIN at 9.30 a.m.

Dress - Marching order.

Arrival in billets to be reported to Bde. Headquarters which will close at 9 a.m. in RUITZ and open at BETHUNE at the same time in RUE VICTOR HUGO (opposite THEATRE).

2. The 15/H. L. I.will move to MAZINGARBE via. NOEUX LES MINES, moving by Companies at 200 yards interval from NOEUX.

The move will be completed by noon 29th July.

The Battalion will be clear of HAILLICOURT by 8.30 a.m.

On arrival at MAZINGARBE it will come under orders of 16th Division.

A billeting party under an Officer will be sent forward to the Town Major on 28th July.

3. 2/Manchester Regt. will move to billets near PREOL and ANNEQUIN NORTH via. K.2.b.5.1. - VAUDRICOURT - VERQUIN - BEUVRY.

2/Manchester Regt. will not pass point K.4.a.56.10. before 10.15 a.m. On arrival at destination it will come under Command of 8th Division.

Billeting parties will be sent on in accordance with instructions already issued in 14/Inf. Bde. letter No. S.G. 150/3 and message No. C.79 dated 27th July.

4. ACKNOWLEDGE.

Captain,
Bde. Major, 14th Inf. Bde.

Issued at. 11.45 a.m.
Copies to :-

No.1 War Diary No.1
2 War Diary No.2
3 G. O. C.
4 File.
5 32/Division 'G'.
6. 1/Dorset Regt.
7. 2/Manchester Regt.
8 19/Lan. Fus.
9 15/H. L. I.
10 14/Bde.M.G.Coy.
11. 2/Coy.32/Divl. Train.
12 Signals 14/Inf. Bde.
13 90/Fd.Ambulance.
14 A.D.M.S. 32/Div.
15 96/Inf. Bde.
16 97/Inf. Bde.
17 8/Division.
18 16/Division.
19 Staff Captain,

Prefix........... Code...........m. | Words | Charge | This message is on a/c of: | Recd. at...........m.

Office of Origin and Service Instructions.

Sent
At.............m.
To.............
By.............

..................Service.

(Signature of "Franking Officer.")

Date.............
From.............
By.............

TO 19/ Lan. Fus.

Sender's Number	Day of Month	In reply to Number	AAA
* C 17	8		

Battalion will be ready to march at 9.0 pm

From 14/ Inf Bde.
Place
Time

The above may be forwarded as now corrected.

(Z)

Censor.

Signature of Addressor or person authorised to telegraph in his name.

[illegible] Capt
Bde Major

* This line should be erased if not required.

(A1) O. Ltd., London— W.14042/M.44. 150,000 Pads. 12/15. Form C.2121.

19th Lancashire Fus.

WAR DIARY – JULY 1916.

APPENDIX I

14th }
96th } Bde. Operation Orders.

Prefix .... Code .... m. | Words | Charge

Office of Origin and Service Instructions.

Sent

Sent At .... m. To .... By ....

This message is on a/c of: War Diary Service.

(Signature of "Franking Officer.")

Recd. at .... m.
Date ....
From ....
By ....

TO

Sender's Number.	Day of Month	In reply to Number	AAA
* SA 215	14		

The 96th Inf Bde less 15th Lan Fus and 16th Lan Fus will be relieved by the 14th Inf Bde in OVILLERS this evening aaa The 1st DORSET Regt will take over from 19th Lan Fus and 16th Lan Fus details of handing over to be arranged between officers commanding concerned aaa The 2nd Manchester Regt will take over from 16th North'd Fus and 2R Innis Fus details of handing over to be arranged between officers commanding concerned aaa On relief the 16th Lan Fus will relieve the 15th HLI at DONNET Post and will be employed on carrying parties aaa 15th Lan Fus will remain in present positions and be in

From
Place
Time

The above may be forwarded as now corrected. (Z)

Censor. Signature of Addressor or person authorised to telegraph in his name.

* This line should be erased if not required.

(4198) Wt. W14042—M44. 300000 Pads. 12/15. Sir J. C. & S.

The Officer Commanding,

16th North'd Fus.
2nd.R.Innis.Fus.
15th Highland Light Infantry.
19th Lans.Fus.
14th Bde.M.G.Co.
14th Bde.T.M.Battery.

S.A, 225.

Reference my S.A.221, the spare Officers and other ranks of the units mentioned above will join their units and march to WARLOY today.

Major.
Brigade Major.
96th Infantry Brigade.

12.50 p.m.

Prefix........Code........m. | Words | Charge

Office of Origin and Service Instructions.

Sent
At........m.
To........
By........

This message is on a/c of:
........*Service.*
(Signature of "Franking Officer.")

Recd. at........m.
Date........
From........
By........

TO
16 Northd Fus — 15th HLI
19th Lan Fus — 14th B MG Coy
2 R Innis Fus — 14th B T M Battery

Sender's Number.	Day of Month	In reply to Number	AAA
* Aa 221	15		

(1) The 96th Brigade with attached units will march to WARLOY this afternoon

(2) Order of march
2 R Innis Fus
16 Northd Fus
15 Highland Light Infantry
19th Lan Fus
14th Bde Machine Gun Coy

(3) Units will pass the starting point W 13 C 3.8 and follow Q route at the following times 2 R Innis Fus 2 pm 16th Northd Fus 2.20 pm 15th Highland Light Infty 2.40 pm 19th Lan Fus 3.0 pm 14th Bde Machine Gun Coy 3.20 pm

From
Place
Time

The above may be forwarded as now corrected. (Z)

........Censor. Signature of Addressor or person authorised to telegraph in his name.

* This line should be erased if not required.

(4298) Wt. W14042—M44. 300000 Pads. 12/15. Sir J. C. & S.

MESSAGES AND SIGNALS. No. of Message

Prefix Code m. | Words | Charge | This message is on a/c of: | Recd. at m.

Office of Origin and Service Instructions.

Sent At m. To By | Service. (Signature of "Franking Officer.") | Date From By

TO (2)

Sender's Number. | Day of Month | In reply to Number | AAA

(4) As much 1st line Transport as units have at present in BOUZINCOURT will march with the units.

Remainder of 1st line transport of units which is near SENLIS will march under the orders of Bde. Transport Officer by the main SENLIS-WARLOY Rd. in the same order of march and at the same time as units leave the starting point.

(5) Small billeting parties will be sent to WARLOY at once to report to Town Major.

6 The 14th Bde. T. M. Battery will move to WARLOY on the arrival of the lorry which has been detailed for them.

From

Place

Time

The above may be forwarded as now corrected. (Z)

Censor. Signature of Addressor or person authorised to telegraph in his name.

* This line should be erased if not required.

(4198) Wt. W14042—M44. 300000 Pads. 12/15. Sir J. C. & S.

Prefix.........Code.........m.	Words	Charge	This message is on a/c of:	Recd. at.........m.
Office of Origin and Service Instructions.	Sent		.........Service.	Date
	At.........m.			From
	To			
	By		(Signature of "Franking Officer.")	By

TO (3)

Sender's Number.	Day of Month	In reply to Number	AAA
*			

(7) Baggage Wagons of units will march from BOUZINCOURT via SENLIS to WARLOY leaving the Hd. Qrs. of their units at the following times:-

2.	R. Innis Fus.	3-30 p.m.
16th	North'd Fus.	3-40 pm.
15	H.L.I.	3-50 pm.
19	Lan. Fus.	4-0 pm.
14	B. M. Coy.	4-10 pm.

Lieut Miller 2 R. Innis. Fus. will be in charge.

(8) Bde. Hd. Qrs. will close at BOUZINCOURT at 2.30 pm and open at WARLOY at 3 pm.

From 96 Inf. Bde.

Place

Time 12 noon

R S Popham Capt

The above may be forwarded as now corrected.

(Z)

Censor

Signature of Addressor or person authorised to telegraph in his name.

* This line should be erased if not required.

(4198) Wt. W14 42—M44. 800000 Pads 12/15. S.r J. C. & S.

SECRET. Copy No......6..

96th INFANTRY BRIGADE ORDER NO.46.

Ref.Map.Sheet 57D.
1/40,000. 15th July 1916.

(1) The 96th Inf.Bde. (less 15th Lanc.Fus., 16th Lanc.Fus., 96th Bde.M.G.Coy., & 96 T.M.Battery) with the following units attached, 19th Lanc. Fus., 15th Highland Light Infantry, 14th Machine Gun Coy., and 14th Trench Mortar Battery will march tomorrow to BEAUVAL.

(2) Route VARENNES - LEALVILLERS - ARQUEVES - RAINCHEVAL - BEAUQUESNE - Road Junction G.30.c. 30.10 - road Junction G.16.d.70.00. - BEAUVAL.

(3) Starting Point, road junction V.19.a.20.20.

(4) The units will pass the Starting Point in the following order at the hour named:-

Bde.Hd.Qrs................	10 a.m.
16th North'd Fus..........	10.5. a.m.
2nd.R.Innis.Fus...........	10.20 a.m.
19th Lanc.Fus.............	10.40 a.m.
15th H.L.I................	11 a.m.
14th Bde.M.G.Coy..........	11.15 a.m.
14th Bde.T.M.Battery......	11.25 a.m.
91st Field Ambulance......	11.35 a.m.

(5) Two hours halt for dinners will be made about O.9.a.c.8.2. the spot will be pointed out by a Staff Officer from the Brigade.

(6)a. The whole of the 1st Line Transport will march with units.

b. The Baggage Wagons will be Brigaded and pass the Starting Point in order of units at 11.45 a.m.

(7) Dress:- Marching order without packs. Waterproof sheets will be worn on the back suspended from the D.s. of the braces. Steel Helmets will be worn. No unauthorised articles will be hung on the person, nor will parcels or packages be carried in the hand.

(8.) Packs and heavy kits will be left by units under a Guard at WARLOY. The billet number where the kits are to be stored is to be forwarded to Bde.Hd.Qrs. tonight. These packs will be packed on lorries by the guard on the 17th July.

(9.) Strictest march discipline will be maintained and every C.O. will detail an Officer and a party of N.C.O.s. and men who will be responsible for bringing in all straglers of their units except those that are placed in the Field Ambulance by the Medical Officer.

(10.) Units will send on billeting parties to arrive not less than two hours before the arrival of their units at BEAUVAL.

(11). Halts will be made at 10 minutes to every hour and units will resume the march at the clock hour, Units will send for Divisional Time to Bde.Hd.Qrs. at 9 a.m. on 16th.

(12). Reports to head of Column till arrival at BEAUVAL.

Arthur a. Johnson
Captain.
for Brigade Major.
96th Infantry Brigade.

Issued at 7 p.m.

Copies Nos.1. & 2. - War Diary.
Copy No.3. - Filed.
Copy No.4. - 16th North'd Fus.
Copy No.5. - 2nd R.Innis Fus
Copy No.6. - 19th Lanc.Fus.
Copy No.7. - 15th H.L.I.
Copy No.8. - 14th Bde.M.G.Coy.
Copy No.9. - 14th Bde.T.M.Battery.
Copy No.10.- No.3. Coy. Divl.Train.
Copy No.11.- 91st Field Ambulance.
Copy No.12.- 32nd.Division.

Work Report Night 16/9/16, 17/9/16

150 yds of trench dug to an average depth of 3ft 6ins between HINDENBURG St & the right of WUNDERWERK.. An R.E officer & sappers directed the work. No work was started before 1 a.m owing to shelling of front line trench.

Graham Brown Lt
i/c B. Coy 19 L. F.

MESSAGES AND SIGNALS. No. of Message..................

Prefix SM Code RLM Words 45
Charges to collect
Service Instructions. LC

Received From LC By Jackman

Sent, or sent out At ......m. To ...... By ......

Office Stamp. 1B 19/9/16

Handed in at ...... Office ......m. Received 11.25Pm.

TO 1. B.

*Sender's Number	Day of Month	In reply to Number	AAA
WMW 1	18		

Work report 17th inst aaa On Trench HINDENBERGH ST To TURK st average depth of 4 ft was obtained along the whole length aaa On 2nd PARALEL Trench was cleared from WEST KOYLI To 50 yds beyond THURSO st

FROM L. B.
PLACE & TIME 10.45Pm

* This line should be erased if not required.

Wt. 432–M437 500,000 Pads. H W V 5 16 Forms C.2123.

Prefix .... Code .... m. | Words | Charge

Office of Origin and Service Instructions.

10th (Service) Battalion Lancashire Fusiliers [stamp]

This message is on a/c of: .... Service.

(Signature of "Franking Officer.")

Sent At .... m. To .... By ....

Recd. at .... m. Date .... From .... By ....

TO Adjutant

Work report Night 18–19/9/16

Sender's Number.	Day of Month	In reply to Number	AAA
* 2.F.S.1.	19		

No. 1 party 100 men B. Co under 2/Lt Match
This party met 2/Lt Moss at Pip Street (R31 d.11.5)
at 9 p.m. At 11.20 p.m. party informed by
2/Lt Moss that work had been completed –
returned to camp 2.30 a.m.

No: 2 party 100 men C. Co: under 2/Lt Hamer
completed trench R.31 d 5.8 to R.31 b.5.1
returned to camp 6.00 a.m.

No: 3 party 50 men C. Co under 2/Lt Hilton

Cleared SECOND PARALLEL 200 YDS: WEST
from Q 24 a 78 35

[signature]

From Work

Place

Time 11 a.m.

O.C. Adjutant 10th Lanc. Fus.

The above may be forwarded as now corrected. (Z)

Censor. Signature of Addressor or person authorised to telegraph in his name.

* This line should be erased if not required.

(688-9) —McC. & Co. Ltd., London.— W 14142/641. 225,000. 4/15. Forms C 2121/10.

Prefix .... Code .... m. | Words | Charge

Office of Origin and Service Instructions.

18th (SERVICE) BATTALION LANCASHIRE FUSILIERS No. G.15/1 Date 20/9/16

Sent At .... m. To .... By ....

This message is on a/c of: .... Service. (Signature of "Franking Officer.")

Recd. at .... m. Date .... From .... By ....

TO — I.B.

Sender's Number.	Day of Month	In reply to Number	AAA
* IBX 1	20		

Work report 19–20/9/16

No: 1 Party 100 men under 2/Lt Barker held up by shelling at foot of PIP ST. until 11 p.m. Returned to camp by order of Officer R.E. at 4.30 A.M.

No: 2 Party 100 men under 2/Lt Graham-Browne held up by shelling at foot of PIP ST until 11 p.m. Returned to camp by order of Officer R.E. at 3.00 A.M.

No: 3 Party 50 men under 2/Lt: George deepening strong points on Lonnisbetty between FIRST and THIRD PARALLEL

From
Place IBX
Time 11 a.m.

[signature] Capt. 19th Lan Fus.

The above may be forwarded as now corrected. (Z)

Censor. Signature of Addressor or person authorised to telegraph in his name.

* This line should be erased if not required.

(6S8-9) —McC. & Co. Ltd., London.— W 14142/641. 225,000. 4/15. Forms C 2121/10.

Prefix........Code..........m. | Words | Charge

Office of Origin and Service Instructions.

Sent
At..........m.
To..........
By..........

This message is on a/c of: ....Service.

(Signature of "Franking Officer.")

Recd. at..........m.
Date..........
From..........
By..........

TO 1 B

Work report 20–21/9/16

Sender's Number.	Day of Month	In reply to Number	AAA
* 1BX 1	21		

Party No: I 100 men under 2/Lt Whittles left camp 6.30 p.m. – Dug new trench in R.31 a from point 55 to point 83 – 4 feet deep. Returned to camp 7.05 a.m.

Party No: II 100 men under 2/Lt Graham-Binnie and 2/Lt Mutch – Cleared lower half of PIP ST: made this passable –

Party III 50 men under 2/Lt: Hamer Deepening trench and strong points at the top of INNISKILLING AVENUE between FIRST and THIRD PARALLEL

C.R.E. has his report direct on separate work report now – Will you still require this report in duplicate

From 1BX

Place G/15/I

Time 7.30 a.m.

Only one copy required

The above may be forwarded as now corrected. (Z)

Censor. Signature of Addressor or person authorised to telegraph in his name.

[Stamp: 9th (SERVICE) BATTALION LANCASHIRE FUSILIERS]

* This line should be erased if not required.

(688-9) —McC. & Co. Ltd., London.— W 14142/641. 225,000. 4/15. Forms C 2121/10.

Prefix .... Code .... m.	Words	Charge	This message is on a/c of:	Recd. at .... m.
Office of Origin and Service Instructions.				Date ....
10th (Service) Battalion Lancashire Fusiliers No. 17/51/1 Date 22.9.16	Sent At .... m. To .... By		.... Service. (Signature of "Franking Officer.")	From .... By ....

TO I.B. Work 21/22/9/16

Sender's Number.	Day of Month	In reply to Number	AAA
* IBX 1	22		

No: I Party Lt. Musker 50 ORS:
clearing German front line from end of trench leading from Russian sap to 100 yds left —

No: II Party 2/Lt. Jones 50 ORS
Cleared trench leading from Russian sap to German front line

No: III Party 2/Lt Elden 100 ORS
Cleared continuation German front line to present front

No: IV Party 2/Lt George 100 ORS
clearing German front line from fifth avenue left —

From IBX
Place
Time 8.30 am

The above may be forwarded as now corrected.

.... Censor.

(Z)

[signature]

Signature of Addressor or person authorised to telegraph in his name.

* This line should be erased if not required.

(688-9) —McC. & Co. Ltd., London.— W 14142/641. 225,000. 4/15. Forms C 2121/10.

Prefix .... Code .... m. | Words | Charge

Office of Origin and Service Instructions.

Sent
At .... m.
To
By

This message is on a/c of:
.... Service.
(Signature of "Franking Officer.")

Recd. at .... m.
Date ....
From ....
By ....

TO { 1.B.

Sender's Number.	Day of Month	In reply to Number	
* 1BX 1	23		AAA

Party No: 13 2/Lt: Yama ½ 100 ORS: clearing old German front line above FIFTH AV: to point 30 The whole of this continuously shelled party stayed there until relieved. —

Party No: 14 2/Lt Smith ½ 100 ORS: deepening trench running from Point 55 to PRINCE ST: above Point 03. in places to 6 feet others to 4 feet —

Party No: 15 2/Lt Shutte 100 ORS: communication trench from old British front line to old German front line at R. 31. a 31. Sunk trench average 2'6" across before relieved. —

No: 14 party did very good work being led straight to its task – the other two parties again got in a muddle but eventually got to their work.

From 1BX
Place 8.30 AM
Time

[signature] Lt

The above may be forwarded as now corrected. (Z)

.... *Censor.* Signature of Addressor or person authorised to telegraph in his name.

* This line should be erased if not required.

(688-9) —McC. & Co. Ltd., London.— W 14142/641. 225,000. 4/15. Forms C 2121/10.

"C" Form (Original). Army Form C. 2123.
(In books of 50's in duplicate.)

MESSAGES AND SIGNALS. No. of Message

Prefix SM Code IFAM Words 26 £ s. d. Charges to collect	Received From TS By OREILLY J.	Sent, or sent out At m. ME To By	Office Stamp. 1B 23/9/16

Service Instructions. TS

Handed in at TRANSPORT LINES Office 9·30A m. Received 9·40A m.

TO 1 B

*Sender's Number	Day of Month	In reply to Number	AAA
	23		

Party	of	100	men	were
led	by	R E	officers	to
an	old	GERMAN	trench	position
unknown	150	yds	of	trench
were	dug	before	being	relieved
by	a	party	of	YORK
AND	LANCS	Hours	of	departure
5·30PM	Hours	of	return	3·50AM

FROM LB

PLACE & TIME

* This line should be erased if not required.

Wt. 432–M437 500,000 Pads. H W V 5 16 Forms C.2123.

"C" Form (Original).

(In books of 50's in duplicate.)

MESSAGES AND SIGNALS. No. of Message

Prefix SM Code ICAM Words 56

£ s. d.

Charges to collect

Received From TS By GAIT A, PTE

Sent, or sent out At m. To By

Office Stamp. 1B 24/9/16

Service Instructions. TS

Handed in at TRANSPORT Office 9.15 m. Received 9.20A m.

TO 1 B

*Sender's Number	Day of Month	In reply to Number	AAA
	24		

The	100	men	of	B
coy	deepened	and	improved	200
yds	of	trench	last	night
from	RUSSIAN	SAP	to	old
german	~~sap~~	trench	correct	map
ref	unknown	We	were	connected
up	with	D	Coy	working
party	on	our	right	RE
supervised	the	work	time	of
departure	9.15pm	time	of	return
6.15AM				

1ST BATTALION, LANCASHIRE FUSILIERS. G15/1 25/9/16

FROM PLACE & TIME LB

* This line should be erased if not required.

Wt. 432—M437 500,000 Pads. H W V 5 16 Forms C.2123.

No I Coy. 1-9-16

Details of Work on 31-8-16.

Lancashire Dump	Martinsart Dump
6.0 AM All MEN ~~working in yard~~ out Collecting Trenches	1. NCO & 6 MEN Repairing Trucks L.D.
11.0. 10. MEN working in Yard.	1 " 6 " Ration Party to " "
	1 " 2 " Repairing Railway " "
12.0. 2 G S Wagon unloaded	
	2 " 33 " Working Party at " "
2.30. 16 MEN Collecting Tins	Remainder working on
4.45 1 G S Wagon unloaded	Dugout & Martinsart Dump
7.30. 1 Truck to Aveluy Dump French Boards	
7.40. Remainder of MEN collecting Picks & Shovels for Fatigue Party	

19th (SERVICE) BATTALION
LANCASHIRE FUSILIERS
No. G 15/1.
Date 2/9/16.

P. West
C. S. M. No I Co.

[illegible] Capt
O. C. No I Co

No. I Coy.

2. 9. 16

Details of work on 1-9-16

Lancashire Dump	Martinsart Dump
10-30. 1 G.S. Wagon unloaded S. Bags	
	1 - NCO & 6 MEN Repairing Trench & L. Dump
11-30 1 " " " Timber	
	1 " 6 " Ration Party to " "
4-30 2 " " "	
8-30 2 Trucks loaded Aveluy	1 " 2 " Repairing Rail " "
11-30 P.M. 2 G.S. Wagons unloaded R	2 " 33 Working Part at " "
4-30 A.M. 2 " " " Rails	Remainder working on Dug out at Martinsart Dump

P. West
C S M

M. C. Maywood - Capt
O C No I Coy

No I Coy 3. 9. 16

Details of Work on 2nd 9. 16

Lancashire Dump	Martinsart Dump
	1 N C O & 6 MEN Repairing Trench L. O.
7-30 4 MEN to Martinsart Dump	
	1 " 6 " Ration Party " "
11-0 2 G. S Wagon unloading Timber	
	1 " 2 " Repairing Road " "
12-30. 2 " " Trench "	
	6 " 41 " Working Party " "
2-30 All MEN Helping FM Barker	Remainder on Pay out Martinsart Dump
4.0 1 G S Wagon unloaded Timber	
4.30 All trench collected from Swamp	
12 MEN on All Night from 8-30 PM	

P West
C S M.
A. Clonsdale 2/Lt for
O C No I Coy

No 1 Coy. [stamp: ...th (SERVICE) BATTALION LANCASHIRE FUSILIERS No. G/15/... Date ...] 4.9.16

Detail of Work on 4.9.16

Lancashire Dump	Martinsart Dump
6-15. 16 Men conveying Truck to Aithwilh	1 NCO & 6 MEN Repairing Track @ L Dp
10-45. 1 G.S. Wagon unloaded Sand Bags	1 " 6 " Ration Party to " "
11-15. 2 Truck with Rail	1 " 2 Repairing Rail " "
12.0 All Men clearing Road	Remainder Working Party @ Lane Dump.
3.30. 1 G.S. Wagon unloaded Timber	
7-30. 1 G.S Wagon Timber	
12 Men awaiting during night for Loads	

P. West
C S M

[signature] Lt 2/1
for Capt
O.C. No 1 Coy

No. Ca/1

1

5.9.16

Details of work on 4-9-16

Lancashire Dump	Martinsart Dump
9.30 3 Truck of Rails for Track	1 N.C.O. + 6 Men Repairing Truck at D
10.45 2 G S Wagon unloaded S Bags	1 " 6 " Ration Party to "
11-30 Collecting Empty Truck	1 " 2 Repairing Rail to "
12-15 2 G S Wagon unloaded S Bags + Rails	Remainder Working Party at Lanc. Dump
2-15 All Men employ on Swamp	
5-45 Finish at Swamp	

pp West
C. S. M.

W G Hainsworth Capt
O C No I Co

No I Coy

6·9·16

Detail of Work on 5·9·16

Lancashire Dump	Martinsart Dump
6·0·AM 6 Wagon for Ovisly Dump	1 N.C.O + 6 MEN Repairing Track L D
11 AM 3 Motor Lorries unloaded	1 " 6 " Ration Party to "
2·30 to 4·30 All Men on Dug Out	1 " 2 " Repairing Rail " "
5 P.M. 2 Motor Lorries Unloaded	
	3 " 30 Working Party " "
Platelayer Usual repair	Remainder on Dug out

C S M.

M W G Marwood Capt
O C No I Co

No I Coy. 7-9-16

Details of Work on 6-9-16

Lancashire Dump	Martinsart Dump
6.0 AM All MEN on Dugout Fatigue	1 NCO x 6 Men Repairing Trench
12.0 1 Motor Lorry Loaded	1 " 2 " " Rails
12.15 1 " " unloaded	1 " 6 " Ration Party L.D.
2.0 to 4.30 All men on dugout	2 " 30 Working Party L. Dump
	Remainder on Dugout
6.30 - 3 G S Wagons unloaded	

O.R.W. C S M

W G Maywood Capt
O.C. No I Coy

No I Coy 8-9-16

Detail of Work 7-9-16

Lancashire Dump	Martinsart Dump
6-0. All MEN on Yard	1 NCO 6 MEN Repairing Trench LD.
11- 2 Motor Lorry unloaded	" 2 Repairing Road to "
12- 1 G.S. Wagon unloaded	1 6 Ration Party " "
20-4.30 All men on Dugout	2 10 Repairing Road & Lan Dump
	2 20 Working Party & Lane Dump
Platelayers road repairs	Remainder on Duty Out
	C Martinsart Dump

19th (SERVICE) BATTALION
No. G.15/1.
Date 8/9/16
LANCASHIRE FUSILIERS

[illegible] C.S.M.

W G Maywood Capt
O.C. No I Coy

No 1 Coy   10·9·16

Detail of Work on 9-9-16

Lancashire Dump	Martinpuich Dump
9-0 to 12.30. 10 MEN carrying fatigue for RE	1 NCO & 6 MEN Repairing Track
8 MEN cutting Brushwood	
1.30 to 4.30 Ditto	1 " 6 Ration Party
2·30 3 G.S Wagon unloaded	1 " 2 Repairing Bail
3·30 2 "	
5·0 2 Motor Lorry "	2 · 30 · Working Party
Platelayer moved Repair	
	Remainder & Pay out

C S M

Capt

O.C No I Coy.

No I Coy 9-9-16

Detail of Work on 8/9/16

Lancashire Dump	Martinsart Dump
9-0 to 12-30 18 men Working on Dugout	1 NCO & 6 MEN Repairing Track
10-30 AM 2 Motor Lorries unloaded	1 " 2 " Repairing Road
9-0 AM to 12-30 1 NCO & 10 men Brushwood Fatigue	1 " 6 Ration Party
2 Pm to 4-30 Pm 10 men Working on Dugout	2 " 12 Repairing Road
" " " Remainder of men unloading 10 G.S. Wagons	2 - 20 Working Party
Platelayers Usual Repairs	Remainder on Dugout

A.P.W. CSM

[illegible] Capt
O.C. No I Coy

/

No I Co. 11-9-16

Detail of work on 10th

Lancashire Dump	Martinsart Dump
6-0 AM All Men Collecting Trench	1 NCO & 6 Men Repairing Trench
9-0 to 12-30 10 MEN RE Fatigue / 10 Carrying Brushwood	1 " 6 " Ration Party to Dump
	1 " 2 " Repairing Rail "
2 to 4.30 10 RE Fatigue Suffolk	2 " 30 Working Party "
7-30. 6 Wagon loaded to Dy.	Remainder on Dug outs
10-30 2 Motor Lurry unloaded	
4.30 1 " " "	
Platelayer usual Repair	

F. West
C S M

W. G. Maywood Capt.
O. C No I Co

No I Coy 12-9-16

Details of Work on 11-9-16

Lancashire Dump.	Martinsart Dump
4-30 AM 5 Truck to Salford Dump	1 N.C.O. & 6 Men Repairing Truck
9-0 AM to 12-30 12 MEN RE Fatigue	1 " 2 " " Rail
10-30 5 Trucks Loaded to Salford Dump	1 " 6 " Ration Party
11-0 AM 2 Motor Lorries unloaded 1 G S Wagon	2 " 30 Working Party L.D
12-15 2 Motor Lorries	2 10 Platelayer "
2-0 to 4-30 12 Men RE Fatigue Remainder on Dugouts	Remainder on Dugouts and Latrines

[illegible] C S M

[illegible] Capt
O C No I Co

No I/Co 13-9-16

Detail of Work on 12-9-16

Lancashire Dump	Martinsart Dump
8 to 12 12 Men working on New Ref	
4 " 12 Men Collecting Trench	1 N C O & 6 M Repairing Track
" 4 " " Shuttles & Picks	
4 Men on Dug Outs	1 " 2 " " Rail
2-30 1 G S Wagon Unloaded	
2 Trucks of Brushwood for Authuille	1 6 Ration Party
All men available clearing roadway.	2- 30 Working Party S. L. D
12 Men work R E Fatigue	2 10 Platelayer L. D
2 G S Wagon Unloaded	
5 Truck Loaded for Talfort	Remainder on Dug out
5 " " Pauley Dump	
Used Platelayers Repair	

C. M. Sheeney
a/c C S M

W. G. Maywood Capt
O C No I Co

No I Co.

14/9/16

Detail of Work on 13th

Lancashire Dump	Martinsart Dump
4-30 AM 5 Truck to Salford	1 N.C.O. & 6 Men Repairing Truck
8-30 Rails brought in from Marsh	1 " 2 " " Rail
Men Collecting Trench	
10.0 2 G.S. Wagons Unloaded	1 " 6 " Ration Party
2-30 7 Men Clearing Roadway	1 " 20 Working Party
3.0 7 " Working on Rails	1 " 20 Rail Work
3-30 9 G.S. Wagon Unloaded	Remainder on Dugout
5-0 2 Motor Lorry "	
7.0 6 Trolley for fatigue Party	
Usual Platelayer Repair	

C.G. [illegible]
C.S.M.

W. G. Haywood Capt.
O.C. No. 1 Co.

A Co 15th/9/16

Details of Work on 14th

Lancashire Dump	Martinsart Dump
8-30. 6 Men 1st Working on Rails Sump	
" 6 " " Causeway	1 N.C.O & 6 Men Rep Tre
10 0. 2 Motor Lorry unloaded	
12-30 1 G S Wagon "	1 " " 2 Men Rep Rails
2-30 2 " " "	
2-45 3 " " "	1 " 6 " Ration Party
3-30 2 Motor Lorry "	
3 Truck for Fatigue Party	1 20 Working Party
2 " Brushwood	1 20 Rating "
	Remainder on Dugouts
Platelayer went Repairs	

CQMS Cherry

M G Haywood Capt
OC A Co

A Co 16-9.16

Detail of Work on 15-9-16

Lancashire Dump	Martinsart Dump
6 Men 1 Sgt Working on Wharf 8-30	
12 " " " " Bridge 8-30	1 NCO & 6 Men Repairing Trench
6 Trollies from Martinsart Dump with trench ladders 10-15	1 " 2 " " Rails
5 G S. Wagons unloading timber 10-30	
2 Motor Lorries " Shot Iron 12-45	1 " 6 " Ration Party
2 G S Wagons " Timber 2-15	
2 Trollies from Martinsart with trench ladders 2-15	2 " 25 " Working Party on Dugouts L. D.
2 Motor Lorries unloading iron 4-0	2 " 20 Repairing Rails
1 " " " trench ladders 6-0	
8 Trollies for Fatigue party 6-30	Remainder on Dugout and Latrine

C G McElhinney.

[illegible] Capt
O.C. A Co

A Co. 17-9-16

Detail of Work on 16-9-16

Lancashire Dump	Martinsart Dump
5 Truck Salford Dump 4-15	1 N.C.O. 6 Repairing Track
6 Men 1 Sgt Working on Dump 9-0	1 " 2 " Roads
2 Motor Lorries unloading sand bags 10-45	1 " 6 Ration Party
2 Trucks for fatigue party 2-0	2 " 24 Working Party L.D.
2 " " Paisley Dump 3-0	1 " 20 " on Roads
2 Motor Lorries unloading iron 5-0	Remainder on Latrines and Dugouts Martinsart
4 Trucks pick & shovels B. H. road 6-0	
3 G.S. Wagons unloading timber 6-15	

C. [G?]. M. Mahoney

W. C. Maynard Capt
O.C. A Co.

A Co

19-9-16

A/15/1

Details of Work on 18th 9-16

Lancashire Dump	Martinsart Dump
1 NCO 10 Men c Installing Dump	1 N.C.O. c 6 MEN Repairing Track
1 " 6 " c Causeway	
1 " 9 " Railway.	1 " 2 " " Road
unloading 1 Motor Lorry	1 " 6 Ration Party
1 N C O & 12 Working on Rd.	2 " 30 Working Party Z D
2 Motor Wagon Unloading	1 " 20 " " "
Platelayers Hand Repair	Remainder on Canteen Dug out.

C W Whaley

W. C. Maywood Capt
O.C. A Co.

A. Coy 20/9/16

Details of Work on the 17th/9/16

Tamsolrire Dump.	Martinsart Dump
18-9-16.	
1 N.C.O + 40 Men Paisley 4.30 AM	1 N.C.O & 6 Men Repairing Trucks
19-9-16.	
1 " " 10 " Inniskilling. 9.0 AM	1 – – 2 – – Rails
	1 – – 6 – Ration Party
1 Motor Waggon Sand Bags. 10.45 AM	2 – – 30 – Working Party
1 " " Sump Boards. 1-30 AM	1 – – 20 – – –
1 " " Pit Props. 5.0 AM	
2 " " Sump Boards 6.0 "	Remainder on Dug Out
1 N.C.O + 4 Men Paisley 6-30 "	
Men working on dugouts	
Platelayers general repairs	

Capt [illegible]

[stamp: (SERVICE) BATTALION ... LANCASHIRE ... No. G 15/1 Date 20/9/16]

[signature] Capt

O.C. A Co.

A Co. 21.9-16

Detail Work on 20-9-16

Lancashire Dump	Martinsart Dump
1 N.C.O. + 4 Men Salford Dump 5.0 AM	1 N.C.O. 6 Men Repairing Track
1 " " 10 " Inniskilling " 9.0 AM	1 " 2 " " Rail
2 Motor Waggons Sumph Bank 11-30	1 " 6 " Ration Party
1 " " " " 1-0 PM	2 " 30 " Working " L.D
1 Sgt + 12 Men Paisley Dump. 7-0 "	1 " 20 " " "
1 Motor Waggon Sand Bags 8-0 "	
Platelayers General repair to line.	Remainder Cleaning Dump

Sgt Ravenscroft

C.Q.M.S. [illegible]

M.G. Maywood Capt
O.C. A Co

A Co

22nd 9-16

Details of Work on 21st.

Lancashire Dump	Martinsart Dump
1 Cpl + 10 Men Inniskilling Dump 9 am	1 N.C.O. 6 Men Repairing Truck
2 Motor Waggons Dump Boards 11-0 am	1 N.C.O. 2 " " Rails
2 Motor Waggons Sand Bags + Iron Pickets 4-0 am	1 " " 3 Rations
2 Motor Waggons Dump Boards 5-15 pm	1 " 30 Working Party
1 Motor Waggon Shovels 4-0 pm	1 " 20 " "
1 Cpl + 12 Men Paisley Dump 4-0 pm	1 N.C.O. 6 Men Burial Party Bouzincourt.

Sgt [illegible]

[illegible] R.M.O. R.A.M.C.

[illegible] Haywood Capt.
O.C. A Co.

A Co

23-9-16

Detail of Work on 22nd

Lancashire Dump	Martinsart Dump
1 Cpl 10 men Immediately Dump	1 N.C.O. 6 Men Repairing Trench
10 motor waggons unloaded.	1 " 2 " " Rails
	1 " 6 Ration Party
1 Cpl 24 men Paisley Dump	1 " 30 Working Party L.D.
Remainder on dug out Construction	1 20 " " "
Platelayers General repairs.	4 Men Making Oven

[illegible signature]

[signature] Capt
OC A Co.

A Coy 24th Sept/16

Detail of Work on 23rd

Lancashire Dump	Martinsart Dump
1 Cpl + 10 Men "Stores" Dump	1 NCO & 6 Men Repairing Trucks
1 Motor Waggon Pikes + Shovels	1 - 2 - - Rails
3 G.S. Waggons + 11 Trucks Dump Boards loaded at Lancs Dump	1 - 6 - Ration Party
	1 - 30 Working Party L.D.
	1 - 20 - - -
1 Sgt + 40 Men Paisley Dump	4 Men Working Oven

19th BATTALION, LANCASHIRE FUSILIERS.
No. G15/1
Date 25/9/16

Sgt. Ravenscroft

B.Q. McSherry

W.G. Haywood Capt
O.C. A Coy

10 + Appx
19 L.F

Work Report for 5/6th Sept.

Party of 1 Off. & 50 O.R. went at 5.30 a.m. to INNISKILLING AV which was cleared from ROSS ST to the bottom.

Party of 2 Offrs & 100 men left MARTINS WOOD at 7 p.m. and cleared and deepened 100 yds of 1st & 2nd parallels to the left of the K.O.Y.L.I.

Party of 1 Offr & 50 O.R. left for work on INNISKILLING AV at 5.30 this morning

Casualties NIL

MARTINSART WOOD
8 a.m.
6/9/16

R. Mush
OC No. 3

Adjt 19 L F

19th (SERVICE) BATTALION LANCASHIRE FUSILIERS
No. G/[illegible]
Date [illegible]

Work Report for Night 4/5.5

Party of [illegible] Offrs and 100 O.R left MARTINSART WOOD at 7 p.m

<u>Work Done</u> About 50 yds of the 1st and 2nd parallels were cleared to the left of K OYLI WEST
Party returned at 3 30 a.m

<u>Casualties</u> NIL

Party of 1 offr and 50 men left MARTINSART WOOD at 5 15 a.m. for work on ELGIN and SANDY AV.
This party has not yet returned

MARTINSART WOOD
10 30 a.m

[illegible]
O.C No 2 Coy
19 L.F

To:- Adjt.
19 L.F.

Work Report for 7th/8th Sept.

Party worked on INNISKILLING AV during morning. The work of deepening is completed as far as BELFAST CITY TRENCH

Night party continued work on the parallels. These have been cleared and deepened for 170 yds of each.

Morning party for INNISKILLING AV. has not yet returned.

Casualties NIL.

MARTINSART WOOD.
8/9/16.
10.45 a.m.

G. Muskee Lt
O.C. No 2 Coy

To – Adjt
19 L F.

Work Report

Morning Party completed clearing of INNISKILLING AV as far as ROSS ST.

Night Party found that a considerable amount of work already done had been blown in.

KOYLI WEST was cleared between the front line and the 2nd parallel. The 2nd Parallel was cleared to within 3 bays of THURSO. Fire bays were started in 6 bays along this parallel.

MARTINSART WOOD.
9/9/16.
11 am.

[illegible]
OC N Coy

To Adjt
19th L.F.

Work Report for 10th/11th Sept

Night party (100 O.R.) continued work on parallels.

In the first parallel we are working to the left to 15 yds to the left of THURSO St. Some places blown in & still need deepening. One body was removed from the floor of the trench.

In the second parallel we are working to 100 yds to the left of THURSO St.

Fire steps are being constructed in 1st parallel

Casualties NIL

MR THIEPVAL WOOD
10.45 a.m

[illegible] Lt
O.C. No. 2 Coy

To Adjt 19th L F

Work Report for 11th/12th Sept

1st Parallel This trench is cleared up to trench beyond THURSO ST to an average depth of 5ft the sides [illegible] straightening with sandbags. This work has been started. The W Ridings were working about 50 yds on our left.

2nd Parallel from W KOYLI to [illegible] ST. A few steps have [illegible] constructed. The [illegible] [illegible] parapet still need further [illegible] [illegible] 30 yds to the left of THURSO ST the clearing and strengthening is still in progress to be connected with W Ridings here also.

THURSO ST to W KOYLI been cleared

Casualties Nil

[illegible] Lt
OC [illegible] Coy

[illegible]

To Adjt 19 L.F

Work Report for 12/13 Sept

1st Parallel deepened and built up [illegible] [illegible]
Sandbagging in progress.

2nd Parallel joined up with W York about 30 yds beyond THURSO ST
[illegible] deepened all along
Have fire-step started

Casualties NIL

[illegible]

MARTINSART WOOD
13/9/16
4 am

OC No 2 Co.

To:- Adjt. 19 L.F.

Work Report for 13th/14th Sept.

Both parallels were sandbagged where necessary. More fire-steps were constructed in 2nd parallel.
Work was discontinued early owing to instructions to be clear by 2 am.

Casualties NIL.

S. A. Palk.
O.C. No 2 Coy
19 L.F.

MARTINSART WOOD
14/9/16
2.0 a.m.

Work done by C & D Coy

Night of 15th & 16th

Work on No 1 Parallel was needed in many places owing to shelling, all parts were cleared & more fire-steps constructed.

No 2 Parallel was cleared & deepened, weak places in sides sand-bagged.

Casualties NIL

S. A. Bulk Capt

O.C. C. Coy

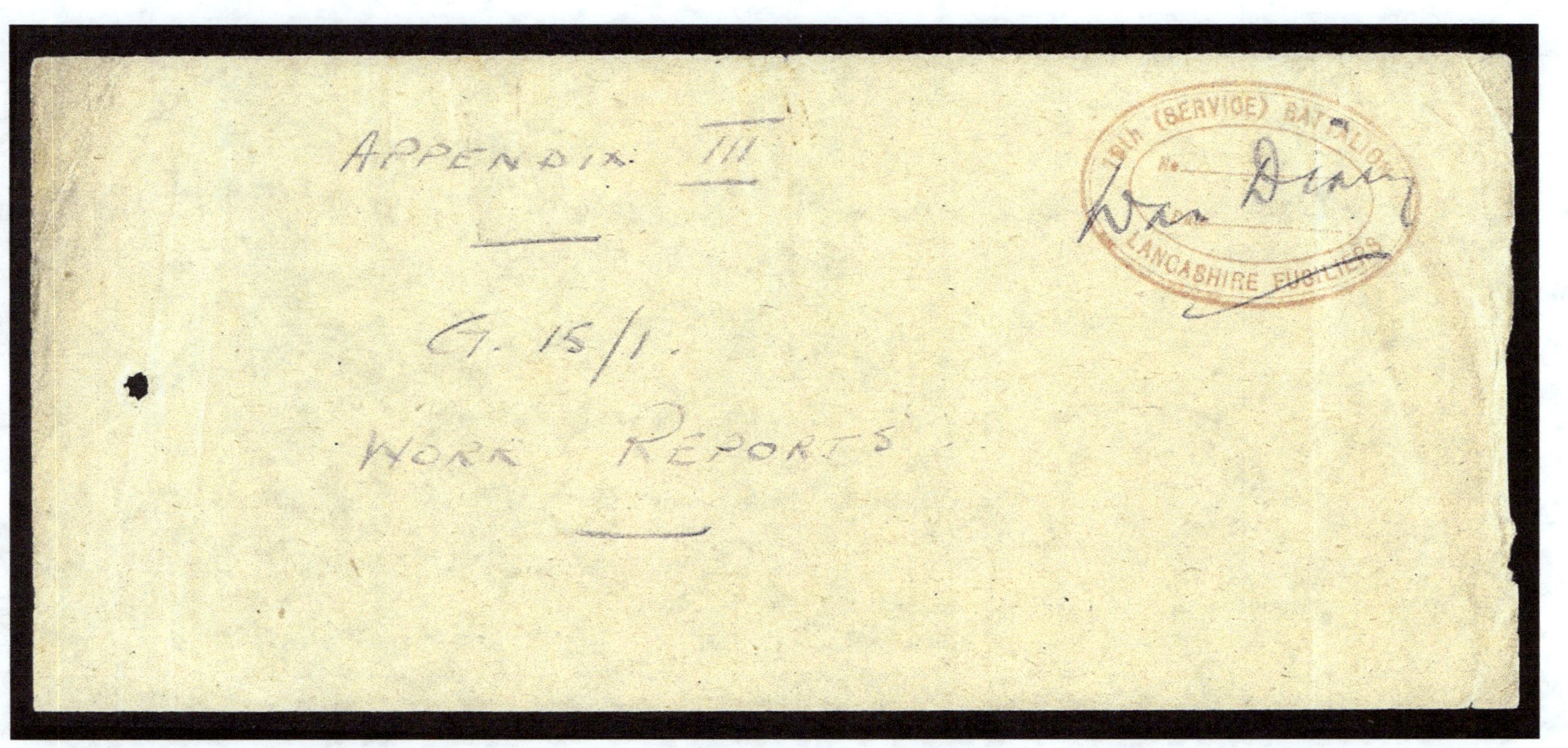
APPENDIX III

G. 15/1.

WORK REPORTS

19th (SERVICE) BATTALION
No.
LANCASHIRE FUSILIERS

War Diary

Report on Op rations   1st to 4th July

Report on Operations

1st/4th July. 1916.

July 1st. 2.0 am. The Battalion arrived BLACKHORSE SHELTERS, drew tools etc. & was ready to move at 3.0 am.

ZERO time for commencement of operations - 7.30 am.

7.10 am. 1st DORSET REGT. (leading Batn. of RIGHT Column) moved off from BLACKHORSE SHELTERS by platoons at 50 yards interval.

7.35 am. Leading platoon of "A" Coy. 19th Lancs. Fus. moved off & followed route as detailed in Operation Order No. 37.

8.10 am Battalion held up by leading Battalion being unable to leave exit of WOOD owing to heavy flanking fire of enemy machine guns. This "hold up" was overcome by advancing in short rushes.

9.35 am Battalion closed into Column of Route on DUMBARTON TRACK, immediately in rear of 1st DORSETS & moved up to the exit of WOOD.

10.30 am. 1st party of "A" Coy. 19th Lancs. Fus. left exit of WOOD followed closely by parties of "B" & "C" Coys. Casualties during this move severe; all caused by machine gun fire.

11.5 am Message from O.C. "A" Coy. with information that BRITISH Front Line trenches were congested with remnants of preceding Battalion and dead & wounded.

C.O. delayed advance of "D" Coy., which was ordered to move up by communication trench - ROCK STREET.

Meanwhile

2

parties of "A" "B" & "C" Coys., under Capt G. HIBBERT advanced to the enemy front line. Which was lightly held by personnel of 1st DORSETS.

11.15 a.m. Troops in front line (British trenches) were organised into their units & prepared to advance in support of troops in enemy trenches, but under orders of G.O.C., 14th Bde. remnants of this Battalion & 11th BORDER REGT. were ordered to withdraw.

1.30 p.m. Battalion took up position in old FRENCH TRENCH by ROCK ST. - NORTH of DUMBARTON TRACK, re-organised into Coys., roll was called and 7 Officers & 182 other ranks were present, remainder killed, wounded, missing or in German trenches.

Estimate of casualties during 1st 6 hours fighting :- 8 Officers 150 other ranks. Lewis Gunners & bombers suffered heavily.

The advance from our own front line was carried out in waves:

1st Wave - lead by 2/Lieut. H. W. Hardy, failed to reach enemy trench owing to heavy casualties.

2nd Wave, under Capt. G. Hibbert, and 3rd Wave - under Lieut. H. Mesken and 2/Lieut. R. L. George succeeded in entering enemy trenches.

Capt. Hibbert took command of men of 19th Lancs. Fus. in German lines and held the RIGHT flank - with 1st DORSET REGT. on Left - by bombing.

3.

Enemy several times attempted bombing counter attacks but were repulsed.

The supply of bombs in these trenches ran short, and Captain Hibbert had to resort to Boche bombs which were used most effectively.

3.30 pm. Lieut. Mucker returned to Battalion H.Q. (via RUSSIAN SAP) and reported situation & position held by our troops. 2nd Manchester Regt. had now come up to occupy this captured portion of the line.

Nothing of importance occurred until

7.30 pm. when Battalion was ordered to withdraw to AUTHUILLE DEFENCES.

This was carried out and completed at 10.30 pm. with the exception of Capt. Hibbert & party, who were relieved at 12.30 am. 2/7/16.

2nd JULY. AUTHUILLE DEFENCES - Coys. were re-organised & casualties estimated at 7 Officers & 375 other ranks.

3.30 pm. to 5 pm. Defences were heavily shelled & "B" Coy suffered further casualties.

9 pm. Battalion moved to relieve 15th H.L.I. in the line - MERSEY ST. to CHEQUERBENT ST. "D" Coy. held the line, with A.B.C. Coys. in support at WOOD POST. Battn. H.Q. at WOOD POST. 2nd Manchester Regiment on our LEFT; 9th Royal Fusiliers on RIGHT.

Relief completed at 11.30 pm. at which time Operation Orders from 14th Inf. Bde.

4 (for attack by 15th H.L.I. at 3.15 am)

were received. Operation Order was

3rd Feb. issued accordingly at 12.15 am.

3 am Enemy heavily bombarded front line trenches & WOOD POST. Great number of Lachrymatory shells used, causing much inconvenience but no serious effect. Casualties during this bombardment – which lasted until 4.30 am. – were slight. Dug-out occupied by Capt. Hibbert Lt. Brown & 2/Lt. Huxley was blown in, causing these Officers to become casualties.

3.10 am Wire from 14th Bde. postponing proposed attack by 15th H.L.I. at 3.15 am to 6.15 am.

6.15 am Postponed attack by 15. H.L.I. carried out & more ground gained.

Remainder of day passed without any infantry action. Artillery kept up continuous bombardment.

11.30 pm Battalion was relieved by 10th Cheshire Regiment & withdrew to Billets at SENLIS.

(Total casualties sustained shown on sheet annexed).

Operation – 1st/4th July 1916.

Casualty List.

Lieut. R. C. Masterman – Killed 1.7.16.
2/Lieut. E. D. Ashton – ditto.
– A. N. Dussee – ditto.
– E. C. E. Chambers – ditto.

Capt. G. Hibbert – wounded 3/7/16.
Lieut. J. Hewitt – wounded 1/7/16
– K. R. Evans – wounded 3.7.16.
2/Lieut. H. W. Huxley – wounded 3.7.16.

2/Lieut. W. R. Nightingale N. 3/7/16.
– L. N. Middleton 1.7.16.
– J. Shields 1.7.16

Summary.

4 Officers killed.
7 Officers wounded.

7 other ranks killed.
234 – wounded.
29 – missing.

Ref. Map.
1/20000.
Sheet 57D. S.E.

Report on Operations carried out by 19th Lancashire Fusiliers from 1st to 4th July, 1916.

At 9.30 p.m. on the evening of the 30th June, 1916, the Battalion left billets at SENLIS and proceeded to BLACKHORSE BRIDGE SHELTERS, arriving there between 1-0 and 2-0 a.m. on the 1st July. Here were assembled the Right Column, consisting of:-

under command of Lieut-Col. J.M.A. Graham D.S.O. 19th Lancs. Fus.

1st DORSET REGIMENT.
14th BDE. T.M. BATTERY (less 2 sections).
4 STOKES GUNS.
19th LANCASHIRE FUS.
1/2 Section 206th COY. R.E.

At 7.10 a.m. the order to advance was given and the column moved off in the above order. The advance was carried out in columns of platoons in fours, with 100 yards interval between platoons.

The line of advance was along the river bed of the ANCRE, left [illegible] across the AVELUY – AUTHUILLE r[illegible] at point W-11-b-7/6, thence [illegible] point W-6-c-55/06 on S. edge [illegible] AUTHUILLE WOOD, along path [illegible] DUNBARTON TRACK, and [illegible] point X-1-c-38/75 on [illegible] of WOOD.

(2). On arrival at WESTERN EDGE of AUTHUILLE WOOD, information was received that the 1st DORSET REGT. was experiencing heavy casualties, emerging from WOOD. The 19th LANCASHIRE FUS. continued to advance until the whole Battalion was in column of route along DUNBARTON TRACK, immediately in rear of 1st DORSET REGT.

Owing to the severe casualties on leaving the WOOD, the O.C. RIGHT COLUMN brought up 2 Trench Mortars to point X.1.C. 35/75, and also established 2 LEWIS GUNS, and under cover of the fire of these guns the advance was continued. The open space in front of point X.1.C. 35/75 was crossed by squads in rushes of 30 to 40 yards – the men taking cover in shell craters.

"A" "B" and half of "C" Companies thus crossed the open space between point X.1.C. 35/75 and our front line trench, heavy enfilade fire being experienced the whole way across, causing many casualties.

At this juncture, a message was received from LIEUT. HUXLEY, Comdg. "A" Coy., stating that the front line trench was so crowded with the remnants of all preceding regiments that it was inadvisable to send any more men across until the congestion was relieved. This having been

3. communicated to H.Q. 14th INF. BDE. the advance was discontinued by the remaining half of 'C' Coy. and 'D' Coy. and orders were given that these Companies were to move round by ROCK STREET to CHEQUERBENT STREET and effect an exit from the head of the latter street; but owing to the excessive crowding in all these front line trenches, it was found impossible to make any progress, and orders were received from BDE. H.Q. to 'STAND FAST'.

In the meanwhile, 'A' 'B' and part of 'C' Coy. had continued their advance from the front line trench in waves of 30 or 40 men. The leading wave, lead by LIEUT. HUXLEY, got within 15 yards of the German Trench but out of forty men only four remained, and they could get no further.

CAPTAIN HIBBERT led the next wave and succeeded in getting into the German trench. He was followed by LIEUT. MUSKER and Lieut. GEORGE with all the men that could be collected. These were the only three officers left with the two and half Companies that had advanced, the remaining officers having been killed or wounded.

The names of those officers killed or wounded in this advance were :-

2/Lieut. H. W. Huxley, (Wounded but remained at duty).
" E. C. E. Chambers. Killed.
" A. N. Pussee. Killed.
" E. D. Ashton. Killed.
Lieut. J. Hewitt. Wounded.
2/Lieut. L. N. Middleton. Wounded.
Lieut. R. C. Misterman. Killed.
2/Lieut. J. Shiels. Wounded.

Captain G. Hibbert then took command of all available men belonging to the Battalion and proceeded to hold the N.W. Angle of the Lemburg Salient, - the Dorset Regt. being on his Right.

Throughout the day this line of German trench was held in spite of continual bombing attacks by the enemy from a large mine crater on the left flank.

The supply of bombs carried over was soon exhausted, and Captain Hibbert very soon found it necessary to make use of all the German bombs in the trench - some 700 or 800 being used.

Seven or eight Germans were found hiding in the dug-outs, and these were sent down in the course of the afternoon to Blackhorse Bridge, by means of making use of the Russian Sap opposite Sanda Street.

At 9.30 p.m. on the evening of the 1st. July orders were received for the 19th Lancashire Fus. to return on Authuille

5. being relieved by the MANCHESTER REGT. All wounded men belonging to the Regiment were brought down, but the withdrawal had to be conducted very slowly owing to the heavy hostile artillery fire on this section of our front line. The remainder of the Battalion retired down DUNBARTON TRACK on to the AVELUY - AUTHUILLE ROAD. AUTHUILLE VILLAGE was reached at 1 a.m. on the morning of the 2nd July, and the Battalion proceeded to man the defences.

On the night of the 2/3 July, the Battalion was ordered to relieve the 15th H.L.I., then holding our front line trench from MERSEY to CHEQUERBENT STREET. The relief was effected by 11 pm and this sector was held by the Battalion until the night of the 3rd July, when it was relieved by the 11th Cheshire Regiment.

During the night of the 2/3. July and throughout the morning of the 3rd July, the line was subjected to an intense bombardment causing several casualties - the following Officers being wounded :-

CAPTAIN G. HIBBERT
LIEUT. K.R. EVANS.
2/LIEUT. H.W. HUXLEY.
" W.R. NIGHTINGALE.

Throughout these operations the Battalion behaved with the greatest steadiness, and the advance was carried out without hesitation on the part of the men - in

6. spite of the intense artillery and machine gun enfilade fire.

The greatest difficulty was experienced in trying to advance from our own front line trench on the morning of the 1st July.

This was due to the fact that when the trench was reached, it was found to be blocked by men of the preceding units of the attacks, and consequently it was found to be almost impossible to keep any direct hold on the men, as they were immediately swallowed up in the melée found in the first line trench, but in spite of this the men moved forward and crossed the trench without hesitation.

The Battalion returned to billets at SENLIS on the night of the 3/4 July.

During these operations the Battalion experienced two hundred and sixty-eight casualties - that is to say, 50% of its fighting strength - having 20 Officers and 577 other ranks when going into action.

Attached is list of Officers who went into action on the morning of the 1st July:-

LIEUT-COL. J.M.A. GRAHAM. D.S.O.
MAJOR J. AMBROSE SMITH
LIEUT. & ADJT. A.R. MOXSY
LIEUT. G.B. SMITH.

7. **'A' Coy.** 2/Lieut. H. W. Huxley.
- E. C. E. Chambers.
- A. N. Dusser.
- E. D. Ashton.

'B' Coy. Capt. G. Hibbert.
Lieut. J. Hewitt.
2/Lieut. R. L. George.
- L. N. Middleton.

'C' Coy. Capt. W. G. Haywood.
Lieut. H. Musker.
- R. C. Masterman.
2/Lieut. G. H. Dykes.

'D' Coy. 2/Lieut. W. R. Nightingale.
- I. Jones.
- H. B. Cartwright.
- J. Shiels.

One Lewis Gun was carried over into the German trenches, but the others, the carriers were either killed or wounded.

Of the bomb-carriers very few got across the fire-swept zone with their buckets. This was due to the fact that the men could not advance quick enough with the loads they had to carry, and they, probably being more conspicuous, were singled out.

The smoke barrage thrown out on our Right flank on the morning of the 1st July considerably aided our advance, and that, together with the machine and Lewis Guns fire from point X.1.C 35/75

8. certainly helped in reducing our casualties.

6th July, 1916. Lieut-Col.

DENOTES {100 BOXES S.A.A. / 100 G.}
THIEPVAL.
30
25
26
35
36
31
32
Q
R
W
X
6
1
5
2
11
12
7
8
HAMILTON
GREENOCK AV.
AUTHUILLE
EVACUATION TRENCH
BURY AV.
22,000 GRENADES
LOMOND CASTLE 100 GALS.
AUTHUILLE WOOD
BLACKPOOL ST.
CHORLEY ST.
THORPE ST
JARDINE BRIDGE
DUMBARTON
RIVER ANCRE
RAILWAY
COMISTON POST.
WENNING ST.
LANCASTER AV.
CRUCIFIX CORNER
AVELUY
R.E. DUMP
SCALE 1/10,000
R.E. DUMPS
FIELD ARTILLERY BRIDGES
PACK MULE BRIDGES
DRESSING STATIONS

Intelligence Report

Operations of 1st to 3rd.

Intelligence Report. July 1st – 3rd. 1916.
Operations

July 1st. 7.30 a.m. The Battn. left BLACK HORSE SHELTERS and proceeded via DUMBARTON TRACK to AUTHUILLE WOOD.
A.B.C. Coys. advanced across open from AUTHUILLE WOOD to our front line at X.1.a.6/4. Owing to hostile M.G. fire the advance was made by short rushes. Casualties were heavy.

11.30 a.m. Orders were received from 14th Bde. to proceed via ROCK ST. to front line. This was done by D Coy. Front line was found to be impassable. D Coy and men of other Coys. still in front line were withdrawn and reformed in AUTHUILLE WOOD.
A portion of A.B.C. Coys had continued to advance to hostile front trench in LEIPZIG SALIENT, about R31 2/1. Here a bombing fight was already in progress. They held the enemy trenches already captured, in support of 1st DORSET REGT., until relieved in the evening. Casualties heavy in "NO MAN'S LAND".

9.30 p.m. Orders were received from 14th Bde. to man AUTHUILLE defences. This was done, and Battn. remained there until evening of July 2nd.

Enemy Artillery There was little hostile shelling encountered before noon July 1st. Enemy artillery then became more active against our front line, AUTHUILLE WOOD and communication trenches, with shrapnel, 5.9 and lachrymatory shells. This continued for the rest of the day.

10–11 p.m. AUTHUILLE was bombarded with shrapnel. ~~about~~ to Some casualties.

July 2nd. 5 p.m. AUTHUILLE defences heavily shelled with 5.9s. Casualties were suffered by "B" Coy.

~~July 3rd~~. 8.30 p.m. D Coy. went into front line from CHEQUERBENT St. to MERSEY St. in relief of 15th H.L.I. A.B. & C. Coys being in reserve at WOOD POST.

July 3rd.
2.30 am. Enemy commenced heavy bombardment of AUTHUILLE WOOD, and trenches leading to front line, with 5.9s, shrapnell and lachrymatory shells. Front line was less heavily shelled, mostly with 77 mm. The bombardment continued intense for about 1½ hours, and was intermittent for the rest of the day.

9 p.m. Bn. relieved. Few casualties throughout the day.

J B Smith
Lt. 19th L.F.
Intelligence Offr.

Prefix.......Code.......m.	Words	Charge	This message is on a/c of:	Recd. at.......m.
Office of Origin and Service Instructions.	Sent At.......m. To....... By.......		.......Service. (Signature of "Franking Officer.")	Date....... From....... By.......

TO

Sender's Number.	Day of Month	In reply to Number	AAA
*			

16th	Northd Fus	[illegible] 2	[illegible] Fus	19th
Lan Fus	and	18th HLI	as relief	[illegible]
forward	[illegible]	[illegible]	in	BAZENTIN [illegible]
Details	96th	Bde MG Coy	& 96	T M Battery
will	be	relieved	under	[illegible]
to	be	[illegible] by	OC	[illegible]
on	[illegible]	[illegible]	18th HLI	[illegible]
on	[illegible]	[illegible]	be	[illegible]
BAZENTIN [illegible]				

From SA.

Place

Time 6 pm

The above may be forwarded as now corrected. (Z) R S [illegible] Major

Censor. Signature of Addressor or person authorised to telegraph in his name.

* This line should be erased if not required.

(4198) Wt. W14042—M44. 300000 Pads. 12/15. Sir J. C. & S.

Intelligence Report. July 11th – 14th
Operations

July 11th Evening. No 1 Coy (Right Coy) took over from 15th H.L.I. a line in trenches X.8.C: 8/8, 7/7, 8/3.

No 2 Coy (Left Coy.) a line X.8.c: 5/4, 6/7, 6/73, 8/83.

Connection between nos. 1 and 2 Coys. was by trenches X.8.C. 6/75, 6/7, 7/7.

Night of July 12th – 13th. 11 p.m – 4.30 a.m. No 1. Coy. attacked up trench X.8.c. 77-18 in cooperation with 2nd S. LANCS. advancing up 34-18. Objective pt. 18. No 1 Coy. made 4 unsuccessful attacks. Casualties from M.G fire and bombs heavy.

13th 6.30 a.m. Pt. 18 taken by 2nd S. LANCS. No 1 Coy. at once got into touch with them, and occupied and consolidated trench 77-18.

9 a.m. 2nd S. LANCS. who had advanced up 18-31-33 were driven back by counter-attack down this trench. Pt. 18 was held with difficulty. Casualties fairly heavy.

---

11 p.m. No 2 Coy. advanced without difficulty up X.8.C. 6/73 – X.8.a. 8/83, to about pt. X.8.a.9.1. This they consolidated. Few casualties, mostly from snipers.

July 13th 8 a.m. 37 of the enemy, ~~mostly~~ belonging to 180th, 186th and G.F. Regts. surrendered to No 2 Coy. These stated that they were lost, nearly surrounded, and hungry and thirsty.

July 14th 3.-6. am. Enemy bombarded his own trenches, especially 77-18, with 77 mm. shells. M.Gs were also very active during this period. Few casualties, as hostile artillery shot badly.

7.0 p.m. Battn. was relieved.

General Enemy artillery was mostly inactive on his own trenches, though the sunken road from OVILLERS to CRUCIFIX CORNER was frequently bombarded, though rarely hit.

Enemy snipers were throughout very active, and caused many casualties.

J.B. Smith

Lt. 19th L.F.

Intelligence Offr.

Report on fighting at OVILLERS

12th to 14th July 1916.

Map No. OVILLERS / 10000

Report on the Fighting in OVILLERS on the 12th 13th 14th July 1916 by the 19th Lancashire Fusiliers

On the 12th July 1916, the 19th Lancashire Fusiliers forming part of the troops occupying the captured German trenches WEST OF OVILLERS were ordered to push further EAST and capture as much ground in the village as possible, particularly strong point 18 almost due SOUTH of the Church.

The Battalion owing to the casualties sustained on the 1st. July only consisted of two companies under the command of Captains Haywood and Palk.

The Battalion occupied the trenches to the SOUTH and part of the trenches to the WEST of the village.

No. 1 Company under Captain Haywood occupying the southern part.

No 2 Company under Captain Palk occuping the western portion.

The 16th Lancashire Fusiliers prolonged the line occupied by No. 2 Company on the west side of OVILLERS.

The 2/ South Lancs. were advancing North down a communication from LA BOISSELLE.

The plan of attack was that at 11 pm. on the 12th, No 1 Coy. 19th Lancs. Fus. should attack point 18 and at the same time No 2 company 19th Lancs. Fus. and also strong patrols from the 16th Lancs. Fusiliers should push EAST and endeavour to gain as much ground in the village as possible. At the same time arrangements were made with the 2/ South Lancs that in the event of No. 1 Coy. 19th Lancs. Fus. being unable to capture Point 18 at 11pm. a further combined assault should be made at 3am. The orders as above set forth were carried out. No 1 Coy pushed on towards point 18, but owing to the trench leading to this point being blocked by fallen trees and other impedimenta, had great difficulty in progressing. However, in spite of these difficulties, the storming parties moved on until they came to the Enemy's barricade. Here they were subjected to heavy machine gun fire and showers of bombs, and forced to retire. Another attempt was made with no better result. In the meanwhile No 2 Company under Captain Pack pushed forward and succeeded in gaining ground almost up to the Church and dug themselves in and further consolidated their advance.

At 3a.m. on the morning of the 13th No 1 Coy. resumed its attack on Point 18, two assaults were delivered and in the last one they succeeded in ~~~~ rushing the barricade, but were immediately overwhelmed by machine gun fire from guns posted a short way in rear of the barricade. In the meanwhile the 2/South Lancs advanced down trench 70-34 and leaving the trench attacked the Enemy's strong point from the rear, this manoeuvre was completely successful and point 18 and some hundred yards of communication trench running EAST were captured. At about 6am. the enemy, having brought up reinforcements, counterattacked driving the 2/South Lancs. back through point 18, but this success was only momentary. The 2/South Lancs. again pushed forward their bombing parties and with the aid of machine gun fire from No. 1 Coy. 19th Lancs. Fus, the enemy were forced back and point 18 was finally seized and held permanently. During these operations a party of the enemy tried to retire across the new front occupied by No 2 Coy just south of the church and coming under the machine gun fire of this company surrendered to Captain Park, who went out personally and brought these men in - although the Germans had begun to turn their own machine guns on to them. Thirty seven prisoners belonging to the Garde Fusiliers Regiment were thus captured by No 2. Coy., the 2/South Lancs. making some more prisoners including an officer.

On the morning of the 14th further counterattacks were made by the enemy but were driven off without any loss of ground.

During the above operations 2/Lieut^s. Longley and Mahoney were killed and 2/Lieut. Young wounded, all belonging to No 1 Coy. Some 40 O.R. were either killed or wounded.

During the four assaults made by No 1. Company on point 18, bombs and rifle grenades were used and nearly all the bombers of this company were either killed or wounded.

The following officers took part in these operations:—

H.Q^{rs}	Lt. Col. J.M.A. Graham, D.S.O.	
	Lt. & Adjt. A.L. Moccey	
	Lieut. G.B. Smith Intelligence Officer	
No 1. Coy.	Capt. Haywood	
	2/Lieut. Young	W
	" Longley	K
	" Cartwright	
	" Mahoney	K
No 2. Coy.	Capt. Park	
	2/Lieut. Dykes	
	" Morrison	W.
	" Graham-Brown	
	" Gowzu	

July 25th 1916.

JMGraham Lt. Col.

Comm^d 19th Lanc. Fus^{rs}

Prefix .... Code .... m.	Words	Charge	This message is on a/c of:	Recd. at .... m.
Office of Origin and Service Instructions.	Sent		.... Service	Date ....
Sent	At .... m.			From ....
	To			By ....
	By		(Signature of "Franking Officer.")	

TO

Sender's Number.	Day of Month	In reply to Number	AAA
*			

X 14. b. 7.5 and X 15. a 2.9 do not fire west of a line through X 8. b. 0.2 – X 8 a. 9.5. (b) that Machine guns sited in positions between X 15. a. 2.9 and X 9. c. 8.2 do not fire west of a line through X 8. b. 3.1 – X 8. b. 1.6 (c) that no Machine gun fire be directed from SW of OVILLERS over the heads of troops in the village (3) At 11 pm July 12th the 7th Brigade has been ordered to attack X 8. b 90/81/71 and 75th Bde to attack X 8. d 24/34 which points are to be consolidated and communications opened to the ALBERT – BAPAUME Rd. add ack and inform later all concerned

From SA

Place

Time 11.50 am

The above may be forwarded as now corrected. (Z) R.S. Popham Major

Censor. Signature of Addressor or person authorised to telegraph in his name.

* This line should be erased if not required.

(4198) Wt. W14042–M14. 300000 Pads. 12/15 Sir J. C. & S

Prefix........Code..........m. | Words | Charge | This message is on a/c of: ....Service. | Recd. at..........m.
Office of Origin and Service Instructions.

Secret

Sent At..........m. To.......... By..........

(Signature of "Franking Officer.") | Date.......... From.......... By..........

TO UW

Sender's Number.	Day of Month	In reply to Number	AAA
* Sa 117	12		

(1) During the night the 7th Inf Bde opened up and consolidated trench X 9. c. 4. 6 to X. 8 b. 9. 0 aaa At the same time the 75th Inf Bde were making good a trench from X 14. b 75. 68 to X 8. d. 7. 0

(2) The 7th Brigade have been ordered to place Machine Guns in trench X 14. b. 7. 5 to X 9. c. 8. 2 to sweep the ground between OVILLERS and the points their troops are holding and between OVILLERS and the following points X 8 b 0. 1. X 9. a. 0. 5. X 8. b. 7. 8. X 8. a 9. 5. but the 25th Div has been asked to arrange that (a) Machine guns sited in position between

From
Place
Time

The above may be forwarded as now corrected. (Z)

Censor. Signature of Addressor or person authorised to telegraph in his name.

* This line should be erased if not required.

(4198) Wt. W14042—M14. 300000 Pads. 12/15. Sir J. C. & S

19th (SERVICE) BATTALION
No. 25
LANCASHIRE FUSILIERS
BLOCK
13.7.16
Ovillers-
la Boisselle
TO OVILLERS POST
AVELUY.
APPROX.*
POSITION
OF
BN HD QRS.
PART OF
LINE OCCUPIED by
19 L.F.
TRENCH CAPTURED
IN CONJUNCTION
WITH.
2. S. LANC. REGT.

L

SHEET 1 49

Army Form C. 2118

WAR DIARY
or
~~INTELLIGENCE SUMMARY~~
(Erase heading not required.)

Instructions regarding War Diaries and Intelligence Summaries are contained in F. S. Regs., Part II. and the Staff Manual respectively. Title Pages will be prepared in manuscript.

19th LANCASHIRE FUS
JULY 1916. VOL 7

Place	Date	Hour	Summary of Events and Information	Remarks and references to Appendices
THIEPVAL AVEHUVLLE WOOD	1 2 3	}	Battn took part in "Attack of 4th ARMY on German Positions" See APP. IV & APP. V. Bn arrived SENLIS at 12.30 am on the night of 3/4 July.	
SENLIS	4		Battn reorganising & re-equipping. 7 officers reinforcements joined see APP	VI
SENLIS – FORCEVILLE	5		Battn moved to FORCEVILLE SEE OP. ORDERS APP. II	
FORCEVILLE	6		Battn continued work of reorganising – Classes for Lewis Gunners Bombers & other specialist formed.	
FORCEVILLE BOUZINCOURT	7		Left FORCEVILLE for BOUZINCOURT at 6 a.m. arrived 7.30 a.m. made preparations to move towards the "Battle area". Bn in huts and billets. Bn organised into 2 Coys under Capts HEYWOOD and PIKE respectively	SEE APP. II
BOUZINCOURT – DONNET POST	8		Bn moved to DONNET POST (in the OVILLERS SECTOR) & relieved 11th MIDDLESEX REGT. No 2 Coy employed in carrying Bombs from CRUCIFIX CORNER to OVILLERS.	SEE APP. II
DONNET POST	9		Battn employed in carrying bombs & clearing up trenches. 2Lt S. MORRISON 15 KINGS LIVERPOOL REGT (attached 19th L F) & 2 O.R. Killed.	

8.X. 4 sheets

VOL

1875 Wt. W593/826 1,000,000 4/15 J.B.C. & A. A.D.S.S./Forms/C. 2118.

Instructions regarding War Diaries and Intelligence Summaries are contained in F. S. Regs., Part II. and the Staff Manual respectively. Title Pages will be prepared in manuscript.

WAR DIARY
or
~~INTELLIGENCE SUMMARY~~
(Erase heading not required.)

SHEET 2

Army Form C. 2118

19. LANC. FUS.

Place	Date (JULY)	Hour	Summary of Events and Information	Remarks and references to Appendices
DONNET POST	10		100 O.Ranks under Capt HEYWOOD went into line at OVILLERS & were placed at the disposal of O.C. 2 MANCHESTER REGT who was commanding troops in that village. No 2 Coy continued carrying Bombs	
DONNET POST – OVILLERS	11.		Battn placed at the disposal of 96th Inf BDE under BRG GEN YATMAN and relieved 15 H.L.I. in line as shown on attached sketch. 16 LANC. FUS on left – 2 SOUTH LANCS on right. No 1 Coy held line ~~along~~ along 82–83–77– to point X with 4 platoons. No 2 Coy held line ZY with 2 platoons and held 2 platoons in reserve along 33–42–84.	
OVILLERS	12 13 14		In action in OVILLERS – Fighting described in APP III. Bn was relieved by 1/DORSET REGT & withdrew BOUZINCOURT. Casualties during these days 2LTs. LONGLEY and MAHONEY – K. 2 LT A.N YOUNG – W. Other ranks 8 K. 41 WOUNDED.	
BOUZINCOURT WARLOY	15.		Bn moved to billets in WARLOY arrived there 5 15 p.m. See OP. order APP. II	

Army Form C. 2118

Instructions regarding War Diaries and Intelligence Summaries are contained in F. S. Regs., Part II. and the Staff Manual respectively. Title Pages will be prepared in manuscript.

WAR DIARY
or
~~INTELLIGENCE SUMMARY~~
(Erase heading not required.)

SHEET 3.

19 LANC FUS

Place	Date (JULY)	Hour	Summary of Events and Information	Remarks and references to Appendices
WARLOY-BEAUVAL	16.		Battn moved to BEAUVAL See Op order App II.	
BEAUVAL-le SOUICH	17		Battn moved le SOUICH See Op order App. II	
le SOUICH	18.		Battn rejoined 14 BDE the HEAD QUARTERS of which moved into le SOUICH.	
le SOUICH MONTS-en-TERNOIS	19		Battn moved to MONTS-en TERNOIS See Op order App. II	
MONTS-en-TERNOIS - MONCHY-BRETON	20		Battn moved to MONCHY-BRETON See Op order App: II	
MONCHY-BRETON CAUCHY-a-la-TOUR	21		Battn moved to CAUCHY-a-la-TOUR See Op order App II.	
CAUCHY-a-la-TOUR	22		Battn spent day cleaning up, clothing re-equipping etc.	
"	23		Battn started Training - Bombing & Lewis gun classes organised	
"	24		C.O. inspected the Battn by Coy.	
	26		Battn continued Training	

1875 Wt. W593/826 1,000,000 4/15 J.B.C. & A. A.D.S.S./Forms/C. 2118.

Instructions regarding War Diaries and Intelligence Summaries are contained in F. S. Regs., Part II. and the Staff Manual respectively. Title Pages will be prepared in manuscript.

WAR DIARY
or
INTELLIGENCE SUMMARY
(Erase heading not required.)

Army Form C. 2118.

SHEET 4

19 LANC FUS

Place	Date	Hour	Summary of Events and Information	Remarks and references to Appendices
	JULY			
CAUCHY-a-la TOUR HOUCHIN	26		Battn moved to HOUCHIN See op. order App. II.	
HOUCHIN	27		Battn was inspected by G.O.C 14 INF. BDE, who expressed himself extremely pleased with the Battn.	
HOUCHIN	28.		Battn along with 14 INF BDE was inspected by Sir CHAS. MUNROE Comdg First Army.	
HOUCHIN - CAPELLE	29		Battn moved to CAPELLE in G.H.Q. TROOPS area with a view to being transformed into a Pioneer Bn. Bn left BETHUNE (where it had entrained 2.14 pm. and arrived HESDIN 6 pm from which place Bn marched to CAPELLE about 3 miles away. arrived 6.45 pm. See op. order App. II.	
CAPELLE	30		Battn cleaning up.	
Do	31		Battn started training in Pioneer work under R.E. N.C.O's	

1/8/16

[signature] Lt Col
Comdg 19th Lanc Fus

2449 Wt. W14957/M90 750,000 1/16 J.B.C. & A. Forms/C.2118/12.

CORRECTION.

With reference to 14th Inf. Bde. Operation Order No. 40., the following alteration will be made,-

In para. 1.(b) lines 5 - 6 read

15th H.L.I. will reach the point where BROOKERS PASS crosses the Railway Line W.11.c.18.18 at 12.35 a.m.

26/6/16.

Captain,
Bde. Major, 14th Inf. Bde.

War Diary 19/Lan Fus.

SECRET

Copy No 4

14th Inf. Bde. Operation Order No 41

1. 14th Inf. Bde Operation Order No 40 paras 1 and 6 are cancelled.

2. (a) On night 30th June/1st July the 1st Dorset Regt will march via main road SENLIS - BOUZINCOURT - NORTHUMBERLAND AVENUE - PIONEER RD. - AVELUY - HAMEL RD. to BLACK HORSE BRIDGE SHELTERS 1/Dorset Regt will clear cross roads W.13.a.5.9. at 9.30 p.m. but will not pass point W.10.c.1.5. till 11.30 p.m.

(b) 19th Lancs. Fusiliers will follow 1st Dorset Regt. to BLACK HORSE BRIDGE SHELTERS passing cross roads W.13.a.5.9. at 9.40 p.m. and ~~reaching~~ passing point W.10.c.1.5. at 11.45 p.m.

(c) 14th Bde M.G. Coy. (less 2 sections) and 14th Inf Bde T.M. Battery (less 8 Guns) will follow 19th Lancs. Fus. to BLACKHORSE BRIDGE SHELTERS, clearing cross roads W.13.a.5.9. at 9.45 p.m. and passing point W.10.c.1.5. at 12.0. midnight.

(d) 2nd Manchester Regt will march via main road SENLIS - BOUZINCOURT - AVELUY - BROOKERS PASS to CRUCIFIX CORNER SHELTERS, clearing the Eastern Barrier of BOUZINCOURT at 10 p.m.

On arrival at BROOKERS PASS guides will be met to lead 2 Companies to relieve 2nd K.O.Y.L.I. in the line from CHOWBENT STREET to MERSEY STREET. Tools will be drawn first as arranged.

(e) 15th H.L.I. will follow 2nd Manchester Regt to CRUCIFIX CORNER clearing Eastern Barrier of BOUZINCOURT at 10.15 p.m.

2/

(f) 2 sections, 14th Inf Bde M. G. Coy. and 8 guns 14/Inf. Bde. T. M. Battery will follow 15th H. L. I. to CRUCIFIX CORNER clearing Casting Barrier of BOUZINCOURT at 10.20 p.m.

(g) 14th Inf Bde Headquarters will move to Battle Headquarters. Report centre will close at SENLIS at 8 p.m. and open at same hour at Battle Headquarters.

3. Paras 2, 3, 4, 5, 7, 8, 9, of Operation Order No 40 will ~~[illegible]~~ hold good.

4. March will be by companies at suitable intervals.

Issued at
30/6/16.

[signature] Capt
Bde Major.
14/Inf Bde.

SECRET. Copy 8

14th INFANTRY BRIGADE OPERATION ORDER No. 44.

5th JULY 1916.

Map Reference - 57 D. S.E. 1/20,000.

1. The Brigade will move from SENLIS to FORCEVILLE to-day via HEDAUVILLE.

2. Starting point will be V.5.c.30.35, and Units will pass in the following order,-

   1st Dorset Regt...............5.15 p.m.
   2nd Manchester Regt...........5.45 p.m.
   19th Lanc. Fus................6.15 p.m.
   15th H. L. I..................6.45 p.m.
   14th Bde. M. G. Coy...........7. - p.m.
   14th Bde. T.M.Battery.........7.15 p.m.

3. Billeting parties will be sent to the Church at FORCEVILLE by 5.30 p.m. where they will be met.

   Parties will be detailed by Units to load Baggage Waggons.

4. Reports, when Units are settled in Billets, to be sent to Bde Hd.Q which will close at SENLIS at 5 p.m. and open at FORCEVILLE at the same time.

5. Acknowledge.

Issued at 3.15 p.m.

[signature] Captain,
Bde. Major, 14th Infantry Brigade.

Copies to,-

1. War Diary No.1
2. War Diary No.2
3. G. O. C.
4. Bde. Major
5. 32nd Division 'G'
6. 1st Dorset Regt.
7. 2nd Manchester Regt.
8. 19th Lanc. Fus.
9. 15th H. L. I.
10. 14th Bde. M.G.Coy
11. 14th Bde. T.M.Battery
12. Town Major, SENLIS.
13. Signals 14th Inf. Bde.
14. No.2 Coy 32nd Div. Train
15. 90th Field Ambulance
16. 96th Inf. Bde.
17. 97th Inf. Bde.
18. Staff Captain.

SECRET. Copy No. 8.......

14th INFANTRY BRIGADE OPERATION ORDER NO. 45.

6th JULY 1916.

MAP REFERENCE - Sheet 57 D. S.E. 1/20,000.

1. The Brigade will move into Corps Reserve tomorrow as follows,-

To BOUZINCOURT. 1st Dorset Regt.
19th Lanc. Fus.
14th Bde. M.G.Coy
Route - Main road via HEDAUVILLE.
Starting point P.27.b.5.6.
Time . 1st Dorset Regt........5.45 a.m.
19th Lanc. Fus.........6. a.m.
14th Bde.M.G.Coy.......6.15 a.m.

To SENLIS. 15th H.L.I.
2nd Manchester Regt.
14th Bde.T.M.Battery
Starting point P.27.b.5.6.
Time. 15th H.L.I..............6.30 a.m.
2nd Manchester Regt.....6.45 a.m.
14th Bde.T.M.Battery....7. a.m.

2. TRANSPORT - with Units.

3. On arrival at destination Units will dump packs and be ready to move at short notice in fighting order.

4. S.A.A., and Grenades to complete will be drawn at BOUZINCOURT and SENLIS.

5. All baggage to be loaded by 5 a.m.

6. Arrival to be reported to Bde Headquarters SENLIS.

7. Acknowledge.

[signature] Captain,
Bde. Major, 14th Inf. Bde.

Issued at 10.30 p.m.

Copies to all concerned.

Prefix............ Code..............m. | Words | Charge | This message is on a/c of: ....Service. (Signature of "Franking Officer.") | Recd. at..................m. Date.......... From.......... By..........

Office of Origin and Service Instructions.

Sent At..............m. To.............. By..............

TO 19/ Lanc. Fus.

* Sender's Number	Day of Month	In reply to Number	AAA
C 12	8		

Copy of telegram received please comply AAA Orders have been received for the 32nd Div to take over 12th Div front from about X13 a 3/5 to left boundary of Div including OVILLERS aaa Have officers ready to reconnoitre the trenches this afternoon on receipt of orders which will be forwarded later

From 14/ Inf Bde
Place
Time 2.50 pm.

The above may be forwarded as now corrected. (Z) Censor.

L. Mulcter Capt Bde Major

Signature of Addressor or person authorised to telegraph in his name.

* This line should be erased if not required.

(A1) O. Ltd., London— W.14042/M.44. 150,000 Pads. 12/15. Form C.2121.

Wo: Diary

SECRET. Copy No.8....

14th Infantry Brigade Operation Order No,46.

8th July 1916.

MAP REFERENCE - 57 D. S.E. 1/20,000.

1. The Brigade will take over the line from DORSET STREET inclusive to 80 yards South of RIVINGTON STREET tonight 8/9th July, from the 36th Inf'Bde.

2. (a) The 1st Dorset Regt., 2nd Manchester Regt., and 15th H.L.I., will hold the captured German line in OVILLERS as follows,-
1 Company 15th H.L.I..........X.8.c.7.7. - X.8.c.58.82.
2nd ManchesterRegt...........X.8.c.58.82. - X.8.a.46.05.
1st Dorset Regt..............X.8.a.46.05. - X.8.c.05.85
1 Company 15th H.L.I. will be in support at a place to be determeined later.
(b) The 19th Lanc. Fus. will be in reserve with Hd.Qrs. at DONNET POST.

3. Guides will be at CRUCIFIX CORNER for Units at 10 p.m. and platoon guides will be at point X.8.c.13.50.

4. The Brigade will move via NORTHUMBERLAND AVENUE - PIONEER ROAD,- AVELUY - CRUCIFIX CORNER.
BROOKER'S PASS will not be used.
1st Dorset Regt. will pass the starting point W.7.c.95.70. at 8 p.m.
15th H.L.I. at 8.30 p.m.
19th Lanc. Fus. at 9 p.m.
14th Bde.T.M.Battery at 9.30 p.m.
The Brigade will be East of the river ANCRE by midnight.

5. The 14th Bde. M.G.Coy will relieve the 36th Bde M.G.Coy tomorrow, arrangements to be made direct between Commanders.

6. Transport will remain in its present position.

7. Rations will be delivered by first line transport on pack ponies tonight at OVILLERS POST.
Lieut. DUNN will see that parties proceed at intervals. Units will send carrying parties for their rations which will be ready there at midnight.

8. Completion of relief will be reported to Bde. Hd.Qrs, which are in RIBBLE STREET, W.12.d.7.0.

9. Acknowledge.

[signature]
~~Major~~ Captain,
Bde. Major, 14th Infantry Brigade.

Issued at 6.15 p.m.
Copies to all concerned.

Secret   Copy no 3

14th Inf Bde Operation Order No 47

11.7.16

1 The Brigade (less 19 Lancs Fus and 15 HLI) will be relieved in the line by the 96 Inf Bde tonight 11/12 July and will on relief withdraw to BOUZINCOURT.

2 The 1st Dorset Regt and 2nd Manchester Regt, in the order named will be relieved by the 16 Lancs Fus and 16 North. Fus. respectively

3 Company guides will be at CRUCIFIX CORNER at 6.30 pm and platoon guides will be at ~~point where~~ OVILLERS ~~[illegible]~~ POST ~~German front line trench~~ at 7.0 pm.

4 The 14 MG Coy and 14 TMB will be relieved by the 96 MG Coy and 96 TMB tomorrow. All details to be arranged by Commanders concerned

5 The 19 Lancs Fus will relieve 15 HLI in the line today as previously ordered. Both these regiments will be under orders of GOC 96 Inf Bde

The 15 HLI will on relief, withdraw to old British ~~front line~~ trenches for carrying and salvage work.

6 Completion of relief and arrival in billets

2

will be reported to Brigade Headquarters which will move to BOUZINCOURT on completion of relief.

7 Units will march to BOUZINCOURT by * sections or platoons (as the occasion demands) at suitable distances. via CRUCIFIX CORNER – main AVELUY–BOUZINCOURT ROAD

8 Acknowledge

Issued at 3.30 pm.

J W Kentish Capt
Bde Major
14 Inf Bde

Copies to all concerned

* Incoming units will march by sections after OVILLERS POST

SECRET. Copy No.8...

14th INFANTRY BRIGADE OPERATION ORDER No.48.

Map Reference - 57 D. S.E. 1/20,000. 14/7/16.

1. The 14th Inf. Bde. (less 19th Lan. Fus. and 15th H.L.I.) will relieve the 96th Inf. Bde. in the OVILLERS Sector today.

2. 1st Dorset Regt. on the right and 2nd Manchester Regt. on the left will take over the OVILLERS trenches.

3. 15th Lan. Fus. and 16th Lan. Fus. will remain in the line and come under the Command of the 14th Inf. Bde. on completion of relief. The 15th Lan. Fus. will be in reserve and the 16th Lan. Fus. will take over carrying duties from the 15th H. L. I.

4. Company Officers of the 1st Dorset Regt. and 2nd Manchester Regt. will report at 96thb Inf. Bde. Headquarters at once and will be shown the line to be held. Platoon guides will meet incoming units at OVILLERS POST at 7 p.m.

5. The 1st Dorset Regt. will pass the 12 " gun at entrance of NORTHUMBERLAND AVENUE at 5.30 p.m. followed by 2nd Manchester Regt. 200 yards will be maintained between Companies and from OVILLERS POST the march will be made by sections.

6. The 14th Bde. M. G. Coy. and 14th Bde. T. M. Bty. will relieve the 96th Bde. M. G. Coy. and 96th Bde. T. M. Bty. during the 15th July.

7. Completion of relief to be reported to Brigade Headquarters which will close at BOUZINCOURT at 8 p.m. and open at RIBBLE STREET at the same hour.

8. ACKNOWLEDGE.

Issued at 4 p.m.

[signature]
Captain,
Brigade Major, 14th Infantry Brigade.

~~Copies to~~ No.1 War Diary No.1.
2 War Diary No.2.
3 G. O. C.
4 File.
5 32nd Division "G".
6 1st Dorset Regt.
7 2nd Manchester Regt.
8 19th Lan. Fus.
9 15th H. L. I.
10 14th Bde. M.G.Coy.
11 14th Bde. T.M.Batty.
12 Signals 14th Inf. Bde.
13 No.2 Coy. 32nd Divl. Train.
14 90th Fd. Ambulance.
15 96th Inf. Bde.
16 97th Inf. Bde.
17 Staff Captain.
18 25th Division.
19 49th Division.
20 C. R. E. 32nd Division.
21 Town Major BOUZINCOURT.

SECRET. Copy No...8...

14th INFANTRY BRIGADE OPERATION ORDER No.53.

MAP REFERENCE - Sheet LENS 1/100,000.

18th JULY 1916.

1. The Brigade will move tomorrow to the area MONTS-EN-TERNOIS - MONCHEUX - SIBIVILLE, by the following route Cross roads point 165 - Cross roads ½ mile N. of ARBRES - ARBRE - LA COUTURE - REBREUVE - HONVAL - SIBIVILLE.

2. The Brigade will be clear of REBREUVE by 10 a.m., and will pass the starting point, cross roads near point 165 as follows,-

Bde. Headquarters	8. 5 a.m.
15th H.L.I	8.10 a.m.
19th Lanc. Fus	8.15 a.m. 7-45
2nd Manchester Regt	8.20 a.m.
1st Dorset Regt	8.25 a.m.
14th Bde. M.G.Coy	8.30 a.m.
14th Bde.T.M.Battery	8.35 a.m.
90th Field Ambulance	8.40 a.m.

3. Transport will accompany Units.

4. Dress - Marching order.

5. Billeting parties will meet the Staff Captain at the Church, SIBIVILLE, at 7.30 a.m.

6. Arrival in Billets will be reported to Bde. Headquarters, which will close at LE SOUICH at 8.30 a.m., and open at the MAIRIE, ~~SIBEVILLE~~ SIBIVILLE, at the same hour

7. Acknowledge.

Rome Baggallay
Captain,
for Bde. Major, 14th Inf. Bde.

Issued at 6.40 p.m.
Copies to,-

No.1 War Diary No.1
2 War Diary No.2
3 G.O.C.
4. File
5. 32nd Division 'G'
6. 1st Dorset Regt.
7. 2nd Manchester Regt.
8. 19th Lanc. Fus.
9. 15th H.L.I.
10. 14th Bde.M.G.Coy
11. 14th Bde.T.M.Battery
12- 96th Inf. Bde.
13. 97th Inf. Bde.
14. Signals 14th Inf. Bde.
15. 90th Field Ambulance
16. A.D.M.S. 32nd Division
17. Town Major LE SOUICH
18. Town Major, SIBIVILLE.
19. Staff Captain

APPENDIX "A" (CONT'D)

THIEPVAL.

There are 66 houses in THIEPVAL, chiefly farms. Most of these have rain water cisterns.

The Chateau, facing West, is an important building the cellars of which are very large and are used by the Germans for lodging soldiers, and are always full.

THIEPVAL farm is used as a grenade store.

The village is in ruins but from latest reports and from aeroplane photographs it may be deduced that many of its less fragile buildings are still so little damaged as to afford valuable protection against attack.

The following are a few particulars of the buildings that may have escaped our gun fire. The rest may be taken as mere flimsy barns of "torches" (unbaked clay and chopped straw).:-

1. GRIBEAUVAL farm. Brick, some cellarage - say 20 men.
2. Maison MORONVAL. A small brick house with cellars for 15 men.
3. Maison OBIN. A "torches" house which, however, has been sandbagged by the Germans, and has good cellars which are protected by barrels of earth. A small fort for about 40 men.
4. Maison CATHELAIN. A large strongly built house (brick) of seven rooms. Its cellars will hold about 50 men and the whole has been fortified.
5. Maison BARNS which has been strengthened by the enemy.
6. Maison The Cures house (presbytery). A substantial little building of brick with cellars in which 62 people lived for 40 days.
7. Maison SOREL. A small farm with indifferent cellarage.
8. Maison BENJAMIN. A brick house with excellent cellars capable of holding 40-50 men.
9. A sandbagged farm.
10. Maison BAUDELOQUE. A poor house which has been fortified. It has cellars for 10-15 men.
11. Maison DARCHEZ. A "torches" farm with cellars for 20-30 men. It has a good well.
12. A cafe burnt down in 1915. Excellent cellars 30-40 men.
13. A small house with a good well.

Tower in THIEPVAL WOOD, 300 metres North of the Chateau and 80 metres S.S.W. of HAIE, the most Westerly building on the THIEPVAL-St. PIERRE DIVION road and North of it, is loopholed and contains an O.P.

It is estimated that there is accommodation for 1500 men underground.

There are 3 wells (communales), depth about 30 metres, containing good water. There are also wells to be found in most of the farm houses. The water supply of the Chateau is considered abundant. The well in the square North of the Church was mined and had a gallery running towards the Church.

There is a deep, walled-in village pond.

<u>Telephones</u>. Behind a wall on the Eastern side of the square by the Church.

PARTICULARS OF ROADS BEHIND THE GERMAN LINES.

From information obtained from Refugees.

THIEPVAL-AUTHUILLE.

Metalled road, about 5 metres wide in all. Metalling 3 metres road.

THIEPVAL-HAMEL.

Metalled. About 5 metres wide. Crosses the R. ANCRE by a brick bridge.

THIEPVAL-POZIERES

5 metres wide (metalled) A 12 foot road leads from it to the FERME DE MOUQUET at Point R.33.a.4.4.

THIEPVAL-GRANDCOURT

Good metalled road, 5 metres wide, 3 metres metalled.

OVILLERS-GRANDCOURT

A cart track (Unmetalled). Leaves OVILLERS N. and passes the THIEPVAL -POZIERES road in R.32.b.

FERME DE MOUQUET-GRANDCOURT

Road unmetalled to R.28.a., thence metalled to GRANDCOURT.

PARTICULARS OF WELLS IN VILLAGES BEHIND THE GERMAN LINES.

From information obtained from Refugees.

THIEPVAL.

There are 3 wells (communales), depth about 30 metres, containing good water, which may be now polluted. There are also wells to be found in most of the farm houses.

FERME DE MOUQUET

The farm contains several wells. There is a pipe line from the FERME DE MOUQUET to THIEPVAL.

APPENDIX "A" (CONTD)

HOSTILE ARTILLERY OPPOSITE 32ND DIVISION FRONT.

SITUATION.	NUMBER & NATURE OF BATTERY.	
POZIERES	(6	77 mm.
	(1	10.5 cm.
	(1	15 cm.
R.21.b.28.22.	1	77 mm Battery
R.21.a.55.60.		- do -
R.27.b.43.13.		- do -
R.28.a.20.70.		- do -
R.28.c.90.00.		- do -
R.28.c.95.50.		- do -
R.33.b.20.23.		- do -
R.34.a.97.64. to) R.34.b.20.45.)		- do -
R.15.c.52.50.		- do -
R.15.d.02.70.		- do -
R.15.b.35.30.	1	15 cm.
R.15.b.38.60.	1	10.5 cm.

APPENDIX "A" (cont'd)

FERME DE MOUQUET.

A large farm belonging to a Belgian.

There are 2 supply dumps and an Artillery dump in it or its vicinity.

There is a pipe line from the FERME DE MOUQUET to THIEPVAL.

The farm contains several wells.

The telephone exchange is situated here.

Under the two barns are 4 big cellars, with windows about a metre square above the ground, from which men standing in the cellars could fire or work Machine Guns (good field of fire). The cellars are capable of holding 40 men.

The Right wing was burnt down in Sept. 1914.

There are several small clusters of trees N., N.W., S.W. and S. of the farm in which batteries are placed.

APPENDIX 'A' (CONT'D)

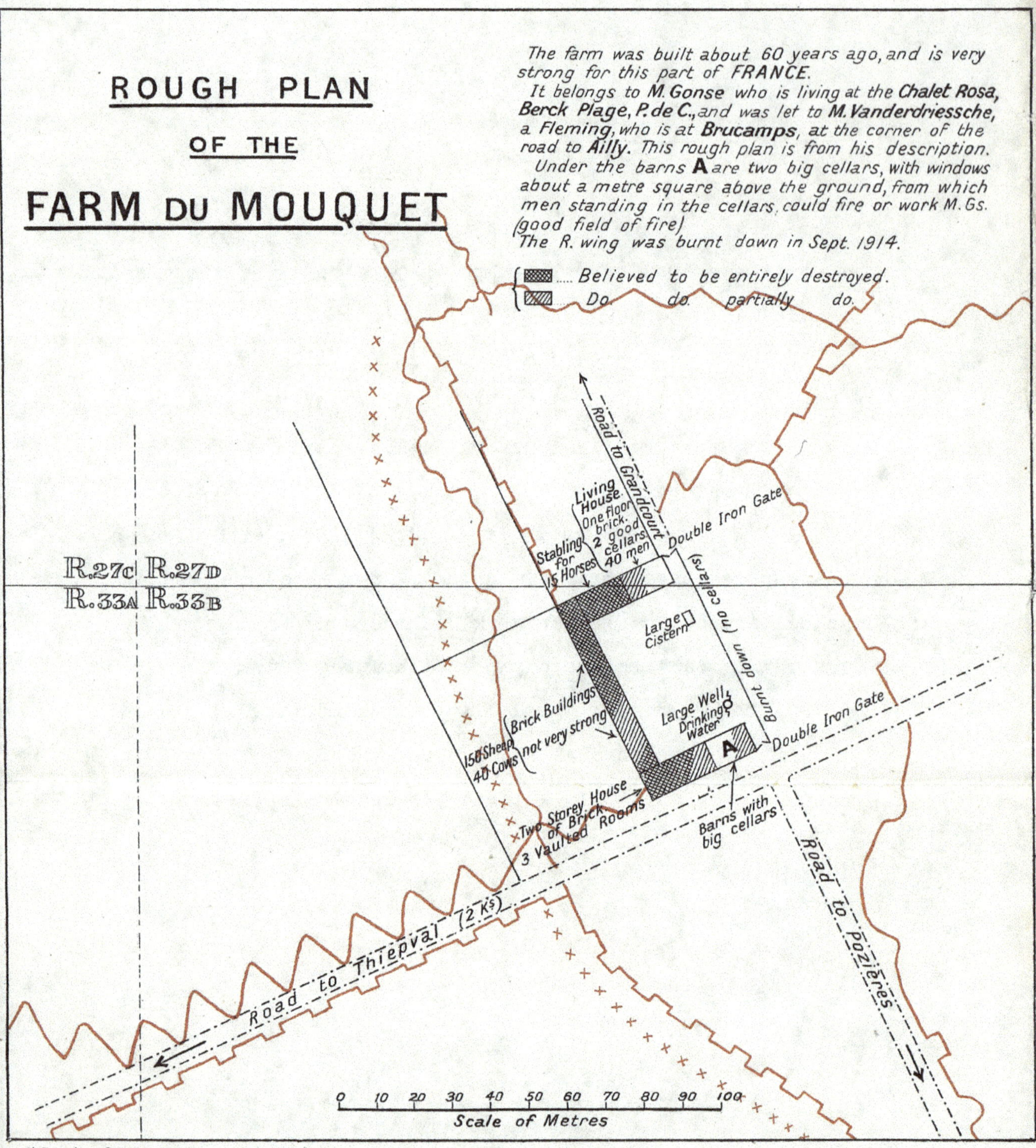

1st Printing Coy R.E. IV Army Sect. (282)

War Diary

The Officer Commanding,

16th North'd Fus.
2nd.R.Innis.Fus.
19th Lanc.Fus.
15th H.L.I.
14th Bde.M.G.Coy.
14th Bde.T.M.Battery.

Reference baggage and Qr.Mr. stores which arrived last night from WARLOY, these must be left herewith a small guard. There are no lorries available for their removal today. You should make arrangements accordingly with the Town Major.

Major.
Brigade Major.
96th Infantry Brigade.

July 17th.1916.

S E C R E T.   Copy No. 6.....

96th INFANTRY BRIGADE ORDER NO.47.

Reference Map. LENS.
1/100,000.   17th July 1916.

(1)(a) The 96th Inf.Bde., less 15th Lanc.Fus. 16th Lanc.Fus. 96th Bde.M.G.Coy. and 96th T.M.Battery will march today to NEUVILLETTE.

(b) The 19th Lanc.Fus., 15th Highland Light Infantry, 14th Bde. M.G.Coy. and 14th Bde. T.M.Battery, attached from 14th Inf.Bde., will march to LE SOUICH.

(2) Route - DOULLENS - Hte. VISEE and thence

(a) for troops of 14th Inf.Bde. via the road passing through TE in Hte VISEE and thence by the road leading through E in BOUQUE MAISON - LE SOUICH.

(b) for troops of 96th Bde. Hte.VISEE and thence by road junction ½ mile N. of Hte.VISEE - NEUVILLETTE.

(3) Starting Point BEAUVAL station on the Main AMIENS - DOULLENS Road.

(4) Units will pass the starting point in the following order at the hour named:-

Bde. Hd.Qrs..................	2 p.m.
15th H. L. I..................	2.5 p.m.
19th Lanc.Fus..................	2.20 p.m.
14th Bde.M.G.Coy..............	2.35 p.m.
14th Bde.T.M.Battery..........	3.0 p.m.
2nd.R.Innis.Fus...............	3.15 p.m.
16th North'd Fus..............	3.35 p.m.
91st Field Ambulance..........	4.0 p.m.

(5)(a) The whole of 1st Line Transport will march with units.

(b) The baggage wagons will be brigaded and pass the Starting Point in order of units at 4.15 p.m.

(6) Dress:- Marching order, with packs. Steel Helmets will be worn.

No unauthorised articles will be worn on the person nor will parcels or packages be carried in the hand.

(7) The strictest march discipline will be maintained and every C.O. will detail an Officer and a party of

N.C.O.s. and men who will march in rear and will be responsible for bringing in all stragglers of their units, except those that are placed in the Field Ambulance by the Medical Officer.

(8) Units will send on billeting parties at once.
In the case of units of 14th Bde. they will meet the Interpreter at the MAIRIE, LE SOUICH.
In the case of 96th Bde. the Staff Captain at the MAIRIE NEUVILLETTE.

(9) Halts will be made at 10 minutes to every hour and the march resumed at the Clock hour.
Units will send for Divisional Time to Bde.Hd.Qrs. at 1.15 p.m.

(10) Units of 14th Inf.Bde. on arrival at LE SOUICH will send two bicycle orderlies to remain at Bde.Hd.Qrs.

(11) Reports to Hd. of Column till Hte.VISEE and after that to NEUVILLETTE.

Major.
Brigade Major.
96th Infantry Brigade.

Issued at ~~XXXXXXX~~ 12 noon.

Copies Nos. 1. & 2. - War Diary.
Copy No.3. - Filed.
Copy No.4. - 16th North'd Fus.
Copy No.5. - 2nd.R.Innis.Fus.
Copy No.6. - 19th Lanc.Fus.
Copy No.7. - 15th H.L.I.
Copy No.8. - 14th Bde.M.G.Coy.
Copy No.9. - 14th Bde. T.M.Battery.
Copy No.10.- No.3.Coy. 32nd.Divl.Train.
Copy No.11.- 91st Field Ambulance.
Copy No.12. - 32nd.Division.

Secret Copy No 1

14th BDE Operation Order 42

1 The 14th INF BDE will continue the attack on the German trenches tomorrow (3rd July) morning

2 Zero time will be notified later

3 The 15th H.L.I. will carry out the attack & will relieve the 2/Manchester Regt in the Nab trenches tonight as already arranged.

~~The left [illegible] will [illegible]~~
~~The [illegible] 15th H.L.I. now~~
~~holding the front line [illegible] only~~
~~[illegible] tonight (2/3rd July)~~

The 2nd Manchesters on relief will take over the trenches now occupied by the 19th Lancs Fus. Details of reliefs to be arranged direct between units concerned.

4 The first objective of the 15th HLI will be the trench running from X1a 59 to R31c 3535

BLACKHORSE BRDGE – PIONEER RD.
– P RD.

5. The march will be made by platoons at 200 yards distance as far as point V.14 b. 88 and after that by companies.

6. 14 Bde. M. G. Coy. will be relieved tonight by the 7th Bde. M G Coy. under arrangements to be made between the commanders, and will march after relief by PIONEER ROAD – P ROAD – SENLIS

7. Completion of relief will be reported at Battle Headquarters and arrival in billets at Bde. Headquarters at SENLIS

8. ACKNOWLEDGE

14/3 Bde
3/7/16

[signature] Capt
Bde Major

SECRET

Copy No 4

14th Inf Bde. Op. Order No. 43

The 14th Bde. will be relieved tonight in the line by the 7th Bde 25th Division.

Arrangements for relief will be as already settled between the units concerned.

The 19/Lan. Fus will be relieved by the 1/Wilts Regt in the line MERSEY STREET — CHEQUERBENT STREET and on relief will march via BROOKERS PASS — PIONEER RD. — P RD to SENLIS.

The 1/Dorset Regt 2/Manchester Regt and 15 H L I will be relieved by the 10/Cheshire Regt in the line CHEQUERBENT STREET — TYNDRUM STREET and the portion of the German line held by 14 Bde and on relief will march to SENLIS by following routes —

Prefix............ Code............m. | Words | Charge | This message is on a/c of: Service. (Signature of "Franking Officer.") | Recd. at.........m. Date......... From......... By.........

Office of Origin and Service Instructions.

Sent At.........m. To......... By.........

TO UW

Sender's Number	Day of Month	In reply to Number	
* BM84	3		AAA

You	will	be	relieved	tonight
aaa	orders	later		

From L R
Place
Time 6 35pm

The above may be forwarded as now corrected. (Z)

Censor. Signature of Addressor or person authorised to telegraph in his name.

* This line should be erased if not required.

(A1) O. Ltd., London— W.14042/M.44. 150,000 Pads. 12/15. Forms C.2121.

The SECOND + final objective will be the trench running from X1a 6085 to R31c 7318 but exclusive of the trench running from X1b 1295 to R31c 5045

5 The 75th INF BDE is simultaneously attacking the German line from about R31c 4370 to R25c 71

The 49th DIV is to attack the German line from about opposite THIEPVAL POINT SOUTH to the R. ANCRE

6 At 15 minutes before zero time an artillery barrage will be established on the 1st objective + will continue until zero time. At zero time the barrage will lift from the northern part of the 1st objective (as arranged by OC right group) and will continue on the Southern part of the 1st objective until 15 minutes after zero when it will lift

to the trench running from XI b 1295 to R31c 5045.

7. The 2nd Manchester Regt will be in Support & will take up a position of readiness in the vicinity of the SANDA SAP, as soon as the last coy of the 15th HLI has ~~[illegible]~~ advanced from our trenches.

8 The 1st DORSET Regt + 19th LANCS FUS will be in reserve & will be ready to move at zero time

9 In order to ensure efficient co-operation very intimate liaison will be established between all units

10 The O.C. 14th BDE MACHINE GUN COY will place one Section at disposal of OC 15th H.L.I. One Section will take up positions to cover the attack remainder of the M.G. Coy. will be in reserve

4

for employment as circumstances dictate.

11 The ~~OC~~ 14th and 97th T.M. BATTYries will come into action in accordance with verbal orders already issued by G.O.C.

12 During the operations yesterday instances occurred of Germans hiding in dugouts until our men had passed & then coming out & attacking with bombs or M. Guns. In this way one BDE suffered very heavy losses. Officers Commanding units will see that sufficiently large mopping up parties are detailed to meet this contingency

13 The O.C 206 Field Coy R.E will detail one section to be in rendezvous to assist in the consolidation of captured trenches. This section will occupy a portion of the AUTHUILLE defences N. of CAMPBELL AVENUE

From 5

14 ~~[illegible]~~ Zero time smoke barrages will be placed on the East of the 14 Bde objective

2.7.16

[signature] Capt
Bde Major
14 Inf Bde

After order

The 19 Lancs Fus will ~~[illegible]~~ take over trenches from MERSEY ST (exclusive) to CHEQUERBENT ST (inclusive). The 1 Dorset Regt will take over from CHEQUERBENT ST (exclusive) to TYNDRUM ST (exclusive)

14/42

"A" Form

Army Form C. 2121

MESSAGES AND SIGNALS.

No. of Message

[P]refix ..... Code ..... m.	Words	Charge	19 Lancs Fus	
[Of]fice of Origin and Service Instructions.	Sent		This message is on a/c of: July 16 Service.	Recd. at ..... m.
	At ..... m.			Date
	To			From
	By		(Signature of "Franking Officer.")	By

TO { War Diary — COPY No. 1

Sender's Number.	Day of Month	In reply to Number	AAA
U.W. 705	30		

Operation Order No. 41 AAA
Ref. Maps 1/40000 Sheet ALBERT 1/5000 Trench Map. AAA

1. Battalion will move to BLACKHORSE SHELTERS to-night 30th June / 1st July 1916 and will parade at 8.50 pm on MILLENCOURT – SENLIS ROAD in order Sigs. A. B. C. D. Coys. Head of "A" Co. to be at JUNCTION of MILLENCOURT – SENLIS & BOUZINCOURT – SENLIS ROADS; and will march via BOUZINCOURT – NORTHUMBERLAND AV. – PIONEER ROAD – ROAD JUNCTION W.16. & .8/ – BLACKHORSE Rd to Shelters AAA.

(2) Advance party of 1 N.C.O. per platoon under LIEUT. G.E. SMITH will [leave] [illegible] SENLIS at 6.30 pm and

[Fr]om			
[Pl]ace		(A).	
[Ti]me			

The above may be forwarded as now corrected. (Z)

Censor. — Signature of Addressor or person authorised to telegraph in his name.

* This line should be erased if not required.

(198) Wt. W14742—M44. 300000 Pads. 12/15. Sir J. C. & S.

"A" Form. Army Form C. 2121

MESSAGES AND SIGNALS. No. of Message

Prefix Code m. | Words | Charge | This message is on a/c of: | Recd. at m.

Office of Origin and Service Instructions. | Sent At m. To By | Service. (Signature of "Franking Officer.") | Date From By

TO (2)

Sender's Number.	Day of Month	In reply to Number	AAA
U.N. 705	30		

moving by above route will take SHELTERS at BLACKHORSE BRIDGE and find R.E. DUMPS etc AAA

(b). Battalion will halt in NORTHUMBERLAND AV for about one hour – & from this point no transport is available, all SIGNALLERS GEAR, BOMBS, LEWIS GUNS & S.A.A. will be carried forward by men AAA

2. Rations for to-morrow will be drawn before leaving SENLIS AAA In order to have hot tea before moving to the attack a small amount of tea and sugar will be carried to each man, who must make arrangements to cook same at BLACKHORSE SHELTERS AAA

From

Place

Time (Cont d)

The above may be forwarded as now corrected. (Z)

Censor. Signature of Addressor or person authorised to telegraph in his name.

* This line should be erased if not required.

(4198) Wt. W14942—M44. 300000 Pads. 12/15. Sir J. C. & S.

"A" Form.

Army Form C. 2121

MESSAGES AND SIGNALS.

No. of Message

efix ... Code ... m.	Words / Charge	This message is on a/c of:	Recd. at ... m.
ice of Origin and Service Instructions.	Sent	... Service.	Date
	At ... m.		From
	To		
	By	(Signature of "Franking Officer.")	By

TO (3)

Sender's Number.	Day of Month	In reply to Number	AAA
U.N. 705	30		

3. O.C. Coys. will render a certificate to the effect that their men are equipped as laid down in Operation Order No 37 - para 11(a) - i.e. with rations, [illegible]. S.A.A. Tube helmets bombs. etc. AAA

4. O.C. Coys. will render to Orderly Room by 6 p.m. to day return showing strength of each platoon & name of platoon commander - this return to include only men who will move with the platoons AAA

5. R.E. tools will be drawn from dump on arrival at BLACKHORSE SHELTERS AAA

(a) O.C. Coys. must see that men keep under shelter as much as possible

(Cont'd) -

from

lace

ime

The above may be forwarded as now corrected.

(Z)

Censor.

Signature of Addressor or person authorised to telegraph in his name.

* This line should be erased if not required.

(4198) Wt. W14042—M44. 300000 Pads. 12/15. Sir J. C. & S.

"A" Form.

Army Form C. 2121

MESSAGES AND SIGNALS.

No. of Message

refix.......Code.......m.	Words	Charge	This message is on a/c of:	Recd. at.......m.
fice of Origin and Service Instructions.	Sent		.......Service.	Date
	At.......m.			From
	To			
	By		(Signature of "Franking Officer.")	By

TO (4)

Sender's Number.	Day of Month	In reply to Number	AAA
U.W. 705	30		

and do not move about in the open AAA.

6. (a) All billets must be left scrupulously clean and O.C. Coys. will inspect them & render certificate to this effect to Adjutant before marching off AAA

(b) [illegible] in shelters will [illegible] be reported immediately AAA.

ACKNOWLEDGE

From H.Q.

Place

Time 3.15 pm

The above may be forwarded as now corrected.

(Z) [illegible] Lieut. & Adjutant

Censor.

Signature of Addressor or person authorised to telegraph in his name.

* This line should be erased if not required.

4198) Wt. W14^42—M44. 300000 Pads. 12/15. Sir J. C. & S.

"A" Form.

Army Form C. 2121

MESSAGES AND SIGNALS.

No. of Message

Prefix Code m. | Words Charge | This message is on a/c of: | Recd. at m.

Office of Origin and Service Instructions. | Sent At m. To By | Service. (Signature of "Franking Officer.") | Date From By

TO Div. Div. COPY No. 1

Sender's Number.	Day of Month	In reply to Number	AAA
U.H. 741.	5		

Operation Order No. 44 AAA.

1/. Battalion will move from SENLIS to FORCEVILLE to-day 5th July 1916 AAA.

(a). Battalion will parade in order B.C.D.A. Coys. at ROAD JUNCTION – MILLENCOURT and BOUZINCOURT – SENLIS ROADS at 5.45 pm. and will march via ROAD-JUNCTION V.10.d 7/7 CROSS ROADS V.5.c. – HEDAUVILLE – FORCEVILLE and take over billets there, for which purpose billeting party of 1 NCO or man per platoon – Transport – etc. will leave Battn. HQ SENLIS at 4.15 pm. & move by above route to CHURCH FORCEVILLE where party will be met AAA.

From

Place

Time

(1)

The above may be forwarded as now corrected. (Z)

Censor. Signature of Addressor or person authorised to telegraph in his name.

* This line should be erased if not required.

(4198) Wt. W14042—M44. 300000 Pads. 12/15. Sir J. C. & S.

"A" Form.

Army Form C. 2121

MESSAGES AND SIGNALS.

No. of Message

Prefix ..... Code ..... m. | Words | Charge

Office of Origin and Service Instructions.

Sent
At .....m.
To .....
By .....

This message is on a/c of:

..... Service.

(Signature of "Franking Officer.")

Recd. at .....m.
Date .....
From .....
By .....

TO (Z).

Sender's Number.	Day of Month	In reply to Number	AAA
U.W. 741	5		

(1). Officers kits will be stacked outside Coy. messes at 4 pm AAA. Mess stuff will be collected at 5 30 pm AAA.

2. Transport will move with Bn. except Mess Cart which will move as soon as possible after loading AAA.

3. All billets will be left scrupulously clean & O.C. Coys. will render certificate to this office before marching off. AAA.

From HQ.
Place
Time 4.45 pm

The above may be forwarded as now corrected. (Z) A. Rupert Hunt Lieut & Adjt.

Censor. Signature of Addressor or person authorised to telegraph in his name.

* This line should be erased if not required.

(4198) Wt. W14^42—M44. 300000 Pads. 12/15. Sir J. C. & S.

"A" Form. Army Form C. 2121.

MESSAGES AND SIGNALS.

No. of Message

Prefix Code m. Office of Origin and Service Instructions.	Words	Charge	This message is on a/c of: Service. (Signature of "Franking Officer.")	Recd. at m.
	Sent At m. To By			Date From By

TO Wm Diary COPY No. 1.

Sender's Number.	Day of Month	In reply to Number	AAA
* G. 10.	8/7/16.		

OPERATION ORDER No. 46 AAA.

1. Battalion will proceed to DONNET POST to-night & will fall in at the HUTS. BOUZINCOURT, in order SIGNALLERS No. 1 COY. No. 2 COY. ready to march off at 9pm. AAA

2. Machine Gun Limbers only will accompany Battalion. AAA

3. Light mess baskets to be dumped at CHURCH. by 8.30pm.

From U.W.

Place

Time 8.5pm.

The above may be forwarded as now corrected. (Z) A Rupert Lunn? Lieut. A/Adjt.

Censor. Signature of Addressor or person authorised to telegraph in his name.

* This line should be erased if not required.

(4198) Wt. W1.042—M44. 300000 Pads. 12/15. Sir J. C. & S.

Prefix........Code........m. | Words | Charge | *This message is on a/c of:* ....Service. (Signature of "Franking Officer.") | Recd. at........m. Date........ From........ By........

Office of Origin and Service Instructions.

Sent At........m. To........ By........

TO War Diary Copy No 1.

Sender's Number.	Day of Month	In reply to Number	AAA
* Cn 536	11.7.16		

Op Order No 46A AAA

1. Bn will relieve 15 H.L.I. in line in OVILLERS tonight 11.7.16 and will placed at the disposal of G.O.C. 96th Bde AAA

2. No 2 Coy will march via SUNKEN ROAD by sections & will take over the left of the line AAA
No 1 Coy will arrange to take over right of line from 15 H.L.I. AAA
Relief to commence at 7.30 pm at which time 1st Section of No 2 Coy will leave DONNET POST AAA.

3. Cooking for Battn will be done at DONNET POST AAA O.C. Coys to arrange carrying parties accordingly AAA

From
Place
Time

The above may be forwarded as now corrected. (Z)

Censor. Signature of Addressor or person authorised to telegraph in his name.

* This line should be erased if not required.

(4.98) Wt. W1.042—M44. 300000 Pads. 12/15. Sir J. C. & S.

Prefix Code m.	Words	Charge	This message is on a/c of:	Recd. at m.
Office of Origin and Service Instructions.	Sent		Service.	Date
	At m.			From
	To			
	By		(Signature of "Franking Officer.")	By

TO 2

Sender's Number.	Day of Month	In reply to Number	AAA
*			

4. Situation Reports to be rendered at 3 am and 3 pm daily AAA. Casualties at 6 am and 2 pm. AAA

5 Relief Complete to be reported AAA

From 15LA

Place

Time 5-35 pm

The above may be forwarded as now corrected.

(Z) [illegible signature] Lt & Adj

Censor. Signature of Addressor or person authorised to telegraph in his name.

* This line should be erased if not required.

(4.98) Wt. W14042—M44. 300000 Pads. 12/15. Sir J. C. & S.

MESSAGES AND SIGNALS. No. of Message

Prefix ... Code ... m. Office of Origin and Service Instructions.	Words	Charge	This message is on a/c of: ... Service. (Signature of "Franking Officer.")	Recd. at ... m. Date ... From ... By ...
	Sent At ... m. To ... By ...			

TO Dar Deary COPY No 1

Sender's Number.	Day of Month	In reply to Number	AAA
* U.W. 116	15		

Operation Order No 47. AAA

Ref Maps 1/40 000 ALBERT.

(i) Battalion will move to WARLOY today 15 7 16 and will parade in order – Signallers No 1 + No 2 Coy at 2 45 pm with head on Billet No 83 and will march via W 13c 37 and Q route to billets for which purpose billeting party of 1 1 NCO per platoon, Head Qrs Transport under Lieut G.B. SMITH will leave BOUZINCOURT at 1·0 pm and will report to TOWN MAJOR WARLOY. AAA

(ii) Lewis Gun limbers, Mess Cart etc will move with Bn Remainder of

From

Place (1)

Time

The above may be forwarded as now corrected. (Z)

Censor. Signature of Addressor or person authorised to telegraph in his name.

* This line should be erased if not required.

(4198) Wt. W14042—M14. 300000 Pads. 12/15. Sir J. C. & S.

MESSAGES AND SIGNALS. No. of Message

Prefix Code m. | Words | Charge | This message is on a/c of: | Recd. at m.

Office of Origin and Service Instructions. | Sent At m. To By | Service. (Signature of "Franking Officer.") | Date From By

TO (2)

Sender's Number.	Day of Month	In reply to Number	AAA
UW. 116	15.		

Transport will move under Bde T.O. AAA Baggage wagons will leave BOUZINCOURT at 4 pm.

(III) O.C. Coys to see that all ranks are clean and dressed alike in usual manner as laid down when carrying packs. There must be NO extra stuff hung on the equipment.

(IV) O.C. Coys will be responsible that all Billets are left perfectly clean and a certificate to this effect will be handed to the Adjutant before vacating.

From H.Q.

Place

Time 1.15 pm

The above may be forwarded as now corrected. (Z) A. Rupert Inness Ker[illegible]

Censor. Signature of Addressor or person authorised to telegraph in his name.

* This line should be erased if not required.

(4198) Wt. W14042—M14. 300,000 Pads. 12/15. Sir J. C. & S.

No. of Message

Prefix .... Code .... m.	Words	Charge	This message is on a/c of:	Recd. at .... m.
Office of Origin and Service Instructions.	Sent		.... Service.	Date
	At .... m.			From
	To			
	By		(Signature of "Franking Officer.")	By

TO O/c No. 1 + No. 2. Coys

Sender's Number.	Day of Month	In reply to Number	AAA
* U.W. 116	15		

Ref Operation Order No 47 herewith and para (D) about billeting party, this will now be formed from Reserve N.C.O.s

From H.B.
Place
Time 1.15 am

[illegible] [illegible]

The above may be forwarded as now corrected. (Z)

Censor. Signature of Addressor or person authorised to telegraph in his name.

* This line should be erased if not required.

(4198) Wt. W14042–M14. 300000 Pads. 12/15. Sir J. C. & S.

MESSAGES AND SIGNALS. No. of Message

Prefix Code m. | Words | Charge | This message is on a/c of: | Recd. at m.

Office of Origin and Service Instructions. | Sent At m. To By | Service. (Signature of "Franking Officer.") | Date From By

TO War Diary

Sender's Number	Day of Month	In reply to Number	AAA
* O.W. 116.	15.		

Ref. Operation Order No 49. herewith and para ① about billeting party, – this will now be formed from Reserve N.C.O's

From H.Q.
Place
Time 1.15 pm.

The above may be forwarded as now corrected. (Z)

Censor. Signature of Addressor or person authorised to telegraph in his name. [signature] Lt & Adjt.

* This line should be erased if not required.

(4198) Wt. W14042–M.14. 300000 Pads. 12/15. Sir J. C. & S.

Prefix.......Code.......m. | Words | Charge | This message is on a/c of: | Recd. at.......m.
Office of Origin and Service Instructions.
Sent At.......m. To....... By.......
.......Service.
(Signature of "Franking Officer.")
Date....... From....... By.......

TO War Diary. Copy No 1

Sender's Number.	Day of Month	In reply to Number	AAA
* U.W. 120.	15		

OPERATION ORDER No 47A AAA.
Ref. Map 1/40000 Sheet 57 D. AAA.

1. Battalion will move to BEAUVAL to-morrow – 16/7/16. AAA.
2. Battalion will parade in order SIGNALLERS – No 2 & No 1 Coys. along the RUE DE MOULIN – facing NORTH – head on ROAD JUNCTION of RUE DU MOULIN & 'R' ROUTE to SENLIS. – at 10-20 a.m. and will march via CROSS ROADS – V. 19. a. 20/20 – VARENNES – LEALVILLERS – ARQUEVES – RAINCHEVAL – BEUUQUESNE – ROAD JUNCTION G. 30. c. 30/0 – ROAD JUNCTION G. 16. a. 70/00 – to billets at BEAUVAL – for which purpose billeting party of 1 N.C.O. per platoon – H.Q. – & Transport

From
Place
Time
(1)

The above may be forwarded as now corrected. (Z)
Censor. Signature of Addressor or person authorised to telegraph in his name.
* This line should be erased if not required.
(4198) Wt. W14 42—M44. 300000 Pads 12/15. Sir J. C. & S.

Prefix	Code	m.	Words	Charge	This message is on a/c of:	Recd. at	m.
Office of Origin and Service Instructions.			Sent		Service.	Date	
			At	m.		From	
			To				
			By		(Signature of "Franking Officer.")	By	

TO (2).

Sender's Number.	Day of Month	In reply to Number	AAA
* U.W. 120.	15		

under Lieut. G. B. SMITH will leave Battn. H.Q. at 9.30 a.m. and proceed via above route AAA.

Billeting party will carry haversack rations AAA.

Battalion will halt for 2 hours at point O. 9. a. 8/2. AAA.

(2). DRESS: MARCHING ORDER – WITHOUT PACKS – Steel helmets to be worn. AAA. Waterproof sheets will be worn on back – suspended from "D's" of braces AAA.

No unauthorised articles etc. to be hung on the person nor will parcels be carried in the hand. AAA.

3. First line Transport will accompany Battalion AAA. Baggage wagons will be brigaded & will pass starting point V.19.a. 20/10

From

Place (Cont'd)

Time

The above may be forwarded as now corrected. (Z)

Censor. Signature of Addressor or person authorised to telegraph in his name.

* This line should be erased if not required.

(4198) Wt. W14 42—M44. 300000 Pads 12/15. Sir J. C. & S.

Prefix........Code........m.	Words	Charge	This message is on a/c of:	Recd. at........m.
Office of Origin and Service Instructions.	Sent		........Service.	Date........
	At........m.			From........
	To........			
	By........		(Signature of "Franking Officer.")	By........

TO (3).

Sender's Number.	Day of Month	In reply to Number	AAA
* U.N.120.	15.		

at 11.45 am AAA.

4. Officers' kits & heavy mess stuff to be at Q.M. Stores by 9.30 am. AAA Mess cart will collect mess baskets at 9.30 am sharp AAA.

5. All men's packs will be handed into Q.M. Stores by 8.30 am. – stacked, & left under a guard detailed by R.S.M. AAA. These packs will be carried by lorries on 17/7/16 AAA.

6. (a) Dinners will be served dining hall – Sergt. COOK to arrange AAA.
(b) SICK PARADE at 7.30 am.

7. Strict march discipline will be maintained AAA. 2nd Lieut. KEIGWIN and 1 N.C.O. per Coy. will move in rear of Battalion & will be responsible

From
Place (cont'd).
Time

The above may be forwarded as now corrected. (Z)

.... Censor. Signature of Addressor or person authorised to telegraph in his name.

* This line should be erased if not required.

(1198) Wt. W14'42—M44. 300000 Pads 12/15. Sir J. C. & S.

Prefix ...... Code ...... m. | Words | Charge | This message is on a/c of: ...... Service. | Recd. at ...... m.

Office of Origin and Service Instructions.

Sent At ...... m. To ...... By ......

(Signature of "Franking Officer.")

Date ...... From ...... By ......

TO (4).

Sender's Number.	Day of Month	In reply to Number	AAA
* U.W. 120.	15		

for bringing in all stragglers AAA.

4. All billets must be left scrupulously clean & certificates to this effect rendered to Adjutants before marching off AAA. No men will be left behind to clean up billets.

From U.W.

Place

Time 10.50 pm.

The above may be forwarded as now corrected.

(Z) A. Rupert Hussey Lieut. & Adjt.

Censor. Signature of Addressor or person authorised to telegraph in his name.

* This line should be erased if not required.

(4198) Wt. W14'42—M44. 300000 Pads. 12/15. Sir J. C. & S.

Prefix .... Code .... m.	Words	Charge	This message is on a/c of:	Recd. at .... m.
Office of Origin and Service Instructions.	Sent		.... Service.	Date
	At .... m.			From
	To			
	By		(Signature of "Franking Officer.")	By

TO Dar Diary. COPY No 1.

Sender's Number.	Day of Month	In reply to Number	AAA
4.H. 766.	17/7/16.		

OPERATION ORDER No. 48 AAA.
Ref. map 1/100.000. Sheet LENS. 11. AAA.

1. Battalion will move to LE SOUICH today and will parade in order. SIGNALLERS. No. 1 + No. 2 Coys. at Battalion HQ. mess facing DOULLENS at 2·5 pm. & will march via DOULLENS - HTE - VISEE - through TE La HTE VISSEE - ROAD through E' in BOUQUE MAISON - to LE SOUICH & take over billets there, for which purpose billeting party of 1 N.C.O. per platoon. Transport & HQ under Lieut. G.B. SMITH will parade Battn. HQ at 12.30 pm & proceed via above route. AAA.
DRESS. Full marching Order ~ Steel helmets to be worn. AAA.

From
Place
Time

(1).

The above may be forwarded as now corrected. (Z)

Censor. Signature of Addressor or person authorised to telegraph in his name.

* This line should be erased if not required.

Wt. W14042—M14. 360000 Pads. 12/15. Sir J. C. & S.

Prefix ______ Code ______ m. | Words | Charge

Office of Origin and Service Instructions.

Sent
At ______ m.
To ______
By ______

This message is on a/c of: ______ *Service.*

(Signature of "Franking Officer.")

Recd. at ______ m.
Date ______
From ______
By ______

TO | | (2). | |

Sender's Number.	Day of Month	In reply to Number	
U.N. 766.	17.		AAA

2. Officers Kits to be at Q.M. Stores at 1 pm. AAA
Mess baskets will be collected at 1.45 pm. AAA

3. Transport will accompany Battalion AAA
Baggage wagons will be brigaded [illegible]
& will pass starting point at 4.15 pm AAA

4. LIEUT MUSKER & 1 N.C.O per Coy.
will march in rear of Battalion to collect stragglers. AAA

5. Billets will be left scrupulously clean & certificates to this effect rendered to Adjutant before leaving. AAA

6. Sergt-Cook to arrange for teas immediately on arrival in billets. AAA

From U.N.
Place
Time 12.40 pm

The above may be forwarded as now corrected.

(Z) A Rupert Musker Lieut.
& Adjt.

Censor. Signature of Addressor or person authorised to telegraph in his name.

* This line should be erased if not required.

(6960) Wt. W14042 – M14. 300000 Pads. 12/15. Sir J. C. & S

Prefix .... Code .... m. | Words | Charge

Office of Origin and Service Instructions.

Sent At .... m. To .... By ....

This message is on a/c of: .... Service.

(Signature of "Franking Officer.")

Recd. at .... m. Date .... From .... By ....

TO — COPY No. 1

Sender's Number.	Day of Month	In reply to Number	AAA
* U.W. 847	27/7/16		

Battalion along with remainder of 14th Inf. Bde., will be inspected tomorrow by General Sir Charles Monro Commanding 1st Army AAA.

1/ Battalion will parade at Camp at 12 noon and will move off at 12.10pm in order SIGNALLERS - No. 1 & No. 2 Coys. via CROSS ROADS K.15.a - ROAD JUNCTION K.13.a.8/4 - ROAD JUNCTION K.13.b.1/6 - CROSS ROADS K.1.d - ROAD JUNCTION J.6.c - to TRACK at point J.6.b.2/3. to Field about J.6.a.7/7. where Battalion will form up, on markers, in mass facing N.E. with 3 paces interval between Coys. AAA.

From

Place

Time

The above may be forwarded as now corrected. (Z)

Censor. Signature of Addressor or person authorised to telegraph in his name.

* This line should be erased if not required.

(4198) Wt. W14042—M14. 300000 Pads. 12/15 S'r J. C. & S

Prefix............Code..................m.	Words	Charge	This message is on a/c of:	Recd. at...................m.
Office of Origin and Service Instructions.	Sent		..................Service.	Date....................
	At..................m.			From....................
	To....................			
	By....................		(Signature of "Franking Officer.")	By....................

TO (2).

Sender's Number.	Day of Month	In reply to Number	AAA
* U.W.847	27/7/16		

2. DRESS: Full marching Order – Steel helmets to be worn AAA. Waterproof Sheets to be neatly folded on top of pack AAA. One gas helmet only to be carried – & will be on Right side – hung over left shoulder AAA. Packs to be well up on the shoulders. belts, braces & all straps of equipment to be tight AAA.

3. Mounted Officers will wear Sam Browne belts AAA. Dismounted Officers will wear fighting kit, & will wear puttees tied off below the knee – On no account will high boots be worn AAA.

4. Transport (loaded) less cookers, watercarts, mess carts & spare horses, will parade on their lines at 12.5 pm and will

From			
Place	(Cont'd).		
Time			

The above may be forwarded as now corrected. (Z)

Censor. Signature of Addressor or person authorised to telegraph in his name.

* This line should be erased if not required.

(T1809) Wt. 14142—641. 45000 pads. 4/15. Sir J. C. & S.

Prefix.........Code.........m.	Words	Charge	This message is on a/c of:	Recd. at.........m.
Office of Origin and Service Instructions.	Sent At.........m. To......... By.........		.........Service. (Signature of "Franking Officer.")	Date......... From......... By.........

TO (3).

Sender's Number.	Day of Month	In reply to Number	AAA
* U.W. 847	27/7/16.		

leave HOUCHIN immediately behind Transport of 1st DORSETS and will come under order of Senior T.O. of the Brigade at Starting point K.13.6.7/6 AAA.
5. No. 1 Coy. will send 4 N.C.O's + No. 2 Coy. 1 N.C.O. as markers to Batt. HQ. at 12.15 pm. AAA
6. Lewis Gunners will be 5 paces in rear of rear platoon of their Coy. — dressed by the Right AAA. L.G. Carts unattended will be in rear of the detachments. AAA.
7. On arrival of the Army Commander the Brig-Genl. will give the caution "The Brigade will come to 'Attention' and 'Slope arms'", action by C.O. will be taken on the bugler sounding

From
Place (Cont'd).
Time

The above may be forwarded as now corrected. (Z)

Censor. Signature of Addressor or person authorised to telegraph in his name.

* This line should be erased if not required.

(T1809) Wt. 14142—641. 45000 pads. 4/15. Sir J. C. & S.

Prefix......Code......m.	Words	Charge	This message is on a/c of:	Recd. at......m.
Office of Origin and Service Instructions.	Sent At......m. To...... By......		......Service. (Signature of "Franking Officer.")	Date...... From...... By......

TO (4).

Sender's Number.	Day of Month	In reply to Number	AAA
* U.W. 847.	27/7/16.		

a "G" AAA. The Brigadier will then give the order to "Present Arms" and the bugler will again sound a "G" AAA.

Buglers of the 19th Lancs. Fus. & 1st Dorsets will sound the General Salute AAA.

On the sound of a third "G" the Brigade will come to the "Slope" AAA.

8. Dinners will be at 11 am. AAA

9. The Buglers of this Battalion with those of the Dorsets – will report to the Adjutant of 1st Dorsets on arrival on parade ground AAA.

10. Spare Officers & N.C.O's will parade in rear of Battalion – position to be decided by Brigade AAA.

From
Place
Time

(Cont'd).

The above may be forwarded as now corrected. (Z)

Censor. Signature of Addressor or person authorised to telegraph in his name.

* This line should be erased if not required.

(T1809) Wt. 14142—641. 45000 pads. 4/15. Sir J. C. & S.

Prefix........Code..........m.	Words	Charge	This message is on a/c of:	Recd. at..........m.
Office of Origin and Service Instructions.	Sent At..........m. To.......... By..........		..........Service. (Signature of "Franking Officer.")	Date.......... From.......... By..........

TO (5).

Sender's Number.	Day of Month	In reply to Number	
* U.W. 847	27/7/16		AAA

U. Grooms of mounted officers to be ready to take their masters' horses when they dismount AAA.

From U.W.

Place

Time 9.20 pm.

The above may be forwarded as now corrected.

(Z) A. Rupert Lewis Lieut & Adjt.

Censor. Signature of Addressor or person authorised to telegraph in his name.

* This line should be erased if not required.

(T1809) Wt. 14142—641. 45000 pads. 4/15. Sir J. C. & S.

"A" Form.

Army Form C. 2121

MESSAGES AND SIGNALS

No. of Message

Prefix Code m. Office of Origin and Service Instructions.	Words	Charge	This message is on a/c of: Service.	Recd. at
	Sent At m. To By		(Signature of "Franking Officer.")	Date From By

TO [illegible]

Sender's Number.	Day of Month	In reply to Number	AAA
U.N. 712.	2.	42	

Operation Order No. 40 AAA.

(1) Battalion will relieve 15. H.L.I. in the line from MERSEY ST. to BOGGART HOLE CLOUGH ~~[illegible]~~ to-day AAA.

(2) 'D' Coy will hold front line & will leave Batt. HQ. AUTHUILLE, at 9 pm. by platoons at 100 yds. interval, and move up by TRENCH RAILWAY to WOOD POST thence into the line. AAA. Remainder of Coys. will follow in order A.B.C. & be in reserve at WOOD POST, accomodation there to be adjusted by O.C. Coys. & their distribution sent to HQ. as soon as possible after arrival AAA. 'WALKER' to be reported immediately.

From HQ.

Place

Time 8 pm.

The above may be forwarded as now corrected.

(Z) [illegible signature] Lieut. & Adjt.

Censor. Signature of Addressor or person authorised to telegraph in his name

* This line should be erased if not required.

(4198) Wt. W14042—M44. 300000 Pads. 12/15. Sir J. C. & S.

"A" Form. Army Form C. 2121.

MESSAGES AND SIGNALS.

No. of Message

Prefix Code m. | Words | Charge | This message is on a/c of: | Recd. at m.

Office of Origin and Service Instructions. | Sent At m. To By | Service. (Signature of "Franking Officer.") | Date From By

TO War Diary. Copy No 1.

Sender's Number.	Day of Month	In reply to Number	AAA
* U.W. 717	3/7/16		

1. 14 Bde will continue attack on GERMAN LINES to day 3rd July AAA
2. 15 HLI will attack the trenches X1a 5/5 to R31c 35/35 AAA 25 Bde will simultaneously attack trenches R31c 43/70 – R25c 7/1 AAA 49th Division will also attack from THIEPVAL POINT SOUTH to R. ANCRE AAA
3. The Battn will hold itself in readiness to move in support of either up on AAA D Coy continuing to hold line MERSEY ST – CHEQUERBENT ST. AAA
4. Zero Time will be 3.15 a.m. AAA
5. OC Coys will arrange to draw bombs & SAA to complete as in Op. Order No 3 – AAA These can be drawn from SAA & Bomb Dump at WOOD POST

From 15 L.F.

Place

Time 12 15 a.m.

The above may be forwarded as now corrected. (Z) A Rupert Murray

Censor. Signature of Addressor or person authorised to telegraph in his name.

* This line should be erased if not required.

(4198) Wt. W14042—M44. 300000 Pads. 12/15. Sir J. C. & S

"A" Form. Army Form C. 2121

MESSAGES AND SIGNALS. No. of Message

Prefix Code m.	Words	Charge	This message is on a/c of:	Recd. at m.
Office of Origin and Service Instructions.	Sent		Service.	Date
	At m.			From
	To			
	By		(Signature of "Franking Officer.")	By

TO O.C. A.B.C. Coy.s.

Sender's Number.	Day of Month	In reply to Number	AAA
* V.W. 726	3		

Op. Order No. ~~44~~ 43

1. Battn will be relieved in the line tonight 3/4 July by 10th Bn Cheshire Regt. Coys will move out as relieved route and destination to be notified later. AAA

2. D. Coy 19 ... will be relieved by A Coy 10th Cheshire Regt, relief will commence at 10 p.m. at which time platoon guides will meet incoming platoons at WOOD POST end of TRAMWAY LINE AAA. D Coy will move out when relieved

3. ABC Coys 19 ... will be relieved by B Coy 10th Cheshire Regt, relief to commence at 9.45 p.m at which time guide detailed by OC 'A' Coy will meet incoming Coy at ~~...~~ WOOD POST end of TRAMWAY LINE AAA

From

Place (1)

Time

The above may be forwarded as now corrected. (Z)

Censor. Signature of Addressor or person authorised to telegraph in his name.

* This line should be erased if not required.

(4198) Wt. W14042—M44. 300000 Pads. 12/15. Sir J. C. & S.

"A" Form.

Army Form C. 2121

MESSAGES AND SIGNALS.

No. of Message

Prefix Code m.	Words	Charge	This message is on a/c of:	Recd. at m
Office of Origin and Service Instructions.	Sent At m. To By		Service. (Signature of "Franking Officer.")	Date From By

TO (2)

Sender's Number.	Day of Month	In reply to Number	AAA
*			

4. H.Q. Bn 15 H.I. will be relieved by H.Q. 10th Cheshire Regt beginning at 5.30 pm at which time R's.H will have joined at Wood Post end of TRAMWAY RAILWAY AAA.

5. C. & D Coys 10th Cheshire Regt will move into AUTHUILLE WOOD & will not relieve any unit of this Bn. AAA

6. Transport for Lewis Guns and M.G.S equipment has been ordered & will meet Bn at place to be notified later. OC Coys will make arrangements to take all available magazines. AAA

7. Relief complete ~~to be reported~~ ~~as soon~~ and arrival in Billets to be reported as soon as possible AAA

From A Rupert Inman Lt (?)

Place

Time 6.45 pm (Cont)

The above may be forwarded as now corrected.

(Z) ~~A Rupert~~

Censor.

Signature of Addressor or person authorised to ~~telegraph in his name.~~

* This line should be erased if not required.

(4193) Wt. W14042—M44. 300000 Pads. 12/15. Sir J. C. & S.

"A" Form.

Army Form C. 2121

MESSAGES AND SIGNALS.

No. of Message

Prefix Code m.	Words	Charge	This message is on a/c of:	Recd. at m.
Office of Origin and Service Instructions.	Sent At m. To By		Service. (Signature of "Franking Officer.")	Date From By

TO O.C. All Coys. - Q.M. - T.O. & H.Q.

Sender's Number.	Day of Month	In reply to Number	AAA
U.N. 756.	6/7/16.		

Operation Order No. 45 AAA.

Ref. maps 1/20000 trench map. AAA

1. Battalion will move from FORCEVILLE to-morrow and will parade in order D.A.B.C. Coys. at 5.40 am with head of 'D' Coy. on CROSS ROADS P.21D. (facing HEDAUVILLE) and will march via HEDAUVILLE to BOUZINCOURT passing point P.27.b.3/4 at 6.0 am AAA.

2. Packs will be carried & will be dumped on arrival at BOUZINCOURT AAA. O.C. Coys. to arrange that all necessary articles are carried in haversack so that Battalion can go forward at short notice in Fighting Kit. AAA.

From
Place
Time

(1)

The above may be forwarded as now corrected. (Z)

Censor. Signature of Addressor or person authorised to telegraph in his name.

* This line should be erased if not required.

(4198) Wt. W14142—M44. 300000 Pads. 12/15. Sir J. C. & S.

"A" Form

Army Form C. 2121

MESSAGES AND SIGNALS.

No. of Message

Prefix .... Code .... m.	Words	Charge	This message is on a/c of:	Recd. at .... m.
Office of Origin and Service Instructions.	Sent		.... Service.	Date
	At .... m.			From
	To			
	By		(Signature of "Franking Officer.")	By

TO (2.)

Sender's Number.	Day of Month	In reply to Number	AAA
* H.W. 756.	6/7/16.		

3. On arrival at destination S.A.A. and bombs to complete will be drawn. AAA.

4. Officers kits will be at Q.M. Stores at 4.45 am AAA. Mess Stuff to be at top of hill by cookers at 5.15 am AAA. T.O. to arrange for Transport to move with Battalion AAA.

5. Reveille at 4.0 am AAA. Breakfast at 4.45 am. AAA. The day's ration to be carried in haversack (as for Fighting kit. AAA.

6. O.C. Coys will see that huts are left clean AAA.

From H.W.

Place

Time 11.15 am

The above may be forwarded as now corrected.

Censor.

(Z) A. R. [illegible] Capt. & Adjt.

Signature of Addressor or person authorised to telegraph in his name.

* This line should be erased if not required.

(4198) Wt. W14942—M44. 300000 Pads. 12/15. Sir J. C. & S.

Prefix .... Code .... m. | Words | Charge

Office of Origin and Service Instructions.

Sent At .... m. To .... By ....

This message is on a/c of: .... Service.

(Signature of "Franking Officer.")

Recd. at .... m. Date .... From .... By ....

TO War Diary. COPY No. 1.

Sender's Number.	Day of Month	In reply to Number	
* U.W. 980.	18.		AAA

OPERATION ORDER No. 49 AAA.

Ref. map 1/100,000. LENS 11. AAA.

1. Battalion will move to area MONTS-EN-TERNOIS – MONCHEAUX – SIBIVILLE, to-morrow & will parade at Battn. H.Q. in order SIGNALLERS – No. 1 & No. 2 Coys. ready to move at 7.45 am. and will march via CROSS ROADS point 165 – CROSS ROADS ½ mile NORTH of Aubres – Aubre – LA COUTRE – REBREUVE – HONVAL – SIBIVILLE, & there take over billets; for which purpose billeting party of 1 Offr. per Coy. & 1 N.C.O. per platoon Transport & H.Q. under Lieut. G. B. SMITH will leave Battn. H.Q. at 5.0 am. & proceed via above route to meet STAFF CAPT. at CHURCH.

From
Place
Time

(1).

The above may be forwarded as now corrected. (Z)

Censor. Signature of Addressor or person authorised to telegraph in his name.

* This line should be erased if not required.

(4198) Wt. W14042—M44. 300000 Pads. 12/15. Sir J. C. & S.

Prefix.................Code..................m. | Words | Charge | This message is on a/c of: ....Service. (Signature of "Franking Officer.") | Recd. at..................m. Date.................. From.................. By..................

Office of Origin and Service Instructions.

Sent At..................m. To.................. By..................

TO (2).

Sender's Number.	Day of Month	In reply to Number	AAA
* G.W. 780	18.		

SIBIVILLE at 7.30 am. AAA.

2. DRESS: Full marching Order – Steel helmets to be worn AAA.

3. Officers kits etc. to be at Q.M. Stores at 6.15 am. AAA. Mess Baskets will be collected at 7.15 am. AAA.

4. Transport to accompany Battalion AAA.

5. Sick Parade at 6-0 am. AAA.

6. Breakfasts will be at 6.30 am. AAA. Sergt Cook to make arrangements for dinners immediately on arrival in billets AAA.

7. Billets will be left scrupulously clean & certificates to this effect rendered to Adjutant before leaving AAA.

From G.W.

Place

Time 8.45 Am.

The above may be forwarded as now corrected. (Z) A Rupert Mossy Lieut. & Adjt.

Censor. Signature of Addressor or person authorised to telegraph in his name.

* This line should be erased if not required.

(4198) Wt. W14042—M44. 300000 Pads. 12/15. Sir J. C. & S.

Prefix	Code	m.	Words	Charge	This message is on a/c of:	Recd. at ___ m.
Office of Origin and Service Instructions.			Sent		___ Service	Date
			At ___ m.			From
			To			
			By		(Signature of "Franking Officer.")	By

TO { Q.M. - T.O. - + H.Q.C. [illegible] 4.

Sender's Number.	Day of Month	In reply to Number	AAA
U.N. 75	19		

Operation Order No. 50 [illegible]

Ref. Map $\frac{1}{100,000}$ Lens 11 [illegible]

1. Battalion will move to area [illegible] [illegible] - [illegible] - [illegible] A Coy will parade in [illegible] [illegible] + No. 2 + No. 4 Coys at junction of Rue [illegible] St. [illegible] and Rue D'Eglise ready to move at 8.40 am and will march via Trans- [illegible] St. [illegible] - [illegible] - [illegible] to take over billets in one of the above villages - for which purpose billeting party of 1 Officer per Coy + 1 N.C.O. per platoon - Transport + H.Q. under Lieut G. B. Smith will leave Battn. H.Q. at 7.0 am + should be able to [illegible] with Staff Capt at Church

(1)

The above may be forwarded as now corrected. (Z)

Censor. Signature of Addressor or person authorised to telegraph in his name.

* This line should be erased if not required.

(1900) Wt. W14042—M14. 300000 Pads. 12/15. Sir J. C. & S.

Office of Origin and Service Instructions.

Sent
At .... m.
To ....
By ....

This message is on a/c of:
.... *Service.*
(Signature of "Franking Officer.")

Recd. at .... m.
Date ....
From ....
By ....

TO (2)

Sender's Number.	Day of Month	In reply to Number	AAA
U.H. 785	19		

1. Marching at 9.0 am AAA
2. Dress: Full Marching Order.
3. Officers kits etc to be at Q.M. Stores at 7.30 am AAA Mess Baskets will be collected at 8.0 am AAA
4. Transport will accompany Battalion AAA
5. Sick Parade will be at 9.0 am AAA
6. Breakfast will be at 7.15 am AAA Sergt. Cook to make arrangements for dinners on arrival in billets AAA
7. Billets will be left scrupulously clean & certificate to this effect rendered to Adjutant before leaving AAA

From U.H.
Place
Time 4.45 pm

The above may be forwarded as now corrected.

(Z)

Censor.

Signature of Addresser or person authorised to telegraph in his name.

Capt. Adjt.

* This line should be erased if not required.

Wt. W14042 -M14. 300000 Pads. 12/16.

Prefix.........Code.........m. | Words | Charge | *This message is on a/c of:* ......Service. (Signature of "Franking Officer.") | Recd. at.........m. Date....... From....... By.......

Office of Origin and Service Instructions.

Sent At.........m. To....... By.......

TO: H.Q. Coy. (w R.S.M.) to be returned to Orderly Room. COPY No 4.

Sender's Number.	Day of Month	In reply to Number	AAA
* 11. W. 790	20/7/16.		

OPERATION ORDER. No 51. AAA. Ref. Map TOO.OOO Sheet HAZEBROUCK 5A. LENS 11 AAA.

1. Battalion will move to area RAIMBERT – CAUCHY-A-LA-TOUR – FLORINGHEM and will parade in order Signallers – No 1 & No 2 Coys at junction of CHELERS – MONCHY and ORLENCOURT – MONCHY ROADS at 7-30 am to-morrow and will march via VALHUON – PERNES & take over billets in above area for which purpose billeting party of one Officer per Coy. & 1 N.C.O. per platoon Transport & HQ under Lieut. A. B. SMITH will leave Q.M. Stores at 5-30 am & moving by above route will report to Staff Captain at CHURCH FLORINGHEM at 9-0 am. AAA.

From
Place (1).
Time

The above may be forwarded as now corrected. (Z)

Censor. Signature of Addressor or person authorised to telegraph in his name.

* This line should be erased if not required.

(4193) Wt. W14042–M14. 300000 Pads. 12/15. Sir J. C. & S

Prefix.................Code.................m. | Words | Charge

Office of Origin and Service Instructions.

Sent
At.................m.
To.................
By.................

This message is on a/c of:
.................Service.
(Signature of "Franking Officer.")

Recd. at.................m.
Date.................
From.................
By.................

TO (2)

Sender's Number.	Day of Month	In reply to Number	AAA
* U.N. 790	20/7/16.		

2. Dress – Full marching Order. AAA.
3. Sick Parade will be at 6-0 a.m. AAA.
4. Breakfasts at 6.15 a.m. AAA
Sergt-Cook to make arrangements for dinners immediately on arrival in billets AAA.
5. Officers kits etc. to be at Q.M. Stores at 6.30 am AAA.
Mess Baskets will be collected at 6.45 am. AAA.
6. Transport will accompany Battalion AAA.
7. Billets will be left scrupulously clean & certificates to this effect rendered to Adjutant before leaving AAA.

From U.N.
Place
Time 7.30 pm

The above may be forwarded as now corrected.

(Z) A. [illegible] Lieut. & Adjut.

Censor. | Signature of Addressor or person authorised to telegraph in his name.

* This line should be erased if not required.

(4193) Wt. W14042—M 4. 300000 Pads. 12/15 Sir J. C. & S

Prefix........ Code........m. | Words | Charge | This message is on a/c of: | Recd. at........m.

Office of Origin and Service Instructions.

War Diary

Sent
At........m.
To........
By........

........Service.

(Signature of "Franking Officer.") | Date........ | From........ | By........

TO: Q.M.
T.O. + H.Q. Mess — COPY No. 1
(last-named to hand to Adjutant).

Sender's Number.	Day of Month	In reply to Number	
* G. 10.	25		AAA

OPERATION ORDER No. 52 AAA.
Ref. map 1/40000 Sheet 36B AAA.

1. Battalion will move to the area RUITZ – HOUCHIN – HAILLINCOURT – tomorrow 26th July, 1916 and will parade in the order SIGNALLERS – No. 2 + No. 1 Coys – at 9-0 am at CROSS ROADS – C.26.6.1/7 and will march via pt. C.21.6.43/30 – AUCHEL – MARLES-LES-MINES – PLACE DE BRUAY – HAILLINCOURT – to take over billets in above area, for which purpose billeting party of 1 Officer per Coy. 1 N.C.O. per platoon, Transport + H.Q. under Lieut. G.B. SMITH will leave Battn. HQ at 8-0 am. + move via above route + report to Staff Capt.

From
Place
Time

(1).

The above may be forwarded as now corrected. (Z)

Censor. Signature of Addressor or person authorised to telegraph in his name.

* This line should be erased if not required.

(4198) Wt. W14042—M14. 300000 Pads. 12/15 S. J. C. & S

Prefix........ Code........m. | Words | Charge

Office of Origin and Service Instructions.

Sent
At........m.
To........
By........

This message is on a/c of:
........Service.
(Signature of "Franking Officer.")

Recd. at........m.
Date........
From........
By........

TO (2).

Sender's Number.	Day of Month	In reply to Number	AAA
* G. 10.	25.		

at CHURCH, HAILLINCOURT, at 11 am AAA.

2. DRESS: Marching Order – Steel helmets to be worn AAA.

3. Sick Parade at 7-0 am.

4. Breakfasts at 7.15 am. AAA. Sergt-Cooks to make arrangements for dinners immediately on arrival in billets. AAA.

5. Officers kits to be at Q.M. Stores at 7.45 am. AAA. Mess Stuff will be collected at 8.15 am. AAA.

6. Transport will accompany Battalion AAA.

7. Billets will be left scrupulously clean & certificates to this effect rendered to Adjutant before leaving AAA.

From U.W.
Place
Time 3.35 pm.

The above may be forwarded as now corrected.

(Z) A Rupert Maxw[ell] Lieut.
A/Adjt.

.... Censor. Signature of Addressor or person authorised to telegraph in his name.

* This line should be erased if not required.

(4198) Wt. W14042—M14. 300000 Pads. 12/15 S r J. C. & S

Prefix........Code........m. | Words | Charge | This message is on a/c of: ....Service. | Recd. at........m. Date........ From........ By........

Office of Origin and Service Instructions.

Sent At........m. To........ By........

(Signature of "Franking Officer.")

TO Dar Diary — COPY No. 1.

Sender's Number.	Day of Month	In reply to Number	
* U. W. 854	28/7/16.		AAA

OPERATION ORDER No. 53 AAA.
Ref. Map 1/40000. Sheet 36 B AAA.

1. Battalion will move to ANNEZIN to-morrow 29.7.16 and will parade in order SIGNALLERS. No. 2 & No. 1 Coys. at 9.25 am along Track leading from Kate with head on ROAD JUNCTION K. 16. a. 7/8 and will march via K. 10. b. 2/9 - K. 4. a. 5/8 - E. 28. C. 0/8 - E. 22. c. 5/9 - E. 10. d. 4/3 - E. 9. b. 8/7 - to take over billets in ANNEZIN, for which purpose billeting party of 1 Officer per Coy. & 1 N.C.O. per platoon. Transport & HQ. ~~under~~ Lieut. G. B. SMITH. will parade Battn. HQ. at 8-0 am. & moving by above route will report

From
Place
Time

(1).

The above may be forwarded as now corrected. (Z)

Censor. Signature of Addressor or person authorised to telegraph in his name.

* This line should be erased if not required.

(T1809) Wt. 14142—641. 45000 pads. 4/15. Sir J. C. & S.

Prefix.......Code.......m.	Words	Charge	This message is on a/c of:	Recd. at.......m.
Office of Origin and Service Instructions.	Sent At.......m. To....... By.......		.......Service. (Signature of "Franking Officer.")	Date....... From....... By.......

TO (2.)

Sender's Number.	Day of Month	In reply to Number	AAA
* U.N. 855	28/7/16		

to Staff Capt at CHURCH, ANNEZIN, at 9.30 am. AAA.

2. DRESS: Full marching Order — Steel helmets to be worn AAA.

3. Sick Parade: will be at 7.0 am AAA

4 Breakfasts at 7.15 am. AAA. Sergt Cook to arrange for dinners to be ready by 12.30 pm AAA.

5. Officers kits to be at QM - Stores by 8.15 am. AAA.

Mess baskets will be collected at 8.40 am AAA.

6. Transport will accompany the Battalion AAA

7. All tents & huts will be left scrupulously clean & certificate to this effect rendered to Adjutant before leaving AAA.

From U.N.
Place
Time 5.40 pm

The above may be forwarded as now corrected.

(Z) A. [illegible] Lieut. for Adjt.

Censor. Signature of Addressor or person authorised to telegraph in his name.

* This line should be erased if not required.

(T1809) Wt. 14142—641. 45000 pads. 4/15. Sir J. C. & S.

Prefix.................Code.....................m. | Words | Charge

Office of Origin and Service Instructions.

Sent
At.........................m.
To.........................
By.........................

This message is on a/c of:
.................................Service.
(Signature of "Franking Officer.")

Recd. at.....................m.
Date.........................
From.........................
By...........................

TO { Div Diary. COPY No. 1.

Sender's Number.	Day of Month	In reply to Number	AAA
* U-W. 861.	28/7/16.		

OPERATION ORDER No. 54 AAA.

Ref. map 1/40000. Sheet 36 B. AAA.

1. This Battalion, who have been selected for conversion to Pioneers, will cease to belong to 14th Inf-Bde. from to-morrow. 29/7/16, and will withdraw to CAPELLE, - in G.H.Q. Troops Area AAA.

2. Battalion will parade in full marching order, with water bottles filled, (steel helmet to be worn), at Tents at 11-40am to-morrow, & will march via CROSS ROADS K-10. 6. 2/8 - VERQUIN - CROSS ROADS E-29. 6. 95/50 - ROAD & TRACK JUNCTION E-[illegible]. 6. 30/05 - RAILWAY STATION - BETHUNE - where Battalion will entrain en route for HESDIN, on arrival at which place

From
Place
Time

(1).

The above may be forwarded as now corrected. (Z)

Censor. Signature of Addressor or person authorised to telegraph in his name.

* This line should be erased if not required.

(4198) Wt. W14042—M44. 300000 Pads. 12/15. Sir J. C. & S.

Prefix .... Code .... m. | Words | Charge

Office of Origin and Service Instructions.

Sent
At .... m.
To ....
By ....

This message is on a/c of: .... Service.

(Signature of "Franking Officer.")

Recd. at ....
Date ....
From ....
By ....

TO (2).

Sender's Number.	Day of Month	In reply to Number	AAA
* U.W. 861	28		

Battalion will detrain & march to CAPELLE. AAA.

3. Transport including baggage wagons but less mess cart & Cookers in use, will leave HOUCHIN at 9.30 am. & moving by above route to STATION, BETHUNE, will entrain there. AAA. T.O. to arrange for Limbers (as required) to be at Q.M. Stores at 6.45 am. & will take surplus stores to Station where same will be dumped, empty limbers will return to HOUCHIN, take up authorised load & move with Transport as above AAA.

4. Supply wagons with rations for 30th. will join Battalion at Station, BETHUNE AAA.

From
Place (Cont'd).
Time

The above may be forwarded as now corrected. (Z)

.... Censor. Signature of Addressor or person authorised to telegraph in his name.

* This line should be erased if not required.

(4198) Wt. W14042—M44. 800000 Pads. 12/15. Sir J. C. & S.

Prefix........Code........m.	Words	Charge	This message is on a/c of:	Recd. at........m.
Office of Origin and Service Instructions.			........Service.	Date........
	Sent			From........
	At........m.			
	To........			
	By........		(Signature of "Franking Officer.")	By........

TO (3).

Sender's Number.	Day of Month	In reply to Number	AAA
* C.W. 861.	28.		

5. Breakfasts will be at 6.30 am. AAA. Dinners will be at 10.45 am. AAA. Remainder of the day's rations will be carried in the haversack AAA.

6. Officers kits to be at Q.M. Stores by 8.30 am. AAA. Mess baskets will be collected at 11.0 am. AAA.

7. Senior N.C.O. or soldier in each compartment will be responsible for the conduct of soldiers in that compartment & will see that no one leaves the train without permission of an Officer AAA. O.C. Coys. will be held responsible for the portion of train occupied by their Coys. & precautions against accidents & fire will be taken AAA.

From

Place (Cont'd).

Time

The above may be forwarded as now corrected. (Z)

Censor. Signature of Addressor or person authorised to telegraph in his name.

* This line should be erased if not required.

(4198) Wt. W14042—M44. 300000 Pads. 12/15. Sir J. C. & S.

Prefix ✓ Code m. | Words | Charge | This message is on a/c of: Service. (Signature of "Franking Officer.") | Recd. at m. Date From By

Office of Origin and Service Instructions.

Sent At m. To By

TO (4).

Sender's Number	Day of Month	In reply to Number	
* O.W. 861.	28.		AAA

8: Tents & huts will be left scrupulously clean, & certificates to this affect will be rendered to Adjutant before leaving AAA.
Accurate Marching-out States to be at Orderly Room at 10.30 am. AAA.

From O.W.
Place
Time 10.55 am.

The above may be forwarded as now corrected.

(Z) A. Rupert Kinney Lieut. & Adjt.

Censor. Signature of Addressor or person authorised to telegraph in his name.

* This line should be erased if not required.

(4198) Wt. W14042—M44. 300000 Pads. 12/15. Sir J. C. & S.

MESSAGES AND SIGNALS. No. of Message

Prefix ... Code ... m. | Words | Charge | This message is on a/c of: | Recd. at ... m.

Office of Origin and Service Instructions. | Sent At ... m. To ... By ... | ... Service. (Signature of "Franking Officer.") | Date ... From ... By ...

TO — Copy No. 4

Sender's Number. * A.W. 835 | Day of Month 26 | In reply to Number | AAA

G.O.C. 1st Inf. Bde. will inspect the Battalion to-morrow AAA.

1. Battalion will parade at huts at 11 am in full marching Order – steel helmets (without covers) to be worn – and will move to field by CRUCIFIX in HOUCHIN where they will form up in mass with Lewis Guns 5 paces in rear of rear platoon of each Coy. – dressed by the Right AAA.
Only the following officers will be mounted:– C.O. Adjutant, SENIOR MAJOR, T.O. AAA.
All dismounted officers will be dressed in fighting kit AAA.

2. Transport will be ready to move at 11 am and will take up position in

From
Place
Time

(1)

The above may be forwarded as now corrected. (Z)

Censor. Signature of Addressor or person authorised to telegraph in his name.

* This line should be erased if not required.

(4198) Wt. W14042—M14. 300000 Pads. 12/15 Sir J. C. & S

MESSAGES AND SIGNALS. No. of Message

Prefix ... Code ... m. | Words | Charge | This message is on a/c of: ... Service. (Signature of "Franking Officer.") | Recd. at ... m. Date ... From ... By ...

Office of Origin and Service Instructions.

Sent At ... m. To ... By ...

TO (2)

Sender's Number.	Day of Month	In reply to Number	AAA
* G.N. 835	26.		

rear of Battalion AAA.

3/ Lewis Gun Handcarts to contain regulation load of guns and S.A.A. AAA. 2 handcarts per Coy. No other handcarts to be on parade AAA.

4/. Wire-cutters will not be carried on rifle, but will be collected and handed in to Q.M. Stores by 10 am to-morrow AAA.

From G.N.

Place

Time 10.20 pm

The above may be forwarded as now corrected. (Z)

Censor. Signature of Addressor or person authorised to telegraph in his name.

* This line should be erased if not required.

19th Lancashire Fus.

WAR DIARY - JULY 1916.

APP: III

Reports on Fighting July 1-4.
11-14.

Precedes W.D.

19th Lancashire Fus

WAR DIARY – JULY – 1916.

APP: IV

Bde. Operation Orders for

Action Operations July 1–4. in

Conformance with Forward movement of 4th Army.

82

Officer Commanding
1st Lancashire Fusiliers

1. On the capture of the enemy's 2nd line defences, patrols will be pushed forward to positions from which they can observe the Western outskirts of COURCELETTE and the valley running SSW from MIRAUMONT (about R22).
2. The time for sending out these patrols will depend, among other things, on our Artillery barrage East of the enemy's 2nd line. This will be controlled by the Division after the completion of the programme of lifts, up to which time all artillery is under control of the Corps.
3. Patrols will be warned to withdraw at once on the approach of any ~~considerab~~ considerable body of hostile troops in order that the Artillery barrage may be put on.
4. The fire of the heavy artillery will be confined to the valley of the R. ANCRE, the gun positions about R10 b & d, and the vicinity of COURCELETTE, so as to leave the space between clear for patrols

C.W. Compton B Genl
Commd. 14th Inf. Bde.

26/6/16.

83.

Officer Commanding
1st Lancashire Fusiliers.

Reference Operation Order No 37 para 16(e).

The SOS signal will be three (3) red rockets by day or red flares by night.

The red flares will only be used when other means of rapid communication have failed.

To indicate the repulse of a counter-attack lamp signalling will be used, or messengers to the nearest working telephone.

Flares should, as far as possible, be lit directly behind the threatened point, but well clear of the troops.

C.W. Compton. Brig. Genl.

26/6/16

Commndg. 14th Infy. Bde.

SECRET. Copy No...7....

14th Infantry Brigade Operation Order No. 37.

Reference Sheet 57 D. S.E. 1/20,000.

1. The 14th Infantry Brigade will take a principal part in an attack on the German positions.

Information. 2. There is no increase in the strength of the enemy opposite us. Details as to the enemy's strength, disposition and artillery are given in Appendix A.

Intention. 3. It is the intention to attack the enemy with the utmost vigour and determination.

Objective. 4. The objective allotted to the Brigade is the German second line from R.34.a.c.9. to 4.21.c.17.

Objectives of neighbouring Units. 5. The objectives of the 97th and 96th Infantry Brigades are MOUQUET FARM - MOUQUET SWITCH - R.27.c.25.75 and MOUQUET SWITCH from R.27.c.25.75 - R.20.c.85.15 respectively. Brigades of the 8th and 36th Divisions are simultaneously attacking objectives on our right and left respectively.

Time of Assault. 6. The exact time of assault will be fixed by higher authority. Zero will be the moment at which the Artillery lifts off the enemy's front line trench.

Artillery. 7. The attack will commence with a steady bombardment of the enemy's positions for four days and nights up to the moment of the Infantry assault on the fifth day (Z day). A detailed programme of Artillery lifts, so far as the 14th Infantry Brigade is concerned is shown in Appendices B.Bi.

Preliminary Moves. 8. (a) On the night T/U the 14th Infantry Brigade will be relieved in the line by the 96th and 97th Infantry Brigades. The relief will be carried out in accordance with a programme to be issued later and the Brigade will be disposed as follows :-

Headquarters	)
14th Inf. Bde. Machine Gun Coy.	)
14th Inf. Bde. Trench Mortar Bty.	)WARLOY.
19th Lancashire Fusiliers	)
2nd Manchester Regt.	BOUZINCOURT
1st Dorset Regt.	W. of SENLIS
15th H.L.I.	near MILLENCOURT - SENLIS road.

(b) On the night X/Y the Brigade will concentrate in AVELUY WOOD.

(c) On the night Y/Z the Brigade will move into its forming up places, the 1st Dorset Regt. and 19th Lancashire Fus. moving to BLACKHORSE SHELTERS, the 2nd Manchester Regt. (less 2 Coys.) and 15th H.L.I. at CRUCIFIX CORNER. 2 Coys. of the 2nd Manchester Regt. will occupy the front line system between MERSEY STREET (exclusive) and CHEQUERBENT STREET (inclusive). The time for taking over the line will be notified later.

Infantry Tasks. 9. The following will be at the disposal of the G.O.C. 14th Infantry Brigade for the attack :-

19th Lancashire Fusiliers
1st Dorset Regt.
2nd Manchester Regt.
15th Highland Light Infantry
14th Inf. Bde. Machine Gun Coy.
14th Inf. Bde. Trench Mortar Battery
Four 4" Stokes Guns for Smoke Barrage
1 Section 206th Field Coy. R.E.

The Brigade will attack the enemy's trenches in two columns :-

Commanding Lt.Col.J.M.Graham, D.S.O. 19th Lancs. Fus.	<u>Right Column.</u>	1st Dorset Regt. 14th Inf.Bde.M.G.Coy.(less 2 sections) 14th Inf. Bde. T.M.Battery (less 8 guns) 4 Stokes Guns for Smoke Barrage 19th Lancs. Fus. Half section 206th Coy.R.E.
Commanding Lt.Col.N. Luxmoore, 2nd Manchester Regt.	<u>Left Column.</u>	2nd Manchester Regt. 1 Section 14th Inf.Bde.M.G.Coy. 4 - 3" Stokes Guns of 14th Inf. Bde. T.M.Battery. Half section 206th Coy. R.E.
Commanding Lt. Col. C.G.Beauchamp, 15th H. L. I.	<u>Support.</u>	15th Highland Light Infantry.
	<u>Reserve.</u>	1 Section 14th Inf.Bde.M.G.Coy. 4 - 3" Stokes Guns of 14th Inf.Bde. T.M.Battery.

<u>The Right column,</u> in the order named, will leave AUTHUILLE WOOD by track No. 1 and will follow the 11th Bn. The Border Regt., the rear Battalion of the 97th Inf. Bde., at 500 yards distance, marching on the gap in the trees just N. of MOUQUET FARM.
Very intimate liaison will be established between the rear Battalion of the 97th Inf. Bde. and the 1st Dorset Regt. At 1.40 after Zero, when the MOUQUET FARM and MOUQUET SWITCH line has been taken by the 97th Inf. Bde. the 1st Dorset Regt. will prepare to attack the German 2nd Line in accordance with time table and sketch attached (Appendices B.Bi) at about point R.27.d.75.50., under cover of a smoke barrage which will be thrown on the line to be attacked.
The smoke barrage will last for 5 minutes during which the 14th Inf. Bde. T.M.Battery will come into action at effective range and fire 30 rounds per gun. As soon as the Stokes Guns are in action a second smoke barrage will be thrown on the German line lasting for 5 minutes, under cover of which the leading Company and Bangalore torpedo party of the 1st Dorset Regt. will advance as closely as possible to the point of attack.
At 2.10 after Zero the Artillery barrage will lift 200 yards. The torpedo party will blow gaps in the wire and the 1st Dorset Regt. will attack and capture the German trenches from R.34.a.o.9. to R.27.b.55.15.
The 19th Lancashire Fusiliers will follow as closely as possible and will capture the German trenches from R.27.b.55.15 to R.27.b.20.75.

<u>The left column,</u> in the order named will follow the right as far as the TRIANGLE, from which point it will be directed on the GOAT REDOUBT, moving with its left on the track running from the TRIANGLE to the REDOUBT.

It will attack and capture the GOAT REDOUBT and the trenches North of it as far as R.21.c.1.7. where connection will be established with the right Brigade of the 36th Division. The line when captured will be consolidated and held at all costs.

The 15th H.L.I. will follow the left column and will advance up the valley East of THIEPVAL until it reaches about the point where the railway crosses the MOUQUET SWITCH. From this point strong patrols will be sent forward towards the German second line. Close touch must be kept with the 2nd Manchester Regt. If it appears that the 2nd Manchester Regt. is unable to advance North of the GOAT REDOUBT the 15th H.L.I. will attack the German trenches North of the GOAT REDOUBT, advancing with its right on the railway.
Otherwise the 15th H.L.I. will not advance, but will be held ready in reserve to repell counter attacks.

The Reserve will remain in AUTHUILLE WOOD at the disposal of the G.O.C. 14th Inf. Bde.

Strong Points.

10. As soon as the German trenches are captured strong points will be established at the following places:

R.28.c.34. (1st Dorset Regt)
R.27.b.81 (19th Lancs. Fus.)
R.27.b.28 (2nd Manchester Regt.)
R.21.c.56 (2nd Manchester Regt, or 15th H.L.I.)

One section 206th Coy.R.E. will be attached to the 14th Infantry Brigade and will accompany the assaulting Battalions to assist in the preliminary work of consolidation. Half the section of the 206th Coy.R.E. will accompany the 1st Dorset Regt., the other half will accompany the 2nd Manchester Regt. to whom they will respectively report on the night Y/Z.
Each strong point will be garrisoned by 2 platoons, with one Vickers and one Lewis Gun.
O.C. Battalions will detail garrisons as follows :-

1st Dorset Regt. 2 platoons
2nd Manchester Regt. 4 platoons
19th Lancs. Fus. 2 platoons
15th H.L.I. 2 platoons

each of these platoons will carry

20 picks
20 shovels
2 hand axes
4 wire cutters
250 sandbags.

3" Stokes Battery.

11. The O.C. 14th Inf. Bde. T.M.Battery will detail 4 guns to accompany the right column to act as described in para. 9. 4 guns will accompany the left column and assist in the attack on the the GOAT REDOUBT, and 4 guns will be held in reserve. The 4 guns with the right column will, after covering the attack on point R.27.d.75.50, move to a position from which they can co-operate with the guns accompanying the left column.
The O.C.14th Inf. Bde. T.M.Battery will arrange to form dumps of ammunition during the advance. Extra carriers will be provided for this purpose (Appendix C).
75 rounds per gun will be carried for the right column.
40 rounds per gun will be carried for the left column.

Dumps of Stokes Ammunition already fused are at
Q.36.d.8.0.
Q.36.d.70.77
Q.30.d.8.0.

Machine Gun Company.

12. 14th Inf. Bde. Machine Gun Coy. (less 2 sections) will accompany the right column and will take up positions to assist the Infantry attack.
One of these sections will be detailed to occupy the strong points, when the objectives have been reached and captured. One section will accompany the 2nd Manchester Regt. to assist in the attack on GOAT REDOUBT and the trenches North of that point.
One section will remain in Brigade Reserve in AUTHUILLE Wood at the disposal of the Brigadier General Commanding.

Smoke.

13. Four 4" Stokes Mortars will accompany the 1st Dorset Regt. for action as in para. 9.
If the wind is favourable the guns will afterwards move to a position from which they can cover the advance of the 2nd Manchester Regt. against the GOAT REDOUBT.

Bombers.

14. Parties will be detailed by Commanding Officers to deal with each section of the enemy's trenches and communication trenches.
The Brigade Grenade Officer and 10 carriers per Battalion will ensure the formation of advanced dumps and a constant supply of bombs to the assaulting Battalions. (Appendix C)
Bombers will not carry extra S.A.A. (see para. 16).

Bangalore Torpedoes.

15. The 1st Dorset Regt. and 2nd Manchester Regt. will carry 3 Bangalore torpedoes each, to deal with wire that remains uncut.

Dress and Special Equipment.

16. (a) Rifle and equipment (less pack)
Water-bottles full.
220 rounds Ammunition (2 bandoliers of S.A.A. in addition to equipment ammunition.)
Waterproof sheet.
2 Sandbags tucked in the belt.
Unexpended portion of day's rations
1 Iron ration.
One 1 lb. tin of Meat and 4 biscuits.
On Y day all packs and greatcoats will be stored at BOUZINCOURT.

(b) Each Officer, N.C.O., and man of Infantry Battalions will carry two fused Mills Grenades in his pocket. Except in the case of bombers these Grenades are not for use by the carriers; they are intended as a means of getting forward large numbers of grenades which will be collected when the objective is reached to replenish bombers ' stocks.

(c) Additional wire cutters will be carried as follows :-

	Mk. V	S.A.Decimals	W.B.	L.H.
1st Dorset R.	20	40	40	15
2nd Manchesters	20	40	40	15
19th Lancs. Fus.)				
15th H.L.I.)	12	24	24	9

(d) 200 Red flares for communication with the contact patrol aeroplane will be carried by each Battalion.

(e) Rockets will be carried by Battalions to call for Artillery support against counter attacks. 5 red rockets fired in quick succession being the S.O.S. signal.

(f) A number of billhooks and axes, hedging gloves, will be carried by each Battalion.

(g) In addition to the tools mentioned in para. 10 each platoon will carry 5 picks and 10 shovels.

Trench Traffic Arrangements. 17. The diagram, (Appendix D) shews the trenches reserved for UP and DOWN traffic and for evacuation of wounded.
Staff Officers and linesmen repairing lines will be allowed to use communication trenches in any direction.

Transport. 18. (a) Detailed instructions are given in the Administrative Orders issued to Battalions for the Transport Lines of Units.

(b) On Z day all Echelon "A" of first line transport viz:- Limbered G.S. wagons for Machine guns, tools, S.A.A., Maltese carts (Medical), pack animals and Officers' Mess carts will be brigaded under Lieut. J. B. DUNN, 15th H.L.I. and will be prepared to move forward to the space South of PIONEER ROAD between W.16.a.8.6. and W.16.b.5.6.

(c) The authorised establishment of baggage and Stores including Officers' kits (35 lbs.) will be packed in the baggage wagons of units on X day.

R.E. Stores Grenades & S.A.A Stores. 19. A diagram is attached (Appendix D) shewing the sites of Magazines and forward dumps of S.A.A. and Grenades.

Medical Arrangements and Water Supply. 20. Diagram (Appendix D) shews the sites of 1st Aid Posts and Evacuation trenches and of the water supply system. There will be difficulty in getting water up to advanced troops. Great care must be taken to husband the supply in water bottles.

Prisoners. 21. Units will send back prisoners with a guard of 10 men per 100. Orders for disposal and collection of information are given in (Appendix F).
Lieut. P. D. KROLIK, 2nd Manchester Regt. will be detailed to attend at the Divisional Collecting Station.

22. (a) All papers and orders are to be destroyed before the advance. No papers will be carried by Officers and men in the attack, except the 1/20,000 Trench Map, shewing German trenches only, the 1/40,000 Map sheet 57 D 57 C, and the LENS sheet of the 1/100,000 series.
All messages and reports will refer to one or the other of these Maps.

(b) Men in the trenches or in the assaulting Brigades will not fall out to bring back wounded.

(c) Any guns captured, which are in danger of being lost again, must be rendered useless by damaging the sights and breech mechanism. Captured Machine Guns must be collected. The C.R.A. will have teams ready to go forward to bring back captured guns.

(d) Attention is drawn to the orders already issued forbidding the collection of souvenirs.

(e) Each Battalion will establish liaison with units on its flanks by means of an Officer or selected N.C.O.

(f) Battalions will keep a reserve of specialists -
(i) A proportion of N.C.O's
(ii) Signallers
(iii) Lewis Gunners
(iv) Machine Gunners.

Veterinary. 23. A Veterinary Collecting Station will be established at W.13.a.2.8.

Communication 24. Arrangements have been made to maintain communication between units and Brigade Headquarters by O.C. 14th Inf. Bde. Signal Section (Appendix G)

Reports 25. Brigade Battle Headquarters will be established at W.12.a.7.7. on X/Y night. The probable line of advance of Headquarters will be up the valley through R.32 central - R.33.a.5.5.

26. A C K N O W L E D G E.

[signature] Captain,
Brigade Major,
14th Infantry Brigade.

22nd June, 1916.

Copy No. 1 War Diary No. 1
2 War Diary No. 2
3 G.O.C.
4 Bde. Major.
5 1st Dorset Regt.
6 2nd Manchester Regt.
7 19th Lancashire Fus.
8 15th H. L. I.
9 14th Inf. Bde. M. G. Coy.
10 14th Inf. Bde. T. M. B.
11 32nd Division
12 96th Inf. Bde.
13 97th Inf. Bde.
14 No. 2 Coy. 32nd Divl. Train.
15 90th Field Ambulance
16 206th Coy. R.E.
17 Town Major, BOUZINCOURT.
18 Town Major, AVELUY.
19 Signals
20 36th Division
21 8th Division
22 No. 1 Coy. No. 5 Battalion, Special Bde. R.E.

APPENDIX 'A'

REGIMENTAL SECTOR:-	X.1.a.5.9. - R.ANCRE. Held by the 99th Res. Regt. of the 26th Res. Div., 14th Res. Corps. The 109th Res. Regt. hold the Sector South of this.
Battalion Boundary:-	R.25. central.
Regimental H.Q.:-	COURCELETTE at R.30.a.5.4.
Battalion H.Q. (Right)	ST PIERRE DIVION, in Reserve lines: large dug-out beside road at Q.24.b. 80.95.
Battalion H.Q. (Left)	Reserve line at R.31.b.25.25.
Battalion H.Q. (when resting)	COURCELETTE R.30.a.95.90.
Company H.Q.:-	(1) West of THIEPVAL at R.25.d.05.92. (2) Support Co. about R.19.d.40.60.
Regimental Rest Billets:-	COURCELETTE.
M.G. Co. Transport and Rest Billets	GREVILLERS.
Command Posts:-	MOUQUET FARM or R.27.b.0.4.
Method of holding line:-	Two battalions in front line & support. 1 Battalion in Rest billets at COURCELETTE. 1 Battalion in Divisional Reserve.
Routes to Trenches:-	(1) COURCELETTE to MOUQUET FARM, thence by communication trenches. (2) COURCELETTE (?) via GRANDCOURT to ST PIERRE DIVION: thence by communication trenches.
Supply Dumps:-	(1) Pioneer Dump S.E. corner of COURCELETTE. (2) Pioneer and Ration Dump, Eastern end of THIEPVAL (ammunition also dumped here). (3) Ration dump and Kitchens in Reserve line at R.19.d.80.50. (4) GRANDCOURT.
Ammunition Dumps:-	THIEPVAL FARM - also Grenade store.
Telephones:-	Telephone Exchange at MOUQUET FARM.
Water Supply:-	Pipe lines into COURCELETTE. From there by water carts to THIEPVAL. This supply is supplemented by well near Church in THIEPVAL.
Railways:-	From COURCELETTE Pioneer Park to THIEPVAL Pioneer Park.
Railhead:-	LE SARS ?

APPENDIX Bi.

TIME TABLE.

Hours:	Min:	Sec:	
0	0	0	Assault by 96th and 97th Infantry Brigades.
1	35	0	18pdr. barrage leaves line G - G and lifts on to I and Ii.
1	40	0	97th Infantry Brigade captures MOUQUET FARM.
2	10	0	18pdr. barrage lifts from Ii to Ji and right column of 14th Infantry Brigade attacks German 2nd line 1st Dorset Regt. leading.
2	15	0	18pdr. barrage lifts from I to J .
2	20	0	18pdr. barrage lifts from Ji to Ki .
2	30	0	18pdr. barrage lifts from J to K .
2	40	0	18pdr. barrage lifts from Hi to Li and 2/Manchester Regt. attacks GOAT REDOUBT.
2	50	0	18pdr. barrage lifts from H to L and 2nd Manchester Regt. take the German trenches N. of GOAT REDOUBT.

APPENDIX C.

Carrying Parties and men withdrawn from units for certain duties.

UNIT.	Carrying For.						TOTAL.
	T.M.Batty.	Bombs.	M.G.Coy.	Runners Bde.H.Q.	Police Control.	Smoke Mortars.	
1st Dorset Regt.	7	10	8*	6	6 & Prov.Sgt.	5	43
2nd Manchester Regt.	7	10	8*	6	6 & Prov.Sgt.	5	43
19th Lan. Fus.	7	10	8*	6	6 & Prov.Sgt.	5	43
15th H. L. I.	7	10	8*	6	6 & Prov.Sgt.	5	43
14th Bde. M.G.Coy.	-	-	-	2	-	-	2
Divl.Cyclist Coy.	20	-	-	-	-	-	20
W/32 T.M.Batty.	24	-	-	-	-	-	24
½ X/49 T.M.Batty.	10	-	-	-	-	-	10
14th Bde T.M.Batty.	-	-	-	2	-	-	2
TOTAL.	82	40	32	28	28	20	230

*In addition to trained men already attached to Bde M.G.Coy.

Appendix. E.

List of substitutes in case of casulties.

Appointment.	Successor.
Brigadier General Commanding. (Brig.General C.W.COMPTON, C.M.G.)	Lt.Col. N.LUXMOORE. 2/Manchester Regt.
Brigade Major. (Captain L.W.KENTISH) Royal Fusiliers.	Captain R.R.C.BAGGALLAY. 11th Hussars.
Staff Captain. (Captain R.R.C.BAGGALLAY) 11th Hussars.	Lieut. K.S.TORRANCE. 2/Manchester Regt.
Bde. Signal Officer. (Lieut. D.F.OSMASTON) Royal Engineers.	
Bde.Grenadier Officer. (Lieut. H.M.MORRIS) 2/Manchester Regt.	Lieut. G.D.A.FLETCHER. 15/H. L. I.
Bde. M.G. Coy. (Captain M.FREEMAN)	Lieut. F.A.HELLABY. Bde. M.G. Coy.
O.C.19/Lancashire Fusiliers. (Lt.Col.J.M.A.GRAHAM, D.S.O.)	Major J.AMBROSE-SMITH. 2/Manchester Regt.
O.C.1/Dorset Regt. (Captain.Temp.Major J.V.SHUTE)	Captain H.G.THWAYTES. 1/Dorset Regt.
O.C.2/Manchester Regt. (Major.Temp.Lt.Col.N.LUXMOORE)	Captain H.G.HARRISON. 2/Manchester Regt.
O.C.15/H. L. I. (Major.Temp.Lt.Col.C.G.BEAUCHAMP)	Major J.GRANT. 15/H. L. I.
O.C. 14/Bde.T.M.Batty. (Lieut. J.G.WHITEHEAD) 19/Lan. Fus.	Lieut E.K.B.PECK. 2/Manchester Regt.

APPENDIX F.

INSTRUCTIONS REGARDING DISPOSAL OF PRISONERS OF WAR AND OF COLLECTION OF INFORMATION FROM PRISONERS, THE DEAD, AND CAPTURED TRENCHES.

---

1. Prisoners will be sent under escort to the Divisional Prisoner Collecting Station at BLACK HORSE BRIDGE, left bank of River ANCRE. Escort must see that prisoners do not destroy documents.

2. An officer (German speaking if possible) will be detailed by the 14th Infantry Brigade and will be posted at the Divisional Collecting Station together with 2 privates (German speaking) who will be detailed by the Division.

3 All information will be handed over by the escort to the officer in charge of the Divisional Collecting Station as to where and by whom the prisoners were captured.

All documents will be collected and a preliminary and rapid examination made.

4. Prisoners will then be sent under escort with as little delay as possible to Corps Prisoner Collecting Station at W.15.b.1/9.

The escort will also hand over all documents to Corps Intelligence Officer.

5. Any important information obtained at Divisional Collecting Station to be sent by quickest means to Divisional H.Q.

6. Railhead for prisoners will be ACHEUX.

* * * * * * * * * * * * *

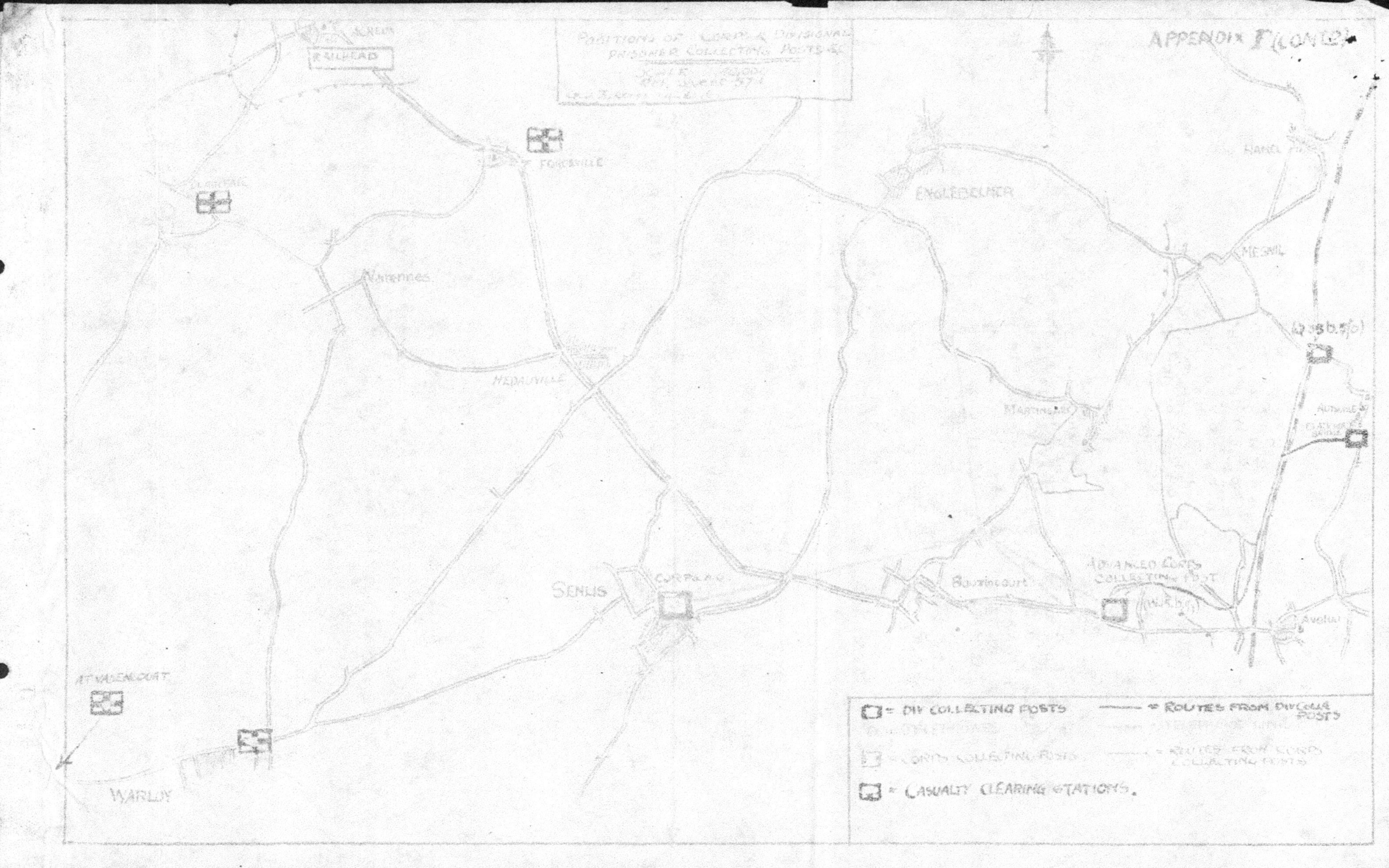
APPENDIX F (CONTD)
POSITIONS OF CORPS & DIVISIONAL PRISONER COLLECTING POSTS &C
RAILHEAD
FORCEVILLE
VARENNES
HEDAUVILLE
ENGLEBELMER
HAMEL
MESNIL
MARTINSART
SENLIS
BOUZINCOURT
ADVANCED CORPS COLLECTING POST
AVELUY
WARLOY
= DIV COLLECTING POSTS
= ROUTES FROM DIV COLL POSTS
= CASUALTY CLEARING STATIONS.

SECRET.

APPENDIX F. (cont'd)

INSTRUCTIONS FOR AND DUTIES OF BRIGADE AND BATTALION INTELLIGENCE OFFICERS.

1. Battalion and Brigade Intelligence officers will be responsible for the collection of letters and documents from the enemy's dead and wounded and from the enemy's dug-outs. The letters and papers found upon the dead and the wounded will, as far as possible, be classified. That is to say, those belonging to Officers and N.C.O's. will be kept apart from the others. Identity discs on dead Germans will be examined and, if the man belongs to a unit which is not normal, the identity disc will be forwarded to Divisional Headquarters. Otherwise they will be left on the body.

2. Intelligence Officers should also be constantly on the look out for fresh identifications by means of shoulder-straps, etc., and the presence of new units should be reported with the least possible delay.

3. Careful search should be made for important documents, maps, etc. These are most likely to be fount on Staff Officers, Regimental Officers or at the Headquarters of units or formations. If any such map or document is found it must be sent to Divisional Headquarters at once through Divisional Prisoner Collecting Post.

4. These instructions are to be considered as supplementary to Appendix F of 32nd Division Operation Order No.24.

* * * * * * * * * * * * * * * * * * *

APPENDIX G

SIGNAL COMMUNICATIONS.

Means Available.

1. The methods of communication for the offensive are as follows:-

(a) Telephone and Telegraph.
(b) Visual (Ground).
(c) Contact Aeroplane.
(d) Wireless.
(e) Despatch Riders and Messengers.
(f) Pigeons.
(g) Visual (Balloon).

Telegraph and Telephone.

2. (a) Buried cables have been extended from 14th, 96th, and 97th Inf. Bde. advanced H.Q. to front at following points:-

(1) Boggart Hole Clough, junction of BURY AVENUE with front line (X.1.4/4) call ST. 14th Inf. Bde.
(2) W. end of Russian Sap off SANDA St. (Q.36.d.9.0.).
(3) W. end of Russian Sap at THIEPVAL Pt.S. (R.25.c.4.3.)
(4) W. end of Russian Sap at THIEPVAL Pt.N. (R.25.c.5.0.)

Signal Offices will be established at each of the above points and messages can be handed in at these points by messengers, thus saving the extra distance between front line and Brigade Advanced H.Q.
The above lines will be extended to the enemy front line immediately that line is captured to enable advanced signal offices to be opened futher forward.

(b) Every unit must go forward with its full establishment of cable.

Cables laid out during an advance must be run outside communication trenches.

When lateral communication cannot be managed by arrangement, the onus of providing the same lies with the Southern unit.

Places should be selected in the enemy's lines where signal offices are to be established, and at least three alternative lines should be run to each.

It is better to have a few points connected by alternative lines than more points connected by only a single line.

Enemy's lines found in the hostile trenches should not be cut by Infantry; they should be left to be dealt with by Signallers.

Sign posts to Signal offices in hostile trenches should be erected as soon as possible.

When a Headquarters moves forward linesman must be left to hand over the lines to the formation in rear taking over.

Should it be necessary to retire from a position that has been reached, any cables that have been run forward to it must be cut.

(c) An advanced station will be opened at THE TRIANGLE as soon as possible.
As each Battalion leaves AUTHUILLE WOOD 3 signallers will be detailed to report to ST.
They will receive DI cable.
1/Dorset Regt., 2/Manchester Regt., and 19/Lan. Fus. will lay lines to TRIANGLE.
Each of these Battalions will find operators at THE TRIANGLE and linesmen to maintain the line.
15/H. L. I. will lay a line along route of its advance and maintain it.
Bde. Signals will lay a D5 cable through point B.2. (R.32.c.4/7) - THE TRIANGLE - MOUQUET QUARRY and maintain it. (~~Attached Sketch.~~)

Visual Groung.

3. (a) A Divisional 'reading' station is established at W.15.b.6.3. call M.L.E. Landmark from the front- between the two Southern trees on MEULES RIDGE. This station will be connected to the Report Centre by wire. Messages will be sent DD - DD three times and no acknowledgement will be sent from the reading station.

There is also a reading station at Q.22.d.8.8. call B.R.K. (36th Division) Landmark from the front - Single tree on MESNIL RIDGE.

There is a third station at Q.29.c.2.4. call 'AVU' Landmark MESNIL CHATEAU (49th Division).

These points should be pointed out to signallers of assaulting infantry who should know how to recognise the direction of the reading stations from the front.

Messages must be limited to those of absolute necessity and be kept as short as possible. Lengthy and unnecessary messages hinder the transmission of other messages, which may be of vital importance.

(b) ST will be ready to receive visual messages. No answers will be sent at first. Messages to be sent through twice. Particular attention must be paid to slow and careful sending.

Contact Aeroplane.

4. The contact aeroplane will ascend at the commencement of the assault. It will be a 'B.E.2.C.' and will have a broad black band under the right bottom plane:-

Communication will be made as follows:-

From Advanced Infantry. By flares or Roman candles denoting 'We are here' and from flashing of mirrors. Three flares or Roman candles will be used fired in a row at 3 or 4 paces interval between each. ½ minute between the firing of each flare.

From Battalion or Brigade Headquarters. By panneau (ground signalling sheet) or lamp. The former will be used in preference to the latter whenever possible.

When wishing to signal, Brigades or Battalions will open ground sheet.

As soon as aeroplane is in position to receive, ground station sends its unit call, meaning "H.Q. are here". This may be followed by one of the following signals:-

NN	meaning	'Short of ammunition'
YY	,,	'Short of Grenades'
OO	,,	'Barrage required'
HH	,,	'Lengthen range'
ZZ	,,	'Held up by wire'
XX	,,	'Held up by Machine Gun Fire'

Each message will be repeated continuously in its entirety.

If necessary the signal may be followed by map location of point or line where barrage is wanted or range needs to be lengthened. No other signals will be used. Aeroplane will acknowledge signals if possible, but will not necessarily do so.

From Aeroplane. White light meaning "Where are you".

Messages received by aeroplane will be transmitted as received (adding time of receipt) by wireless simultaneously to Corps Headquarters and to the Artillery Report Centres of each Division in the line or by dropping message bag at Corps Hd. Qrs.

In cases of great urgency messages may be dropped from a low altitude at Divisional, Brigade or Battalion Hd. Qrs.

Pigeons. 5. (a) The number of pigeons is very limited and should only be used when all other means of communication have failed and then only for great urgency.

Birds should not be kept in small baskets for more than 48 hours.

(b) Pigeons cannot fly at night and must therefore be released int time to reach Headquarters before dark.

1/Dorset Regt. 2/Manchester Regt. and 15/H. L. I. will each have a pair of pigeons.

Balloon. 6. The SENLIS Balloon will be up night and day(weather permitting). This balloon will take messages from Brigade Headquarters by lamp or helios. It will fly a red and white streamer below the basket when it is ready to take messages and at night will flash a lamp every now and then to five directions. The procedure will be the same as signalling to aeroplanes. The balloon will answer by lamp as follows:-

RD - Message understood.
I.M.I. - Repeat,

preceded in each case by Brigade or Battalion code letter. Lamps must be dircted on the basket not on the balloon.

Code Calls. 7. The amended list of code calls issued under G.91/5/7 will be used on all occasions during operations.

The code call will be used as a station call and also as a code name to denote a unit in the 'address to', 'text' or 'address from' of a message.

The writer of any message emanating from or going into the forward area, and also of any message to be sent by visual wireless or pigeon will be responsible for inserting the code name in his message.

Location of advnaced Report Centre ST

Sketch attached.

8. (a) General direction from line of advance of all columns given by fallen tree at N.end of AUTHUILLE WOOD (X.1.a.1/0).

(b) Exact position will then be found by following means.

Signposts painted in two patterns will be placed in lines radially from Brigade office as centre.

Each radial line marked with two or three posts of same pattern spaced about 60 yards apart.

Neighbouring radial lines marked with different pattern posts.

An orderly seeing a post walks to it then looks for next one of same pattern. He then keeps in a direct line with these two posts.

See figs. (1) and (2).

Messengers. 9. (a) Until columns move from AUTHUILLE WOOD, messengers shod be sent direct to Brigade H.Q.

(b) As soon as Battalion leaves wood messenger will be sent to ST and not to Brigade H.Q. direct.

(c) When Battalions have passed THE TRIANGLE messengers should to point B.2. (road corner) If telephone is then through to Brigade H.Q. message will be telegraphed, if not messenger will be sent on to ST.

(d) During attack and subsequently messengers to be sent to THE TRIANGLE where they will be dealt with as in (c).

PTO

Moving Stations. 10. When a station has been established it must not move without informing Bde. H.Q.:-

(1) That it is moving.
(2) next position
(3) leave a guide at old H.Q.

It is better to have a station whose position is known several hundred yards away from H.Q. than one continually moving and losing touch.

fig (1)

fig (2)

19th Lancashire Fus.

WAR DIARY – JULY 1916

APP: V.

Battalion Operation Orders for attack in conformance with forward movement of 4th Army

SECRET.

19th Lancashire Fusiliers. War Di

OPERATION ORDER No. 37.

Ref. Maps. Sheet 57D S.E. 1/10000

1. The 19th Lancashire Fusiliers will take a part in an attack on the GERMAN positions.

INTENTION. 2. It is the intention to attack the enemy with the utmost vigour and determination.

OBJECTIVE. 3. The objective allotted to this Battalion is GERMAN SECOND LINE from R.27.b.55/15 - to - R.27.b.20/75.

Objectives of 1st DORSETS and 2nd MANCHESTER REGT are R.34.a.0/9 to R.27.b.55/15 and GOAT'S REDOUBT to R.21.c.1/7 respectively.

15th H.L.I. will move up RAILWAY VALLEY in support.

TIME. 4. The letter Z is allotted to the day of attack; preceding days will be designated by letters of the alphabet preceding the above letter.

ZERO Time will be the moment the artillery lifts off the enemy's front line, which time will be arranged by Higher Authority.

PRELIMINARY MOVES. 5. (a) On night X/Y, Battalion will move into Shelter trenches No. 16-20 in AVELUY WOOD.

(b) On the night Y/Z, Battalion will move into BLACKHORSE SHELTERS, part of which will also be occupied by 1st DORSETS.

DISTRIBUTION. 6. (a) Brigade will attack enemy's trenches in two columns, with 16th H.L.I. in support.

RIGHT COLUMN:-

UNDER COMMAND OF Lt-Col. J.M.A. GRAHAM D.S.O. 19th LANCS. FUS.

1st DORSETS.
14 Bde. M.G. Coy. (less 2 sections)
14 Bde. T.M. Bty. (less 2 guns).
4 Stokes Guns for Smoke Barrage.
19th LANCASHIRE FUS.
Half SECTION 206 Coy. R.E.

TASK OF BATTALION. 7.

At time notified later, Battalion will leave BLACKHORSE SHELTERS in the order A.B.C.D. Coys. – move S. along River ANCRE and left-wheeling cross AVELUY – AUTHUILLE ROAD at W.11.b. 7/6. – thence to Point W.6.c. 55/06 on S. edge of AUTHUILLE WOOD, along path to DUMBARTON TRACK – leave WOOD by this TRACK at X.1.c. 35/75. Each Coy. will then advance in one line of 4 platoons in fours at 50 yards interval between platoons, and 100 yards distance between lines, ~~[illegible]~~ 1st DORSET REGT. directing (on gap in trees on ROAD running N. from FERME DU MOUQUET), each Coy ~~[illegible]~~ gradually reducing distance between lines to 50 YDS. as they near point of attack.

At Z – 10 mins after ZERO time 1st DORSETS make gap in wire and attack trenches about POINT R.27.D. 75/50 and will take up position R.34.a. 0/9 to R.27.b. 55/15.

'A' Coy. 19th Lancs. Fus., will follow about 50 YDS. behind rear platoon of 1st DORSETS, move through gap and forming LEFT will take up the attack and clear trenches from Point where 1st DORSETS leave off. Sufficient trench will be cleared to give necessary frontage; Coy. will then form to the RIGHT and take up position R.27.b. 55/15 to R.27.b. 51/25, protecting the advance of 'B' Coy.

'B' Coy. following close on 'A' Coy. will continue clearing trench until there is sufficient trench cleared to give necessary frontage, will RIGHT FORM and take up position with RIGHT resting on 'A' Coy's LEFT and LEFT about point R.27.b. 40/45 protecting the advance of 'C' Coy.

'C' Coy. will carry out similar movement and then take up position with RIGHT on LEFT of 'B' Coy. and LEFT about point R.27.b. 30/60.

'D' Coy. will follow 'C' Coy. and after clearing trenches will form to the RIGHT with LEFT FLANK well thrown back until 2nd MANCHESTER REGT. come up & pass through to the attack on GOATS REDOUBT when 'D' Coy. will take up position with its LEFT about point R.27.b. 70/95.

Each Coy. on taking up position will immediately entrench itself, protected by its Lewis Guns.

STRONG POINTS. 8. As soon as German trenches are captured, 'A' Coy. will establish strong points on ROAD at R.27.b.8/1, for garrison of which, O.C. Coy. will detail two platoons and one Lewis Gun.

1 Vickers Gun will be supplied from 11th Bde. M.G. Coy.

Each of these two platoons, which will be as strong as possible, will carry the following, or a proportion in accordance with the strength of platoons:-

20 Shovels
20 picks.
2 Hand axes
4 Wire cutters.
250 Sandbags.

LEWIS GUNS. 9. Will be under Coy. arrangements. O.C. 'A' Coy. to detail 1 gun for strong point.

(a) Each man of teams except No. 1 will carry bucket containing 6 full magazine pans, & will wear the additional 100 rounds S.A.A. in bandoliers.

The magazine pans with the gun (in action) will be filled from these bandoliers, and O.C. Coys. will arrange Ammunition Carriers to replenish this supply from Dumps.

BOMBERS. 10. (a). O.C. Coys. will arrange to have 12 bombers on LEFT flank of LEFT platoon; these will mop up all trenches and will move with Coy. to final position.

(b). Battalion Bombers will be attached to LEFT flank platoon of 'A' Coy., & will mop up trenches, and will continue this until 'B' Coy. is in position, when they will move to Battalion HQ.

(c) Each bomber will carry bomb bag containing 12 bombs but will not carry extra S.A.A. as detailed in para 11(a).

DRESS: 11. (a) Fighting kit will be worn, the mess tin to be inside the Haversack, and to contain part of iron rations.

Steel Helmets.
Water bottles filled.
2 Bandoliers S.A.A. (100) in addition to 120 rounds carried in pouches.
Waterproof Sheet.
2 Sandbags under flap of haversack.
Unexpended portion of days rations.
1 Iron Ration.
1 Tin meat and 4 biscuits.

(b). Two gas helmets will be worn, one attached to shirt as already demonstrated, the other slung over left shoulder in the usual manner. The satchel for gas helmet attached to shirt, will be placed in the haversack.

The top 3 buttons and hooks of the Tunic will be left undone, so as to facilitate the adjustment of helmets.

(C) On X day all packs containing greatcoats will be stored at BOUZINCOURT along with Officers surplus kits and mess stuff.

(d) Each Officer, N.C.O. and man will carry 2 detonated bombs (No. 5) in his pockets. Except in the case of Bombers, these bombs will not be used by the carrier but will be dumped under platoon arrangements, when the final position has been taken up. From this dump, the Bombers will replenish their supply.

EXTRAS TO BE CARRIED 12. (a) Wire cutters will be issued as follows:–

	Regl. Supply.	Mk. V.	S.A.D.	W.B.	L.H.
'A' Coy.	28	3	6	6	3
'B' Coy.	16	3	6	6	2
'C' Coy.	16	3	6	6	2
'D' Coy.	16	3	6	6	2

O.C. Coys. will arrange distribution in their Coys.

12 (f). 9 Red flares will be issued per Coy. & H.Q. O.C. Coys. will issue orders for carrying these so that they can be lighted in 3's as detailed in 14. Bde. S.G. 104 dated 14.5.16 and 29.5.16. Contact aeroplane will be distinguished by black band on RIGHT plane.

(g.) Red Rockets will be issued and will be carried 5 in a sandbag (with lighters), the sticks being tied together in bundles.

3 rockets fired in quick succession is the S.O.S. Signal to be used for artillery support against enemy counter attacks.

(h) O.C. Coys. will make arrangements to carry as many 1" Very pistols (with ammunition) as possible.

(i) Each platoon (less 2 platoons of A Coy) will carry 5 picks & 10 shovels, which will be drawn at BLACKHORSE SHELTERS and carried as demonstrated by A Coy. on last field day.

(j) All hedging gloves will be carried. O.C. Coys to make arrangements.

DRESS - OFFICERS. 13. (a) Officers will be dressed and equipped as much like the men as possible & will carry one Iron Ration and 1 lb. tin of beef & 4 biscuits.

(b) Each Officer will carry the following:-

(i) Maps $\frac{1}{10000}$ Trench Map - $\frac{1}{40000}$ ALBERT - $\frac{1}{10000}$ - LENS 11. All other orders, maps & papers referring to this attack will be destroyed before going into action.

(ii) Compass (prismatic)
Message book - obtainable from Orderly Room.
Revolver - (ammunition from R.S.M.)

WATER. 14. There will be great difficulty in obtaining water and all Officers must ensure that this is used sparingly.

S.A.A. STORES & GRENADES. 15. S.A.A. and GRENADE STORES are situated at
WOOD POST
JUNCTION, BURY AVENUE and HOUGH STREET
CAMPBELL POST
TOBERMORY and KILBERRY STREETS.

S.A.A. CARRIERS. 16. On taking up position O.C. Coys will arrange to send back S.A.A. Carriers at the rate of 3 per platoon. These men will fetch S.A.A. from DUMPS.

SIGNALS. 17. Special Instructions.

LIAISON 18. 'A' Coy will keep in close touch with 1st DORSETS. For this purpose arrangements have been made to send orderlies to that Battn. Strict liaison must be kept up between Coys. & Bn. H.Q.

OFFICERS DISTRIBUTION 19. See Appendix 'A'

N.C.O's & MEN LEFT BEHIND 20. See Appendix B

PRISONERS 21. Intelligence Officers will make a hasty search of all prisoners wounded, & will send any important information to Head Qrs. at once, from where it will be forwarded to Bde. H.Q.
GUARDS for prisoners will be furnished at the rate of 1 man per 10 prisoners. Guards to see that prisoners do not destroy any papers. On no account must advancing troops leave unguarded prisoners behind them.

TRANSPORT 22 (a) On Z day transport ECHELON will be brigaded under Lieut. J.B. DUNN, 15th H.L.I. & will be prepared to move forward to space south of PIONEER ROAD between W.16.a.8/6 & W.16.b.3/6.
(b) Authorised establishment of baggage stores including officers' kits (35 lbs) will be packed in baggage wag on X day.

MEDICAL ARRANGEMENTS 23. Under arrangements made by M.O's of 1st DORSETS and this Battalion, stretcher bearers will follow up the Battalion and collect wounded.
On no account whatever will advancing troops fall out to help or bring back wounded.

MEN FOR SPECIAL DUTIES 24. (Detailed in appendix) will report to Bn. H.Q. at noon on Y day.

BATTN. HEAD QRS. 25. Will move forward with 'C' Coy. line, and will take up a position about centre of line held & slightly in rear. On first arrival the vicinity of BN. HQ. will be marked by a flag.

CASUALTY REPORT 26. Correct casualty returns at 6.0 a.m. and 3.0 p.m.

ISSUED AT. 7 p.m.
26. 6. 16.

A. Rupert ... [illegible] Adjutant
19th Lancs. Fus.

App. A.

List of Officers to accompany Battn. into Action.

H.Q.

Lieut. Col. J. M. A. Graham D.S.O. — C.O.
Major J. Ambrose Smith — 2nd in Command
Lieut. & Adjt. A. R. Moxsey
Lieut. G. B. Smith — Intelligence Officer.

"A" Coy.

2/Lieut. H. W. Huxley O.C. — W. 3.7.16
" E. C. E. Chambers. — K. 1.7.16
" A. N. Dussee — K. 1.7.16
" E. D. Ashton — K. 1.7.16

"B" Coy

Capt. G. Hibbert O.C. — W. 3.7.16
Lieut. J. Hewitt — W. 1.7.16
2/Lieut. L. L. Middleton — W. 1.7.16
" R. L. George.

"C" Coy.

Capt. W. G. Heywood O.C.
Lieut. H. Musker
" R. C. Masterman — K. 1.7.16
2/Lieut. G. H. Dykes.

"D" Coy.

2/Lieut. W. R. Nightingale O.C. — W. 2.7.16
" H. B. Cartwright
" G. Jowke
" J. Shiels — W. 1.7.16

Officers not to accompany Battalion.

Captain G. A. Palk
" J. L. Freeman
Lieut. K. R. Evans
" H. A. Smith
2/Lieut. L. B. Midgley
" L. Whittles
" H. C. Young
" A. G. Vaughan
" H. B. Kilgwin
" D. Graham Brown.

OFFICERS & N.C.O's LEFT IN RESERVE.

'A' Coy.		'B' Coy.		'C' Coy.		'D' Coy.	
Officers	N.C.O's	Officers	N.C.O's	Officers	N.C.O's	Officers	N.C.O's
2/Lieut. H.C. Young. " H.D. Kieghin	Sgt. Ravenscroft. Sgt. Mulraney. Sgt. Yipond. L/Cpl. Braithwaite. L/Cpl. Cheney. L/Cpl. Grimes.	2/Lieut. L.E. Mabey " N. Whittles " D. German-Reed	Sgt. Knight. Sgt. Chapman. L/Sgt. Magee. Cpl. Potts.	✠ Capt. S.A. Palk. Lieut. K.R. Evans 2/Lieut. A.G. Vaughan	Sgt. McCormick. Sgt. Smith T. Sgt. Parkinson. Cpl. Purcell.	Capt. J.L. Freeman	Sgt. Locker. Sgt. Nuttall. Sgt. Gilligan. L/Sgt. Jones. A.E
Lewis Gunners.							
–	Pte Bell. " Bridge.	–	Pte F. Dawson. " J. Healy.	✠ Lieut. H.A. Smith	Cpl. Maughan. Cpl. Rose. L/Cpl. Lewis. Pte Rawlinson.	–	Pte Griffiths. " Reynolds.

✠. On Course of Instruction.

A Rupert Morris Lieut. & Adjt.
for Lieut-Col.
Commanding 19th Service Bn.
Lancashire Fusiliers

APPENDIX. B

N.C.O's and men remaining behind in reserve.

COMPANY.	Sgts	Cpls.	La. Cpls	Lewis Gunners		Bombers.		Signallers.		TOTAL.
				N.C.O's	MEN	N.C.O's	MEN	N.C.O's	MEN	
A	3	-	3	-	2	-	-	-	-	8.
B	4	1	-	-	2	-	-	-	-	7.
C	4	1	2	2	1	-	-	-	-	10
D.	4	-	-	-	2	-	-	-	-	6.
TOTAL.	15	2	5	2	7.	-	-	-	-	31.

APPENDIX B1

TIME TABLE

HOUR	MIN	SEC	
0	0	0	Assault by 96th and 97th Infantry Brigades
1	35	0	18 pdr. barrage leaves line G–G and lifts on to I to I1.
1	40	0	97th Infantry Brigade captures MOUQUET FARM
2	10	0	18 pdr. barrage lifts from I1 to J1 and right column of 14th Infantry Brigade attacks GERMAN 2nd line 1st DORSET REGT. leading.
2	15	0	18 pdr. barrage lifts from I to J.
2	20	0	18 pdr barrage lifts from J1 to K1
2	30	0	18 pdr. barrage lifts from J to K.
2	40	0	18 pdr. barrage lifts from H1 to L1 and 2nd. MANCHESTER REGT. attacks GOAT REDOUBT.
2	50	0	18 pdr. barrage lifts from H to L and 2nd. MANCHESTER REGT. take the German trenches N. of GOAT REDOUBT

App. B.

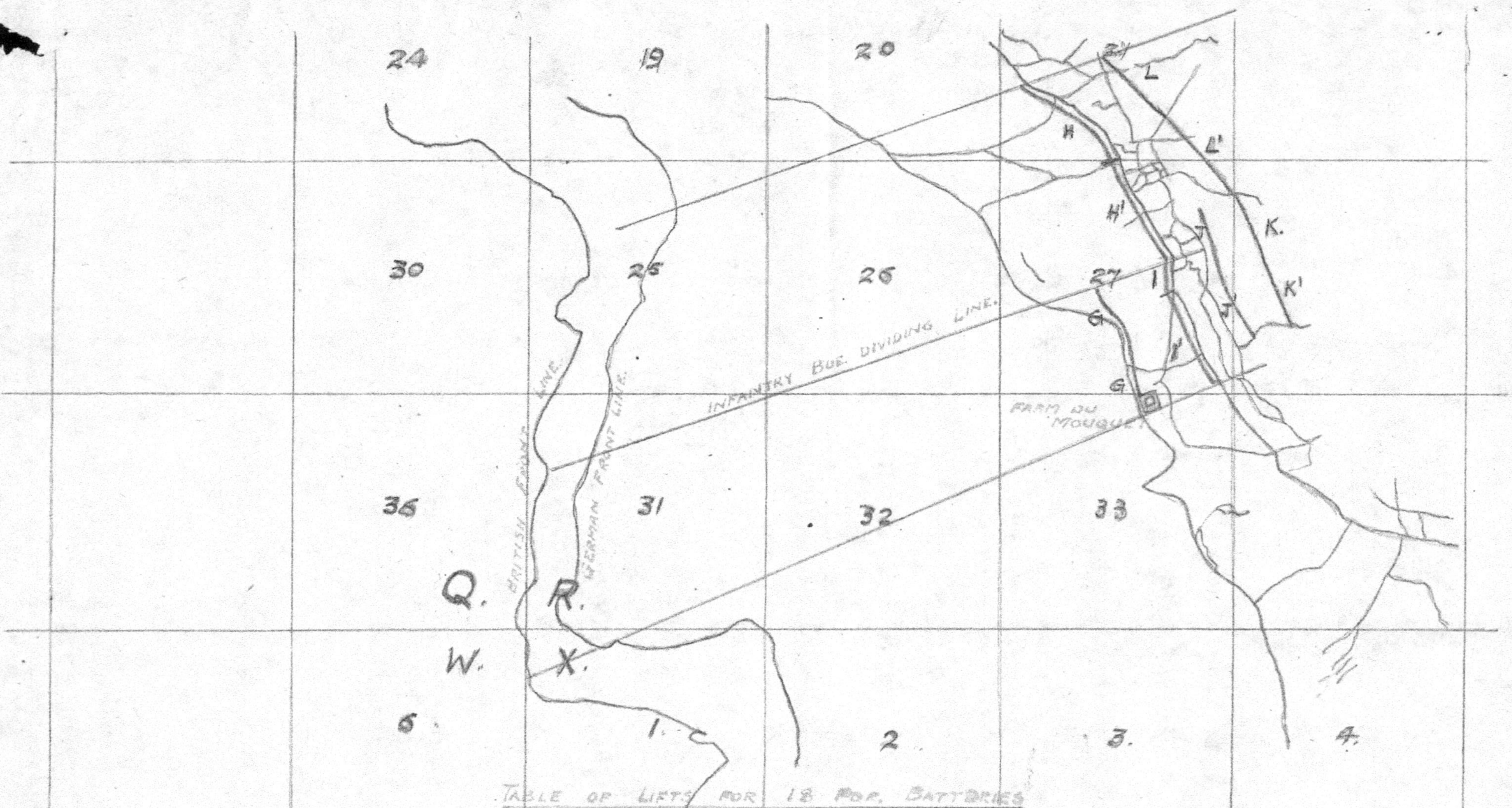

TABLE OF LIFTS FOR 18 PDR. BATTERIES

	Line		Moves to	At
The barrage leaves the line	G	and moves to	I·I'	1 - 35 - 0
"	I'	"	J'	2 - 10 - 0
"	I	"	J	2 - 15 - 0
"	J'	"	K'	2 - 20 - 0
"	J	"	K	2 - 30 - 0
"	H'	"	L'	2 - 40 - 0
"	H	"	L	2 - 50 - 0

Appendix C.

Carrying Parties and men withdrawn from Coys. for certain duties

	CARRYING FOR.						TOTAL.
	T. M. Battery	Bombs	M. G. Coy.	Runners Bn. Hd.	Police	Smoke Mortars	
A	2	3	2	3	-	2	12
B.	1	3	2	3	1	2	12
C.	2	2	2	3	-	3	12
D.	2	2	2	3	-	3	12
H.Q.	-	-	-	-	Regt.[l] Police	-	6
TOTAL.	7	10	8	12	7.	10	54

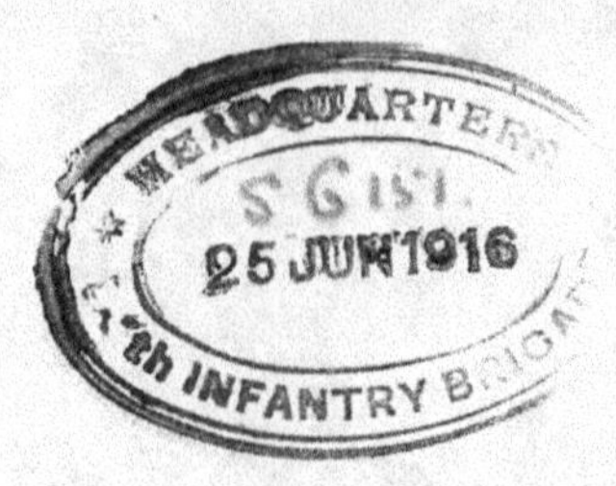

19th Lancs Fusiliers
~~1st Dorset Regt~~
~~2nd Manchester Regt~~
~~15th H L I~~

It has been found necessary to alter the position of units in the assembly trenches.
Maps are attached showing the position of units

<u>19th Lancs Fus</u> Trenches 16–20 (inclusive)

<u>1st Dorset Regt</u> Trenches 21–24 (inclusive)

<u>2nd Manchester Regt</u> Trenches 5, 6, 6a, 7, 7a, 8, 8a, 9, 9a (inclusive)

<u>15 H L I</u> Trenches 10, 10a, 11, 11a, 12, 13, 14, 15 (inclusive)

[illegible] Capt, Bde Major
14th Inf Bde

24.6.16

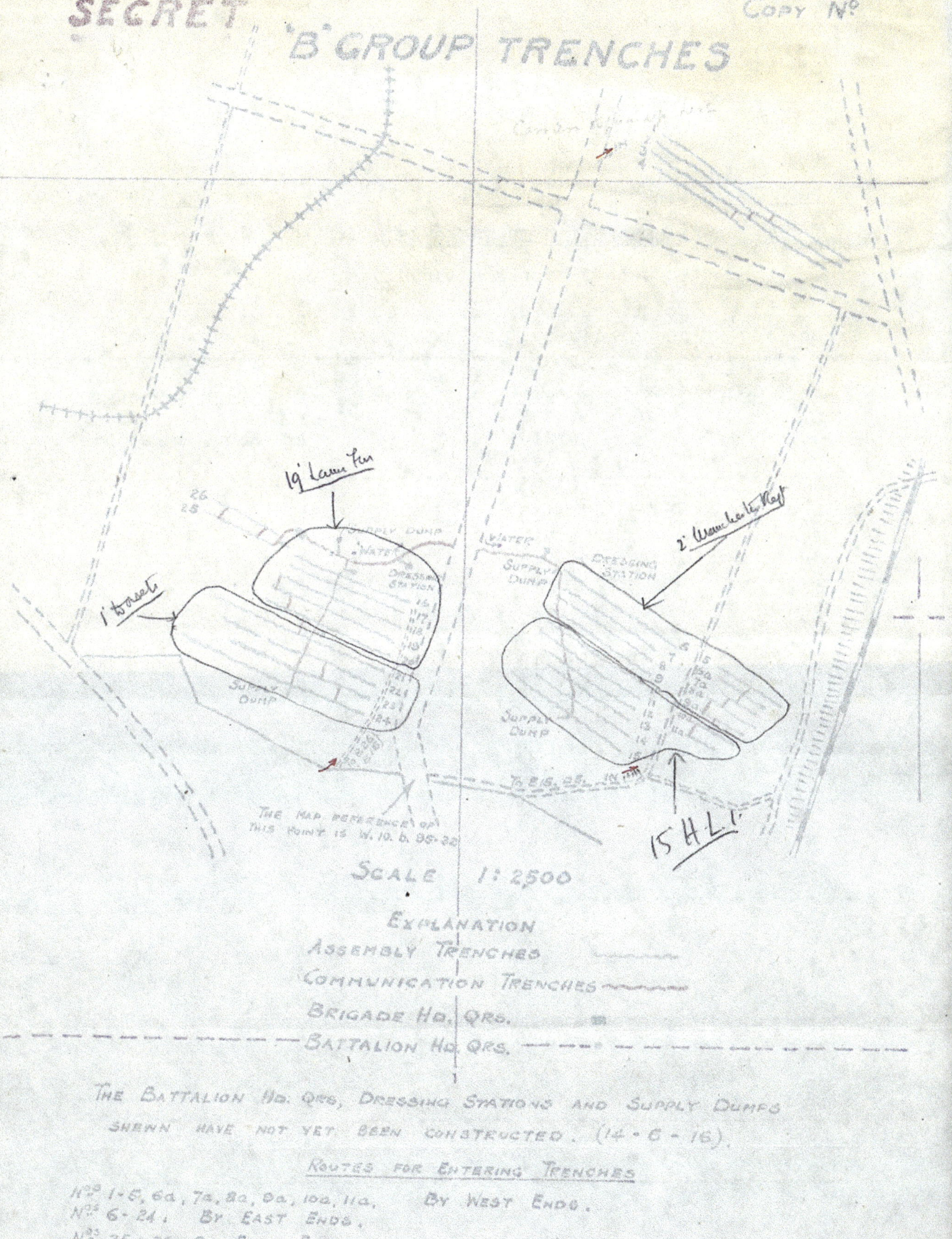

THE BATTALION HQ. QRS, DRESSING STATIONS AND SUPPLY DUMPS SHEWN HAVE NOT YET BEEN CONSTRUCTED. (14-6-16).

<u>ROUTES FOR ENTERING TRENCHES</u>

Nos 1-5, 6a, 7a, 8a, 9a, 10a, 11a. BY WEST ENDS.
Nos 6-24. BY EAST ENDS.
Nos 25 & 26 BY EAST ENDS, APPROACHING THRO' No 16.

<u>ROUTES FOR LEAVING TRENCHES.</u>

Nos 1-4 BY WEST ENDS ON TO MAIN ROAD.
Nos 5, 6a, 7a, 8a, 9a, 10a, & 11a, BY EAST ENDS ON TO TRACK ALONGSIDE RAILWAY.
Nos 6-11, BY EAST ENDS AND THEN THRO'. Nos 6a-11a.
Nos 12-15, BY EAST ENDS ON TO TRACK, FOLLOWING IT SOUTHWARDS, AND EASTWARDS TOWARDS RAILWAY.
Nos 16-24. BY EAST ENDS ON TO MAIN ROAD.
Nos 25-26, BY MOST CONVENIENT ROUTE.

SECRET. "B" GROUP. Copy No.

ACCOMODATION IN TRENCHES.

(2 feet of trench allowed per man).

Trench No.	Accommodation (all ranks)	Remarks.
1	247	) SPARE TRENCHES.
2.	278	)
3.	210	) = 855 (1 Battalion.)
4.	120	)
5.	100	)
6.	137	)
6a	93	)
7.	108	)
7a.	77	) = 871. (1 Battalion)
8.	122.	)
8a.	78	)
9.	112	)
9a.	44	)
10.	126	)
10a.	71	)
11.	148	)
11a.	65	) = 939. (1 Battalion)
12.	138	)
13.	118	)
14.	136	)
15.	137	)
16.	190	)
17.	150	)
18.	186	) = 879. (1 Battalion.)
19.	183	)
20.	170	)
21.	250	)
22.	230	)
23.	230	) = 959. (1 Battalion.)
24.	249.	)
25.	70	) = 140 (1 Field Coy.R.E.
26.	70	)

APP. VI.

Following Officers reported for duty with Battalion 4th July, 1916.

2/Lieut. S. MORRISON - 15th Kings' (Liverpool) Regt.
" L. G. LONGLEY - ditto.
" T. G. MAHONEY - ditto.
" C. QUAYLE ditto.

2/Lieut. H. C. LONSDALE 2nd Lancashire Fus.
" R. A. GOURLEY 2nd Lancashire Fus.
" R. P. S. Eaden - 3rd Lancashire Fus.

Operations 1 – 14 July 1916

Officers accompanying Battalion into action.

Lt-Colonel John A. Graham, D.S.O.
Lieut. & Adjt. A. R. Maxey.
Lieut. G. B. Smith (Intelligence Officer).

No. 1 Coy.

Capt. W. G. Haywood
2/Lieut. H. B. Cartwright
" H. C. Young. (Wounded)
" L. G. Langley. (Killed)
" T. G. Mahony. (Killed)

No. 2 Coy.

Capt. S. A. Park.
2/Lieut. D. Graham-Brown.
" G. H. Dykes.
" S. Morrison (Killed).
" A. G. Vaughan.
" R. A. George.

In Reserve.

Major J. Ambrose Smith
Capt. J. L. Freeman
Lieut. H. Husker.
2/Lieut. L. B. Midgley.
" H. Whittles.
" R.P.S. Eddin
" C. Bungle
" H. C. Lonsdale
" H. D. Keysom.

On Courses.

Lieut. H. A. Smith
2/Lieut. R. L. George.

www.ingramcontent.com/pod-product-compliance
Lightning Source LLC
Chambersburg PA
CBHW080837010526
44114CB00017B/2322
* 9 7 8 1 4 7 4 5 2 4 8 6 5 *